MICROSOFT®

MICROSOFT®

Works

ON THE APPLE® MACINTOSH™

CHARLES RUBIN

PUBLISHED BY

Microsoft Press
A Division of Microsoft Corporation
16011 N.E. 36th Way, Box 97017, Redmond, Washington 98073-9717

Library of Congress Cataloging in Publication Data
Rubin, Charles, 1953–
Microsoft Works.
Includes index.
1. Macintosh (Computer)—Programming. 2. Microsoft Works (Computer program) I. Title.
QA76.8.M3R83 1986 005.36′5 86-17953

ISBN 0-914845-67-5

Printed and bound in the United States of America.

7 8 9 FGFG 8 9 0 9 8

Distributed to the book trade in the United States by Harper & Row.

Distributed to the book trade in Canada by General Publishing Company, Ltd.

Distributed to the book trade outside the United States and Canada by Penguin Books Ltd.

Penguin Books Ltd., Harmondsworth, Middlesex, England
Penguin Books Australia Ltd., Ringwood, Victoria, Australia
Penguin Books N.Z. Ltd., 182-190 Wairau Road, Auckland 10, New Zealand

British Cataloging in Publication Data available

CONTENTS

ACKNOWLEDGMENTS

This book was begun in the spring of 1985, when Microsoft Works was barely a prototype. Writing a book about a product that doesn't yet exist is like painting a picture of an object shrouded in fog, and it wouldn't have been possible without help from a number of people who kept the project going as Microsoft Works and the book took shape together.

At Microsoft, I would like to thank Ron Lamb, my editor, who was extremely patient during a lot of stormy times. I am also grateful to Tracy Smith and Claudette Moore for suggesting this project to me in the first place; to Salley Oberlin, who kept the book on schedule; to Jody Snodgrass, who was never too busy to answer questions; to Darcie Furlan, who did a marvelous design; and to Lia Matteson and Linda Pennington, who facilitated everything. I would also like to thank Kearney Rietmann, who was the book's technical editor.

Of course, this book would also have been impossible without Bob Lissner, who began the original version of Microsoft Works, or Don Williams, who took Bob Lissner's original idea and made it a reality. Although Don was busy coordinating a far-flung team of programmers, he was always available—and cheerfully so—for some telephone advice. Don and Bob are two of those rare individuals who are as pleasant as they are talented and hard-working, and I feel fortunate in having worked with them.

Finally, I want to thank Michael Rogers, Lon Poole, Jeffrey Young, Brad Roth, and especially Doris and Daniel Rubin, who made all the difference during a year's worth of scheduling conflicts, hardware problems, software problems, and attacks of anxiety and frustration.

Charles Rubin
Oakland, California
August 1986

INTRODUCTION

This book is for people who want to make the most of Microsoft Works on the Macintosh.

WHY THE APPLE MACINTOSH?

The Macintosh is a natural choice for those of us who want to become more productive with a personal computer, but don't want to spend weeks or months becoming a computer expert. The Mac is far simpler to learn and use than other personal computers, and it delivers this ease of use without sacrificing computing performance. While it's true that some Macs are sold to computing professionals, most Macs are sold to regular, hardworking people from all industries and professions who don't know much or anything about computers. This book assumes that you are using a Macintosh and that you may have thumbed through the manual, but it doesn't assume that you are intimately familiar with all of the Mac's features and operations. Since Microsoft Works requires at least a 512K Macintosh with at least one 400K or 800K disk drive, the book also assumes you have this type of hardware. However, you'll find that you spend much less time swapping disks if you use Works with at least two 400K disk drives or one 800K drive.

WHY MICROSOFT WORKS?

Microsoft Works is an excellent software choice for the majority of Mac users, because it was specifically designed to give you a lot of computing power without requiring a lot of computing expertise. Microsoft Works delivers the four major personal computer functions—word processing, spreadsheet analysis, database management, and communications—in one reasonably priced package. Works is powerful enough to handle most personal and business tasks, and is simple to learn and use.

In this book, we'll assume that you've spent a little time with Works, and that you've at least browsed through the introductory information and lessons supplied with the Works program disk. We'll also assume that your primary goal in having Works and a Mac is to get something done, rather than to embark on a detailed study of computer hardware and software. This book is designed to help you use Microsoft Works and the Mac to handle real-life business and personal data, to use the power of advanced personal computer hardware and software to make your life easier and more productive.

A REALISTIC SCENARIO: AL'S VIDEORAMA

Throughout this book, we'll be tackling the business and personal computing tasks of Al Chroma, the proprietor of Al's Videorama. Al is a retired motion picture projectionist who has opened his own videotape rental store in a fictional California city. We'll use Works and the Mac to help Al organize his business records, prepare custom sales materials, analyze his profits, and perform other typical business tasks. In one case, we'll even help Al's wife, Claudia, with her job.

We'll also help Al with some personal computing activities. He has recently been named secretary-treasurer of the Classic Film Club, and this job brings with it some record-keeping and reporting duties of its own. And of course, Al has his own personal records to keep, letters to write, and decisions to make. We'll see how Works can help with all of them.

As we help Al with each activity, you'll see step-by-step descriptions of how Works handles the job. Reading these descriptions serves two purposes: It shows Works' features in a detailed, real-life context; and it gives you ideas about how to apply Works' power in your life.

HOW THIS BOOK IS ORGANIZED

As an orientation to Microsoft Works, we'll begin in Chapter 1 with a general description of how Works and the Mac make it easier to get things done. We'll look at basic features of the Mac and Works that make them a simple, yet powerful, computing combination.

The second part of the book, Chapters 2 through 8, gets into the specifics of each Works tool—the word processor, spreadsheet, database, and communications programs, in that order. Chapters 2, 4, 6, and 8 spell out the specific features of each Works tool and show you how, in general, to get the most out of them. Each of these chapters is divided into several sections:

- A section on basics gives a general description of the tool at hand (the word processor, for example), and how it is used.
- A quick tour of the tool's menus details each command and how it is used.
- A discussion of the advantages of the Works word processor, spreadsheet, database, or communications program compares Works with other Macintosh programs that perform the same functions.
- A look at some limitations of Works includes some techniques for overcoming these limitations.
- A section on general operating tips will help you use each tool as effectively as possible.
- Finally, a list of each tool's specifications gives detailed information such as the maximum size of a file, or the maximum width of a printed document.

In Chapters 3, 5, and 7, we'll use the tool discussed in the preceding chapter to solve personal and business problems for Al Chroma and Al's Videorama. The projects in these chapters will show you most or all of Works' word-processing, spreadsheet, and database-management features at work in the real world. (The real-world applications of the communications tool are included in Chapter 8.)

In Chapter 9, we'll consolidate what we've learned about each individual Works tool, using the program to combine data from various documents and to move data between Works and other programs. After discussing the basics of these data-movement features, we'll use them to handle some more business and personal tasks for Al and his Videorama.

Works has a lot of power all by itself, but there are some other hardware and software products that will expand its capabilities. The Appendix, which follows Chapter 9, presents some Works enhancement products. It explains the general features of these products, and then offers some specific examples of products you can buy.

ON YOUR WORKS, GET SET . . .

Microsoft Works comes with an excellent set of lessons that show you the program's main features, and its reference manual fills in the specific details you'll need as you build your experience. But knowing how to operate a program isn't the same as knowing what to do with it.

Many computer novices think that computers are magic, and that by pushing a button or two, they can get an answer to any question they may have. Actually, making a computer work for you isn't a matter of plunking down some money and plugging in a machine. Rather, it's a journey during which you learn to use a tool, and then you discover how to apply that tool in your life.

During this journey, there will certainly be moments when you don't understand something and you wonder if you'll ever learn it all; but there will also be many moments when you'll wonder how you ever got along without a computer. The Macintosh and Microsoft Works are far simpler to learn and use than most other computing products you could have chosen, but when something can make as much of a difference in your life as a Macintosh and Microsoft Works, it's only natural that the change won't happen overnight. As you'll soon see, however, the journey is well worth taking. So, turn to Chapter 1 and let's take the first steps.

CHAPTER 1

Microsoft Works in Perspective

In this chapter, we'll look at the two general features that make Works and the Macintosh such a useful team: the Mac's simple user interface and Works' integration of four major applications in one package.

WHAT'S A USER INTERFACE?

An interface is the method by which you work with a computer—the means of interaction between man and machine. Before the Macintosh came along, user interfaces for personal computers were clumsy and difficult to learn. Typically, there was a blank screen with a single, blinking rectangle (the cursor) on it, and the computer waited for you to type in the proper command to do something. Computer commands were often difficult to learn, and most computers needed hundreds of different commands to do all of the things they could do.

Instead of presenting you with a blank screen and waiting for you to type some complex command, the Macintosh uses graphics and words to show you the various things you can do at any time. All you have to do is choose the operation you want to perform.

Along with being easier to learn and use, the Mac's interface also helps take the anxiety out of computing. With a traditional computer, you may be afraid of typing the wrong command inadvertently. If you don't understand something on the Mac, you can pull down a menu to see a list of commands. If you're about to do something irreversible, the Mac warns you. The Mac supplies you with the information you need to work it as you need that information, so you can concentrate on getting your work done.

This simple Macintosh interface is available whenever you run a program or application. (Different computer programs, such as word-processing programs, spreadsheet programs, and so on, are often called applications, because they each apply the computer differently. They tell the computer to work with information differently. A spreadsheet program usually tells the Mac to treat the character 5 as a specific numeric value that can be calculated, for example, while a word-processing program tells the Mac to treat it as a text symbol like any other letter or number.) Whatever type of program you run on a Mac, the interface—the way you tell the Mac to do things—always remains the same.

WHAT IS INTEGRATED SOFTWARE?

What makes Works different from other programs on the Mac is that it combines, or integrates, four different applications (or tools) into one program. Other programs let you work with data just one way (as words or numbers), while Works lets you work with data in four different ways. Works contains a word-processing program for working with text, a spreadsheet program for working with numbers, a database program for working with groups of facts, and a communications program for transmitting data between your Mac and other computers.

Now, you could use four separate programs to work with data in different ways, but it's much easier to have all four applications integrated into one package. Here's why:

Integrated software is easier to learn

If you used four different programs to work with data, you would have to learn four different sets of commands. With Works, many of the commands are the same in every application, so you have to learn them only once.

Integrated software is easier and faster to use

With four different programs, you may have to change program disks each time you want to do something different. Works combines all four applications on one disk, so you don't have to change disks when you want to work with data in a different way.

Integrated software lets you transfer data more easily

Many times, you'll want to move data from one application into another application. You might want to copy some spreadsheet figures into a word-processor report, for example. Running two different programs, you would have to switch disks and perhaps even convert the data from one program's format to the other program's format. Different programs store and represent data differently. A spreadsheet stores numbers in rows and columns, while a word processor usually keeps text in sentences and paragraphs. With Works, you can copy data between programs directly, without switching disks or converting the data format.

THE MAC + WORKS = TRANSPARENT COMPUTING

When you combine the Mac's simple interface with the flexible data-handling of Works' integrated programs, you have a very powerful and transparent computing tool. It's transparent because you can "see through" the computing tool itself and focus on the work you want to do. You don't have to think much about how you're going to do your work on a Mac—you just do it.

Transparency has long been a goal of personal computing. As with any tool, the productivity you get from a personal computer is proportionate to the ease with which you can use it. It's the same with any piece of equipment. When you pick up a telephone and call somebody, you don't have to know anything about how your call gets from your phone to another person's; all you need to know is how to dial the number. You can concentrate on the message you want to give, rather than the process of getting it there. With a personal computer, transparency means making a computer work more like your mind does: effortlessly.

When you need to recall a fact from your mind, for example, the process is usually very quick and simple: You don't have to think about how you get the fact you want to recall, you just recall it. If somebody describes something to you, you can imagine it quickly and effortlessly. Your mind is not only fast and easy, it's also extremely flexible. It can switch from a color picture of a place to a mathematical formula in a second, without much conscious effort from you.

Typically, computers haven't been very transparent, because they require conscious effort to do things. They aren't as fast as our minds, and they aren't as flexible. To recall a fact that's stored in a traditional computer system, you might have to type a series of commands, and then remember something about the fact you wanted to recall and type it into the computer as well. On the Mac, you could simply point to a command, and then point to the fact to retrieve it from a long file. Because it's simpler to use, the Mac interface removes a lot of the conscious effort from computing.

As mentioned earlier, Works makes computing a lot more flexible, because it lets you work with data in different ways.

Because it is an integrated software package, Works makes it easier to convert data to different formats. The four integrated applications on the Works disk allow you to take the number 7 from the spreadsheet and quickly convert it to a text 7 in the word processor. You can also convert a series of spreadsheet numbers easily to sections of a pie chart with the Works chart feature. And you can take a customer record from the database file and move it into the spreadsheet for additional calculations.

As we'll see later in this book, being able to move data around in this way also means you can reuse data. If you've already entered inventory data into the spreadsheet, you can convert that data to a database file, and then manipulate the data differently without typing the same data into the computer again. As with your mind, once you have stored the information, you can convert it to different formats, rather than storing it in different formats over and over again.

Thanks to a better interface and integrated software, the Mac and Works are more transparent than other computer and software combinations. They're not nearly as transparent as the human mind, but they're definitely a step in the right direction.

Now, let's look at some specific features that are present in all four Works applications.

FEATURES COMMON TO ALL FOUR WORKS APPLICATIONS

Works makes computing transparent by unifying the commands for the four different programs as much as possible, and by making it simple to move data from one program to another, or even between Works and outside programs.

The opening screen

When you start Works, the program's opening screen appears.

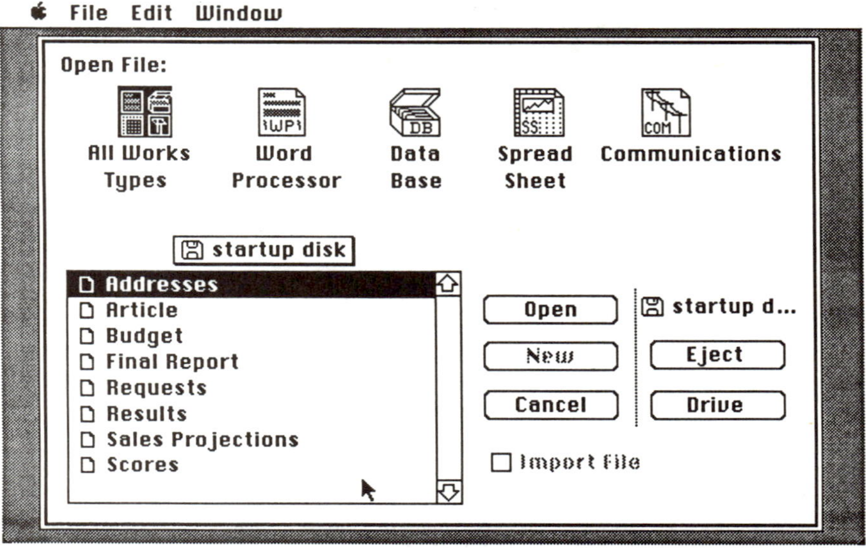

This screen lets you create new documents or open existing documents for any of the four Works applications. The four applications are represented by icons. You select an icon to indicate the type of document you want to open or create, and then you point to and click on either the New or Open button below.

If you are opening a file from a disk, the list of files that appears when you click the Open button will contain only those files for the application you have selected. If you click on the Word Processor icon, for example, and then choose the Open... command from the File menu, the list of available files will contain only word-processor files. If you want to show all the Works files on a disk, you can choose the All Works Types icon.

Works shows you only the Works files on a disk. If you have Multiplan files, MacWrite files, or MacPaint files on a disk, Works doesn't show you the names of these files because you can't open them.

You see non-Works files on a disk listed only when you use the Import File feature. (Microsoft Works, like many programs, creates files in its own special format. When you convert files in other formats for use with Works, you are importing them, and when you convert Works files to other formats for use with other programs, you are exporting them.) You can import files from certain other programs into Works by clicking the Import File box on the main program screen. If you click the Import File box, you'll see the names of files you can import into a Works application along with files created in Works.

Notice that the name of the disk containing the files you are viewing also appears, above the list of files. The type of icon beside the name tells you the type of disk: a floppy disk or hard disk. If you want to look at the files on a disk in a different disk drive, you click the Drive button. If you want to eject the current disk and insert another disk, you click the Eject button.

So, instead of presenting you with a blank screen, Works starts off by showing you a lot of things you need in order to use it in an economical and intuitive way. It's economical because it conveys a lot of information about how to use the program with just a few icons and labels. It's intuitive because you can point to things you want to do, and pointing is one of the most natural human ways of expressing what you want.

The menus

Along with icons, buttons, and file listings, there are also four menu labels in the menu bar at the top of the opening screen. Each Works application has its own menus when you're working with a particular document, but the four menus shown on the opening screen are common to every Works application.

The Apple menu contains a set of desk accessories you can use as you work. These desk accessories are a standard feature in every Macintosh program, and may include an alarm clock, a calculator, the Note Pad, the Scrapbook, an accessory that lets you select the type of printer you're working with, and others. The one accessory that is unique to Works is the first one on the menu, About MS-Works.... When you choose this accessory, you see a box that contains the copyright and other information about the program.

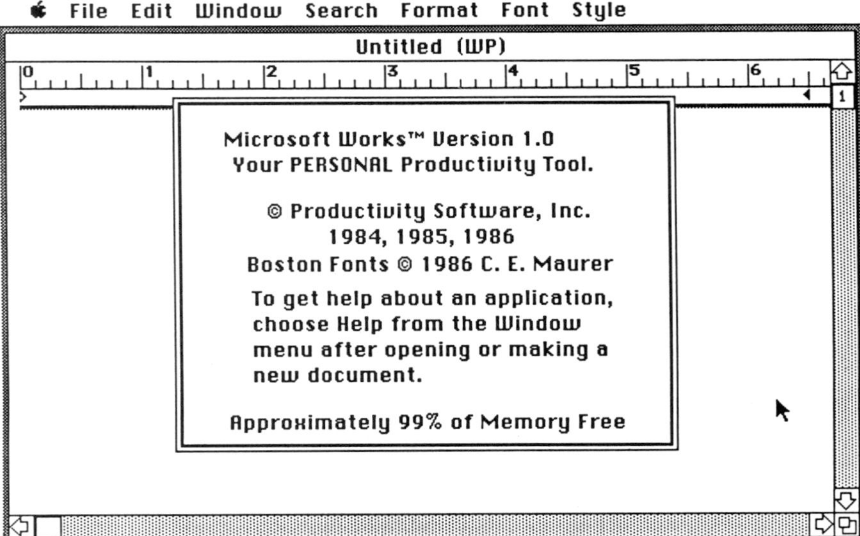

The most useful thing about this screen is that it tells you, at the bottom, the amount of memory you currently have available in your Macintosh. The amount of available memory diminishes as you create larger and larger files with Works and keep them open on the desktop. If you're working with large files, you may want to check the About MS-Works... accessory periodically to make sure you have enough memory to continue working.

Most of the commands on the File, Edit, and Window menus are common to every Works application. The File menu lets you open and save files, create new files, and print files. These procedures are basically the same for every Works application, so you only have to learn about them once to perform these functions with all four programs.

The Edit menu controls cutting and pasting of information between applications, or between one application and the Clipboard (we'll learn more about the Clipboard a little later in this chapter). This process is basically the same in every Works application. The Edit menu may also contain commands that are specific to the application you are working with.

The Window Menu lets you select different documents to work with from those currently open on the Desktop. It also lets you view the contents of the Clipboard. These procedures are identical in every Works application.

By using four common menus, then, Works lets you understand how to do many filing, printing, and editing tasks in every one of its applications without learning four different sets of commands.

The Works desktop

Works uses a desktop metaphor to make computing as transparent and flexible as possible. Having files in memory is like having a group of paper documents on top of a desk. You can have several different paper documents on a desk at a time, and you might move from one document to another as you go through your day. If you want to move information from one document to another, you cut and paste it with a scissors and tape. When you are using Works, you can open up to ten different documents at a time, and then select one or the other to work with by choosing it from the Window menu. You can also move data between documents easily. The Works desktop is really your Mac's memory. You have as much room on the desktop for files as your Mac's available memory allows.

The Clipboard

Along with several files, the desktop also makes use of the Clipboard, which is a document supported by almost all Mac software where you can put data you want to move from one place to another. Using the Edit menu's Cut or Copy command, for example, you can cut or copy data from any Works document and put it on the Clipboard. Using the Paste command from the Edit menu, you can move any data from the Clipboard into another document, or to another place in the same document.

The Clipboard is the main Macintosh feature that lets you use data from one application in a different application. With the Works desktop's multiple-file capability and the Clipboard, you have a powerful environment for working with data the way you want. If you want to move some spreadsheet data into a word-processor document, you can choose the spreadsheet document from the Window menu, copy the data to the Clipboard, choose the word-processor document from the Window menu, and paste the data from the Clipboard into the document. This process, which might require swapping disks, restarting programs, and perhaps even converting data formats if you were using two different programs, is very fast and easy with Works.

File compatibility—importing and exporting

The final feature that makes Works a powerful computing tool is its ability to easily share files with other programs. When you create Works files, they're stored in a data format unique to Works, and you can't share them directly with other programs. But Works lets you use files created by other programs, and lets other programs use files created by Works.

Works can import and export files in two different formats. The first is the text, or ASCII, format, which is the industry standard for data interchange. Most personal computer programs can create or use text files. The Works word processor, database, and spreadsheet can all export their data as text files, so the data can be used in other programs, and they can also import text data from other programs. This means you can share Works data with most other computers and computer programs, and you can make use of most other programs' files within Works.

The second format is called SYLK (for SYmbolic LinK), which was created by Microsoft Corporation to facilitate data interchange among its own programs. The SYLK format lets you transfer a spreadsheet file from one Microsoft program to another while maintaining all the formatting and formulas from the original file (ASCII format doesn't preserve formats and formulas). With the SYLK format, you can transfer Works spreadsheet files to Multiplan or Microsoft Excel, or you can use Multiplan or Microsoft Excel files in the Works spreadsheet. Many Microsoft programs, whether for the Macintosh, Apple II, or IBM PC, use the SYLK data-interchange format. (Some restrictions apply to these transfers. See Chapter 9 for further information.)

A third way Works can share files with other programs is through automatic conversions. Files created with the two most popular Macintosh word-processing programs, MacWrite and Microsoft Word, can be imported directly into Works. While other word-processing programs have to store their files in the text format before Works can use them, Works can load standard MacWrite or Word files and automatically convert them to its own word processor's format.

This feature also works when you're exporting files with the Works communications program. Whenever you transmit a Works word-processor, spreadsheet, or database file with the Send File command in the Works communications program, the file is automatically converted from Works' internal data format into standard-text format.

So by using Works' file import, export, and conversion features, you can make use of just about any kind of data from any source you can imagine. Works becomes a simple, fast tool that allows you to combine data from different sources, convert data to different formats, and use four different tools to work with it flexibly.

PUTTING WORKS TO WORK

As you've seen so far, Microsoft Works and the Mac are a simple, flexible, and relatively transparent personal-computing team. In the chapters that follow, you'll see how you can put this power to good use.

CHAPTER 2

Using the Word Processor

Word processing is the most popular personal computer application because nearly everyone needs to put a few words down on paper from time to time, and most people who've used typewriters find it fairly easy to make the conceptual transition to a word-processing program. In both cases, you type at a keyboard, and what you type appears in front of you. But a word processor has an important advantage over a typewriter: You can store what you've typed and change it later.

In this chapter, we'll look at the advantages of word processing on a Macintosh in general (and with Works in particular). After that, we'll explore each of the menus that are available in the Works word processor. Finally, we'll cover some basic tips that can help make the word processor a more effective writing tool.

WORD PROCESSING ON THE MAC

The Macintosh is ideally suited for word processing because its light gray screen and black letters look a lot like the output from a typewriter. But there are a number of other Mac-related advantages for those who work with words.

What you see is what you get

When you put words on a Macintosh screen, they appear exactly as they will appear on paper. The margins, line spacing, indentations, and justification you apply to your text will show up faithfully on the screen, so you don't have to guess at how your finished document will look. While these particular format settings are common to every word-processing program, the Macintosh allows you to set them more easily—you can point to markings on a ruler to set margins, and you can select a portion of a document if you want to use a different format in just one place.

You get more formatting options

With other computers, you are at the mercy of your printer when it comes to selecting the type font, size, and style that will be printed on paper. Every Macintosh word processor offers a variety of type fonts, and you can embellish them by using a range of type styles and sizes. With an ImageWriter, LaserWriter, or other Macintosh-compatible printer, you can reproduce any type font, style, or size you can display on the Macintosh screen.

You can include drawings or graphs in a document

Thanks to the Macintosh Clipboard, you can easily move drawings or graphs created with MacPaint, Microsoft Chart, MacDraw, or other programs into word-processor documents. Instead of trying to describe a new building or the design of a new product, you can show it right in your letter or report.

These features are hallmarks of word processing on the Mac, regardless of the word-processing program you're using. Microsoft Works adds several important items to the list. To familiarize you with these features, let's look at the commands Works offers.

A QUICK TOUR OF WORKS' WORD-PROCESSOR MENUS

As you do in every Mac application, you access Works commands primarily via pull-down menus in the menu bar at the top of the screen. (You can also issue many Works commands directly from the keyboard by pressing the Command key in combination with a letter key. Keyboard commands are explained in detail later in this chapter, but every menu command that has a keyboard equivalent shows that equivalent next to the command name on the menu.)

Each Works application has a different set of pull-down menus, but, as mentioned in Chapter 1, the first four menus from the left side of the screen are substantially the same in every application.

The Apple menu

As we learned in Chapter 1, the Apple menu contains desk accessories and system information about the program you're currently running on your Mac, and is the same in each Works application.

The File menu

As in other Mac programs, the File menu controls file-management options in Works—opening, closing, deleting, and making new files, as well as printing files and quitting the program. The menu is divided into sections for adding files to the desktop (the New... command and the Open... command), removing and naming files (the Close, Save, Save As..., and Delete... commands), printing (the Page Setup..., Print..., Print Window, Eject Page, and Print Merge... commands), and quitting (the Quit command).

Notice that the Open..., Save, Print..., and Quit commands have keyboard alternatives. Also, notice that some of the commands have an ellipsis (...) after their names. An ellipsis tells you that choosing this command will produce a dialog box on the screen (where you must make further choices before the command is executed) rather than executing the command right away. When you choose the Quit command, for example, you immediately exit Microsoft Works and return to the Finder desktop. When you choose Save As..., on the other hand, a dialog box appears, asking you where to save the file and giving you a chance to rename the file before saving it.

Most of the File menu's commands in Works function the same as they do in other Mac programs, so we won't go into those commands here. But there are some File commands unique to Works. Delete..., for instance, lets you delete a file on disk by selecting from a list of the files on the current disk drive. When you choose Delete..., a dialog box appears, displaying a list of files on the current disk drive. If you want to view the files on another drive, click the Drive button. You select a file to delete either by double-clicking the file's name or by clicking the Delete button. You can delete a file that is currently open on the desktop, but the file will be erased only from the disk—it will remain open on the desktop. To delete the desktop file, close the file without saving the changes.

The Print Window command prints the currently active window. It doesn't print the entire file in that window, only the text or graphics that are shown on the screen. Print Window is the command you use to make hard copies of spreadsheet graphs.

The Eject Page command advances the paper in an ImageWriter printer to the top of the next sheet. You use this command primarily when you want to start printing again on a new sheet of paper after you've used the Print Window command. Print Window uses no more than half a sheet of standard-size paper to print a window, and it stops the printer in the middle of the page when there is only one window on the page. Thus, you could print two windows on one piece of paper. But if you want to print only one window on a page, you can choose the Eject Page command.

The Print Merge... command tells Works that you want to print a form letter or some other type of word-processor document that will contain data merged from a database. When printing a form letter, you must use Print Merge... (rather than Print) so Works knows that it must pull data from a database file. If you use the Print command instead, Works will print one copy of the document with the merge field names (rather than the actual merge data). Chapter 3 contains an example of Print Merge... in action.

The Edit menu

The Edit menu should be familiar to people who have used other Mac programs. Its commands allow you to cut, paste, move, and copy text to and from the Clipboard. In Works, however, this menu has a number of additional items.

The Undo command lets you cancel the previous command you issued. This command is especially helpful for recovering text immediately after you've deleted it, or for undoing a major formatting action you've changed your mind about.

The Select All command does just that—it selects an entire document. This is handy when you want to copy an entire document to the Clipboard, or when you want to apply a format (for example, line spacing or a different font) to a whole document.

The Select Picture command selects graphics in a word-processor document, whether they're drawings you made with Works' Draw... command or pictures you've made with another program and copied into a Works document. Once you select a picture, you can move it around within the document window or change its size. If more than one drawing is displayed on the screen, Select Picture selects drawings one at a time in the order in which you made them. If there are two drawings side by side, for example, choosing Select Picture once highlights the first drawing, choosing Select Picture again highlights the second drawing, and choosing Select Picture a third time highlights the first drawing again. We'll explore this option more in Chapter 3.

The Draw... and Draw Off commands let you draw lines and boxes directly on word-processor documents. Anything you draw with this feature is treated as a picture by Works, and pictures are independent of text. If you draw a box around some text, for example, and then use Select Picture to move the box, only the box will move—the text will stay where it is. (To move text, you employ conventional text-movement techniques, using such tools as the Cut and Paste commands, the spacebar, the Delete key, and the Tab key.) You can change a picture after you've drawn it by either using the Undo command immediately after you draw the picture, or by selecting the picture and then choosing the Clear command to delete it. We'll put the Draw feature to work in Chapter 3.

Prepare to Merge... is the command you use when selecting database files and specific fields to merge into a word-processor document. When you select a field to merge, a box (called a merge box) appears at the insertion point displaying the database file name and the field name. A pair of merge boxes in the salutation of a letter might look like this:

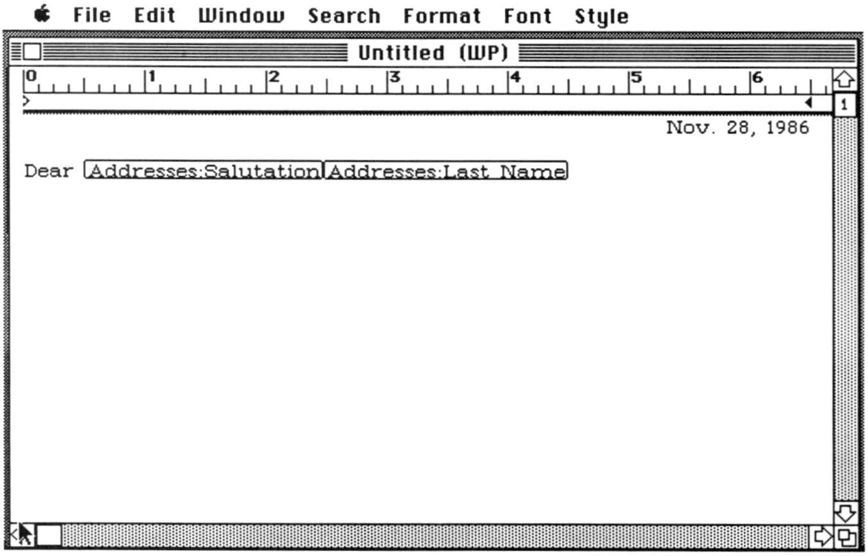

File Edit Window Search Format Font Style
Untitled (WP)
Nov. 28, 1986
Dear Addresses:Salutation Addresses:Last Name

The actual length of a merge box will depend on the length of the database file and field names. Merge boxes appear at the location of the insertion point when you choose the Prepare to Merge... command. Once a merge box is displayed in a word-processor document, you can delete it, move it, or copy it just as you would ordinary text. If you want to see actual data (the contents of a database record to which a merge box refers) in the merge box, instead of the file and field name, choose the Show Field Data option.

The Window menu

Using the commands on the Window menu, you can control what you see on the Works screen.

Normally, documents appear in a full-sized window. You can make a window smaller or larger by dragging the size box in its lower-right corner. The Full Window (or Small Window) command at the top of the menu lets you toggle between the small window size and the full window size, or you can simply double-click on the window's size box to toggle between window sizes.

Other commands on the Window menu let you view the contents of the Clipboard (Show Clipboard), access on-line instructions about how to use Works (Help), and activate different windows on the desktop (the names of all open files are listed at the bottom of the menu). The listing of open files tells you how large each desktop file is and which Works application was used to create it.

The last four menus on our tour are unique to the word processor.

The Search menu

The Search menu lets you find text (the Find... command), find text and replace it with text you supply (Replace...), and jump to a particular page number (Go To Page #...). All of these commands have keyboard alternatives.

You can use the Find... command to locate one occurrence of text at a time. The Replace... command lets you find and replace text one occurrence at a time, or all at once throughout the entire document. These two commands search an entire document, regardless of where the insertion point is positioned at the time.

The Go To Page #... command helps you move to a specific page quickly. Works displays page numbers in the right scroll box, but you can also use this command to determine which page you're on. When you choose the Go To Page #... command, the page-number window in the dialog box that appears always shows the current page number. To move to a different page, enter a new number, click the OK button, and Works will jump to that page.

The Format menu

The Format menu controls all format options except headers, footers, and margins (which you control by using the Page Setup... command from the File menu).

The Hide Ruler command lets you remove the line-length ruler that normally appears at the top of a document window. Hiding the ruler creates enough room in the window for two extra lines of text. If you want to change the line length or insert tabs or indents, however, the ruler must be displayed. To redisplay the ruler, choose the Show Ruler command, which appears on the Format menu in place of Hide Ruler when the ruler isn't displayed.

The Spacing... command controls line spacing. The Spacing dialog box lets you choose single, one-and-a-half, or double spacing for your documents. Text is displayed on the screen and printed according to this setting. The Left, Centered, Right, and Justify options control the justification of text on the page. Left means text is aligned flush along the left margin; Centered means it's centered between the left and right margins; Right means text is aligned flush along the right margin; and Justify means text is aligned with both the left and the right margins, and spaces are inserted between words to make the length of each line the same.

The Copy Format command lets you copy the line-spacing, indentation, justification, tabs, font, style, and font-size settings from one part of a document to another. Copy Format copies the format settings from the line or paragraph containing the insertion point. Once you copy a format, you can duplicate the format at a new location by clicking a new insertion point and choosing the Paste Format command.

Insert Page Break tells Works to begin a new page at the insertion point. You can insert page breaks only before Works' automatic page breaks occur; otherwise, you are asking Works to print a page with more lines than the other pages around it. When you insert a new page break, the automatic page breaks on the following pages are adjusted so that all the pages are the same length. Whenever your insertion point is on the line below a page break that you have manually inserted, Remove Page Break replaces Insert Page Break on the Format menu. You can use Insert Page Break to keep long tables or groups of drawings together on the same page by inserting a page break before and after the material you want to appear on the same page.

The Title Page command tells Works not to print a page number on the first page of a document. You might want to use this command when the first page of your document is a cover sheet or an introductory section that shouldn't be numbered.

The Set Page #... command lets you start the numbering of pages anywhere from 1 to 99,999. This command is useful when you have two files that are part of the same project, such as chapters of a book or sections of a report.

The Font menu

The Font menu contains the names of fonts you can use with the Works word processor.

You can use a font other than 10-point Boston, Works' default font, for new or existing text. To change to a different font for new text, just choose that font before you start typing. To change the font of some existing text, you must first select the text you want to work with, and then choose the new font from the Font menu. The text will change automatically. The font names that appear on the menu are the fonts you have on your current system disk. The Works system disk comes with Boston, Athens, Geneva, Chicago, and Monaco in the sizes described later in this chapter. But you can add or remove fonts and font sizes from your system disk by using the Font/DA Mover program that comes on the system disk. Keep in mind, though, that any fonts you add will be available only in the word processor—you can't change fonts in Works' spreadsheet, database, and communications applications.

One reason you might want to add more sizes of existing fonts in Works is so you can print high-quality characters in larger sizes. When you choose the High quality option from the Print dialog box, your Mac uses a font twice as large as the size you've specified to produce the high quality. If you want to print Boston 12 in high-quality mode, for example, your Mac actually uses the Boston 24 font to print it. If the double-size font isn't available when you want to print a font in high-quality mode, your Mac will scale an available font to the size you specified. So if, for example, you wanted to print Chicago 12 in high-quality mode, you would have to add the Chicago 24 font to your Works Program disk.

One of the benefits of having a Mac is being able to use fonts (either from Apple or from other developers) other than the ones that come on the system disk.

To use the Font/DA Mover, follow the instructions supplied with the Font/DA Mover program.

The Style menu

The Style menu lets you embellish your text by making it bold, italic, underlined, outlined, shadowed, superscript, or subscript. You can also change the size of the current font.

The sizes available for each font vary; the range of sizes for each of the five standard fonts is shown in Figure 2-1. To change the style or the size of a font, you must first select the text you want to change, then choose an option from the Style menu.

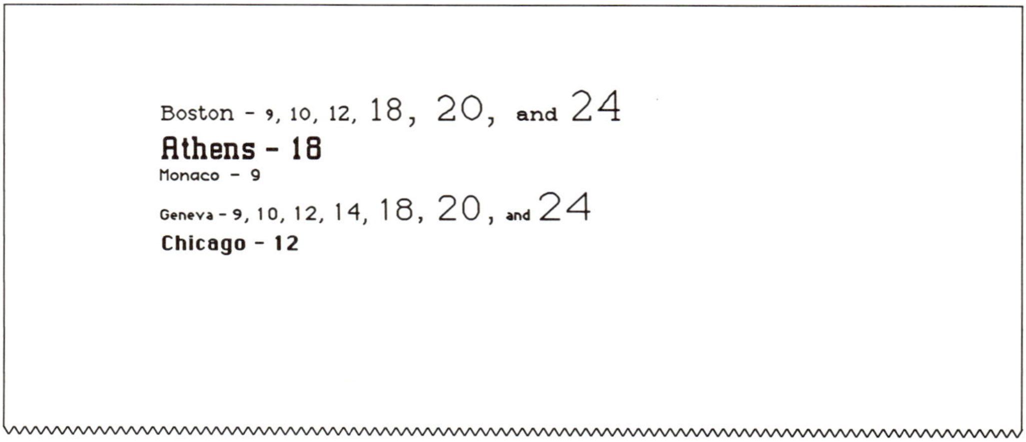

Boston - 9, 10, 12, 18, 20, and 24
Athens - 18
Monaco - 9
Geneva - 9, 10, 12, 14, 18, 20, and 24
Chicago - 12

Figure 2-1. *The standard fonts and sizes in the Works word processor offer a range of options.*

Now that you've looked at the commands Works' word processor offers, let's explore a few of the advantages of using Works for word processing.

ADVANTAGES OF ENTERING AND EDITING TEXT WITH THE WORKS WORD PROCESSOR

Works' word processor has a number of advantages over other word-processing applications for the Mac. Let's first look at what it can do for you when you're creating and editing text.

Works is fast

When you create a document with Microsoft Word or later versions of MacWrite, while you're working on it, most of the document is stored on disk, rather than in your Mac's memory. This feature is called virtual memory. Because of virtual memory, your document can be as large as the amount of available disk space will allow, which is usually more than the amount of available memory space. But you have to trade operating speed for the ability to create larger documents—when you scroll through a document with MacWrite or Word, you often have to wait while the program gets the next portion of the document from the disk. Each portion of a file must be read from your disk as you display it, so you have to wait for the disk drive to work as you move through a file.

Works, on the other hand, maintains your entire word-processing document in random-access memory (RAM), so you don't have to wait for new portions of a document to load as you scroll along. But your documents are limited in size to what can be stored in memory. Since any writing project, no matter how extensive, can be logically divided into chapters, sections, or other increments, each of which can be stored in a separate file, it's extremely unlikely that you'll ever come even close to needing all that room in memory for a single document.

You can have several files open at once

Works speeds up text editing by allowing you to have up to ten files open on the desktop at a time. This significantly improves your ability to cut and paste data quickly from one file or application to another via the Clipboard. Suppose you're using MacWrite to work on file A, for example, and you want to insert some text from file B. With MacWrite, you have to:

- ☐ Save file A.
- ☐ Close file A.
- ☐ Open file B.
- ☐ Copy the text from file B to the Clipboard.
- ☐ Close file B.
- ☐ Open file A.
- ☐ Paste the text from the Clipboard to file A.

If you have both files open on the Works desktop, however, you can make things much simpler:

- Activate the file B window by selecting it from the Window menu.
- Copy the text from file B to the Clipboard.
- Activate the file A window by selecting it from the Window menu.
- Paste the text from the Clipboard to file A.

You can undo mistakes

With Works, if you make a mistake or change your mind about a formatting or editing action, you don't need to go through the same steps to restore the original—just choose the Undo command. Suppose you change the font of several paragraphs from Monaco to Geneva and then decide you liked Monaco better. In MacWrite, you would have to:

- Re-select the affected paragraphs.
- Choose the Monaco font from the Font menu.

With Works, you would:

- Choose the Undo option from the Edit menu, or press Command-Z on the keyboard. Your last instruction (changing the font) is automatically canceled.

You can merge database data with a word-processor document

The ability to merge database information into form letters is important to most business users. Yet many Mac word processors either lack this feature or make it unnecessarily complicated. Works has a fast, simple method of merging data. The following steps are general procedures. If you want to practice the steps here, use the Addresses database on the Works Startup disk.

- Open your form letter file and the database file from which you want to merge information.

- Make your form letter the active window by choosing its file name from the Window menu.
- Move the insertion point to the place where you want the merged information to appear.
- Choose the Prepare To Merge... command from the Edit menu, or press Command-M from the keyboard.
- In the Prepare To Merge dialog box, select the database file containing the information you want merged. (If you have only one database file open, that file is automatically selected.)
- Select the specific field in that file from which you want to take your merged data.
- Click the Merge button at the bottom of the Prepare To Merge dialog box. The merge box will appear at the insertion point in your word-processing document.
- Repeat the previous five steps for each additional field you want to merge.

Once you have specified merged data and the merge boxes appear in your word-processing document, you can move, delete, or copy merge boxes just as you would ordinary text.

Each time you use the Prepare To Merge... command, you can select fields from up to nine database files, assuming they are all on the desktop. (Whether or not you can actually have nine database files on the desktop at once depends on how large the files are and how much memory you have available. You can always find out how much memory you have available by selecting the About MS-Works... command from the Apple menu.) Since one database file can contain as many as 60 fields, there really are no practical limits on how many data fields you can merge in a word-processor document.

Once you've selected fields for merging and inserted them into a document, you can use the Show Field Data command on the Edit menu to see what the actual data will look like in the document before you print it:

- Make sure your form letter is the active window.
- Choose the Show Field Data command from the Edit menu. The data from the first or currently selected record in your

merge database file will appear inside the merge boxes in your form letter, replacing the file and field names.

You can convert files from other programs

Most other Mac word-processing programs work only with MacWrite and standard text files. Works can also make use of Microsoft Word files. In fact, you can load a Word file into Works and convert it to the Works format faster than you can load a Word file into Word.

Along with these major features are many minor ones that enhance your ability to edit text with Works. By moving the pointer to the left margin of a document and clicking, for example, you can select one line of text. You can delete a file from disk by selecting an option from the File menu, instead of having to return to the Finder. We'll explore these and other editing shortcuts later in this chapter and in Chapter 3.

ADVANTAGES OF FORMATTING WITH THE WORKS WORD PROCESSOR

Most developers of word-processing programs have made excellent use of the formatting power and ease of use offered by the Mac's interface, but Works adds some touches of its own.

You can draw

Every Macintosh word processor lets you copy MacPaint drawings or other graphics into documents, but Works lets you draw directly inside the documents themselves. As mentioned earlier in this chapter, you can use Works' Draw... command to make lines and boxes directly on top of or around text. The Draw... command is also handy for drawing simple diagrams, for designing business forms or flow charts, for editing someone else's work and pointing out mistakes, or for embellishing a report by putting a box around the title. In Chapter 3, we'll use the Draw... command to make an organizational chart and a simple floor plan.

You can work with wide documents

Works accommodates documents up to 15 inches or 256 characters wide. (If you're using a small font size, you may reach the 256-character limit before you've hit the 15-inch width limit, which is why this is an either/or situation.) You can create charts much wider than with other word processors, and of course, you can print your extra-wide creations sideways on standard paper by selecting the Wide orientation option with the Page Setup command. To make a document accept wider lines:

- ☐ Point to the left-pointing triangle at the right side of the ruler at the top of the screen.
- ☐ Drag the triangle to the new line-width mark you want (drag to the 10-inch mark for 10-inch lines of text, for example).

The line-width setting affects only the current line or the currently selected portion of the document. To make the lines wider in one paragraph, for example, you must select that paragraph before dragging the triangle. To widen the lines throughout an entire document, select the whole document with the Select All command from the Edit menu first.

Once you've widened a document's lines beyond 8½ inches, they will no longer fit on standard-width paper. To print a document sideways (so you can accommodate lines up to 11 inches wide):

- ☐ Choose the Page Setup command from the File menu.
- ☐ Click the Wide icon under the Orientation selections.

You can copy formats

Other word-processing programs allow you to copy formats by copying the ruler that determines the margins, indents, and line spacing. (If you change formats frequently in MacWrite, all those rulers can clutter up your document considerably.) But Works' Copy Format command lets you copy formats easily, and without having to insert a new ruler in your document. To copy a format in Works:

- ☐ Move the insertion point to any line that contains the format you want to copy.

☐ Choose the Copy Format command from the Format menu.

☐ Move the insertion point to where you want the copied format to appear.

☐ Choose the Paste Format command from the Format menu.

WHAT THE WORD PROCESSOR WON'T DO AND WHAT TO DO ABOUT IT

The Works word processor offers many advantages over other such products for the Mac, but it also has a few deficiencies. Specific deficiencies, such as the ones described below, will probably become apparent as you work and gain experience with the word processor. But if you're aware of them in advance, you can plan some strategies to work around them.

There's no true file chaining

Long writing projects (such as reports or books) will often consist of more than one file, and when you're finished you'll want to print out all the files to assemble the whole project. But Works doesn't link any information in separate files. If you're printing files A and B, for example, the header, footer, or page numbering you specify for file A won't carry over into file B. If file A's page numbering ends at 25, file B's page numbering won't automatically begin at 26.

To remedy this problem, you can manually make the appropriate links among data in multiple files using the header or footer option. You specify headers and footers for documents in Works with the Page Setup... command from the File menu. The Page Setup dialog box, which appears when you choose the Page Setup... command, contains entry bars for header and footer text. When you type text into either the header or footer entry bar, that text will be printed at the top or bottom of the document you're working with.

Along with typing header and footer text, you use special header and footer formatting commands to specify how you want text, page numbers, dates, and times to appear in your header or footer. The header and footer commands must precede the text you want them to affect. These are the header and footer formatting commands:

Command	***Formatting action***
&L	Left justify text that follows
&C	Center text that follows
&R	Right justify text that follows
&P	Print the page number in the header
&D	Print the current data in the header
&T	Print the current time in the header
&F	Print the name of the document in the header
&B	Print the text that follows in boldface
&I	Print the text that follows in italics
&&	Print an ampersand (&) in the header

You can combine as many of these formatting commands in a header or footer as you like (as long as it contains no more than 99 characters, Works' limit). If you wanted to center a header and include the current date and the page number, for example, you might type:

&CThis Is The Header - &D - Page &P

With this header information entered, the header text, This Is The Header, would be centered (because the &C command precedes it), and the date (the &D command) and page number (the &Pcommand) would follow between dashes. When printed in the document, this header would look like this:

This Is The Header - [Current Date] - Page [Page Number]

When dealing with the problem of two different files that you want to have consecutive page numbers, you can use &P in a header to print page numbers, then use the Set Page #... command from the word processor's Format menu, like this:

- ☐ Make sure the header in file B is exactly the same as the header in file A.
- ☐ Activate the file A window and move the cursor to the end of the file.
- ☐ Check the page number by looking in the vertical scroll box to the right of the window. Alternatively, you can choose the

Go To Page #... command from the Search menu, or press Command-G from the keyboard to see the current page number displayed in the window of the Go To Page # dialog box.

- ☐ Activate the file B window.
- ☐ Choose the Set Page #... command from the Format menu, and enter the page number that follows the last page number of file A.

Thus, for example, if file A's page numbers end at 25, you can set file B's page numbers so they begin at 26. When the two documents are printed, the page numbers will be continuous.

You can't split the viewing window

High-powered word processors such as Microsoft Word let you divide the viewing window into two parts, each of which can be scrolled independently. This lets you view two different parts of a long file in the same window at once. Works provides this feature in the spreadsheet and database, but not, unfortunately, in the word processor. You can create the same effect, however, by making two copies of a document and displaying them in separate windows:

- ☐ Open the document you want to work with.
- ☐ Choose the Select All command from the Edit menu.
- ☐ Choose Copy from the Edit menu to copy the document to the Clipboard.
- ☐ Choose New from the File menu to open a new document.
- ☐ Choose Paste from the Edit menu to paste the copied document from the Clipboard into the new document.
- ☐ Resize the original document and new document windows so each occupies half of the screen.
- ☐ Move one of the windows so the two windows appear on top of each other.

With these two files showing in half-screen windows, you can easily activate one file or the other by clicking on its window, and you can then scroll each window independently to view different parts of the file.

Page numbering must begin on the first or second page

When you number a document using the &P command in a header or footer, page numbering usually begins on the first printed page of the document. (See the Works Reference Manual for more information about &P and other header options.) If you want page numbering to begin on the second page of a document:

☐ Choose the Title Page command from the Format Menu.

This will cancel printing of the page number (and any other header or footer information) on the first page, and the second page will be numbered 2 (unless you set a different starting page number).

You may encounter situations, however, in which you don't want to put numbers or headers on the first two or three pages of a document. For example, if your report has a cover sheet with a title, a copyright page, and a table of contents page, you might not want headers or footers and page numbering to begin until the second page of the body of the document, which might be the fifth sheet of paper from the front cover. The way to achieve this with the Works word processor is to set up and print two separate files, one containing the cover sheet, copyright page, and table of contents without headers or footers, and the other containing the actual text with page numbers beginning where you want them to.

Headers or footers can be only one line

With MacWrite and Word, you can create headers or footers several lines long. But with Works, you're limited to one line of header or footer text. The only alternative is to use both a header and a footer, placing some of your running title information in each line.

Headers and footers always print in the same place

In Works, you can't adjust the vertical position of headers and footers—they always appear half an inch below the top edge or above the bottom edge of a page, and they are always followed (or preceded) by your document's text on the next or previous line. If you want to create more space between a header and your text, for example, you must manually insert blank space between the top of the page and your text:

- Move the insertion point to the beginning of the first line of text on each page (the line just below each page break).
- Press the Return key to insert a blank line between the first text line and the page break. (Press Return more than once to add extra blank lines.) The blank lines will appear between the header and the text.

If you want to put blank lines between a footer and your text, move the insertion point to the end of the last printed line at the bottom of the page (the last line before a page break), and press Return.

BASIC WORD-PROCESSOR TIPS

It's not too hard to learn to use the basic features of the Works word processor, but there are a number of techniques that will help you work more quickly and efficiently. Some of the methods apply to all the Works applications (and to most other Macintosh programs, as well), and others are specific to the word processor.

Enter and edit text first, format last

A cardinal rule of working with any word-processing or spreadsheet program is: Wait until you've finished creating your document before you format it. Works has a lot of powerful formatting options you can use to dress up your documents, but most of them require you to move one of your hands from the keyboard to the mouse, pull down a menu, select an option, and sometimes specify a value. It's very disruptive trying to do all of that while you're in the middle of typing or editing text. You can get so distracted by format options that you lose the flow of the text. This is especially important when you're first entering text and you're trying to put words in a logical order, but it's also true when you're reading over text you've already entered. It's impossible to judge the flow of a letter if you're constantly interrupting that flow by fiddling with the Format, Font, and Style menus.

Along with disrupting your creative mood, formatting a document before you're satisfied with its contents can also be a plain old waste of time. You may not be able to judge how you want a document to look until you know exactly which words it will contain. This is especially true with documents that have complex formats, such as business forms, flyers, or lengthy reports. Nine times out of ten, you'll end up adjusting the format of a document just before you print it, so why not wait and make all your formatting choices then?

Another argument for the "Edit first, format later" method is that it lets you work faster. It's fine to want a document to be double-spaced, but if you apply double spacing when you're still editing the text, you'll have to scroll twice as many times to see the same amount of text. For the same reason, if you plan to include drawings in your document, it's best to wait until you've finished typing before you add them. Drawings take up lots of space on the screen and in your Mac's memory, and make scrolling that much slower.

Use the keyboard as much as possible

Using the keyboard, rather than the mouse, is a matter of efficiency. Being able to point to commands with the mouse is convenient when you're just learning, but word processing is primarily a matter of typing at the keyboard. The less your hands leave the keyboard, the more efficient your word processing will be. Apple added a set of cursor-movement keys to the Mac Plus for exactly this reason. So, if you have a Mac Plus, you can use the cursor keys to move through a document and to select small amounts of text.

Whether you have a Mac Plus or an older Mac, when you're moving over a lot of text (say from one end of the document to the other), you can use the Go To Page #... command by pressing Command-G on the keyboard and then entering the number of the page where you want to go.

Naturally, there are some editing and formatting tasks that are faster with the mouse, such as selecting odd amounts of text, but if you set yourself the goal of sticking to the keyboard as much as possible, you'll find your data-entry and editing speed improving dramatically.

Along with selecting text and moving around in a document, the keyboard can be used to issue 19 different word-processor commands. These commands are listed in the table in Figure 2-2 on the following page. For help in remembering them, you might want to make a copy of the list and tape it to the front of your Mac for quick reference.

Action	*Command*	*Menu*	*Keyboard equivalent*
Open a file	Open...	File	Command-O
Save a file	Save	File	Command-S
Print a file	Print...	File	Command-P
Quit Works	Quit	File	Command-Q
Undo a command	Undo	Edit	Command-Z
Cut text	Cut	Edit	Command-X
Copy text	Copy	Edit	Command-C
Paste text	Paste	Edit	Command-V
Prepare document for Print Merge	Prepare to Merge...	Edit	Command-M
Change window size	Full Window/ Small Window	Window	Command-W
Find text	Find...	Search	Command-F
Replace text	Replace...	Search	Command-R
Go to a page	Go To Page #...	Search	Command-G
Copy a format	Copy Format	Format	Command-K
Paste a format	Paste Format	Format	Command-Y
Normal text style	Normal Text	Style	Command-N
Boldface text	Bold	Style	Command-B
Italic text	Italic	Style	Command-I
Underlined text	Underline	Style	Command-U

Figure 2-2. *Works offers keyboard equivalents for 18 word-processor commands.*

As you'll notice, most of these commands are mnemonic—that is, the letter key assignment helps you remember the command that the key combination carries out. To help yourself remember the letter key for the Cut and Paste commands, think of cutting as crossing out, or X-ing, text, and think of pasting as inserting text, which typographers and proofreaders specify by a caret (^) symbol.

It isn't hard to remember these commands, and once you begin using them regularly, you'll get things done much more quickly.

Store custom formats for common documents

The word processor uses certain default formats for every new document, as indicated in the specifications section at the end of this chapter. These defaults are fine if you always use standard paper and want 1-inch margins all around your documents, but they're not so fine if you don't. If you want settings other than these defaults, you can either change them every time you format a new document, or you can create a blank document with the custom formats you prefer and then store that document as a template for your future work.

Suppose, for example, that you normally work with U.S. legal-size paper (8½ by 14 inches), and want a 2-inch bottom margin. To store and reuse this custom format:

- ☐ Open a new document.
- ☐ Choose the Page Setup... command from the File menu.
- ☐ Change the bottom margin setting from 1 inch to 2 inches.
- ☐ Change the Paper option to US Legal.
- ☐ Save these changes by clicking the OK box or pressing the Return key.
- ☐ Choose the Save As... command from the File menu, and save the document with a name, such as Format, that helps you remember this file contains your formatting preferences.

This blank file containing the format options you want will now be available on disk whenever you want to begin a new file. When you want to start a new file:

- ☐ Open the document called Format.
- ☐ Enter your text.
- ☐ When you're ready to save your work, use the Save As... option on the File menu and save the document with a name other than Format.

This way, the original, blank Format document remains unchanged on disk, and the custom-formatted document with your new work in it will be saved with a different name.

Recycle text when possible

Just as you can make a dummy document containing custom formats, you can also save sections of actual text you use repeatedly. If you're a lawyer, for example, you might enter a number of boilerplate legal paragraphs into the file Boilerplate, and then copy the relevant paragraphs as needed into new documents. You may have to make some minor changes in the boilerplate paragraphs to suit each specific document, but that will be much faster than retyping entire paragraphs from scratch each time.

If you're a salesperson, you could save your monthly sales report and then recycle parts of it each successive month. You would simply load the old report, make the changes to update it, and then save the changed document under a different name with the Save As... command. This would leave your original report intact and store a copy of the new one as well.

The ability to store and recycle text is probably the major advantage of using a word processor over using a typewriter, and it can save you hours of extra work. The two examples just mentioned are only the beginning. You could recycle invitations, letters, babysitting notes, invoices, progress reports—anything you have to write more than once that contains roughly the same text as something you did before.

Use windows to work with more than one file

For all but the shortest word-processing projects, chances are that you maintain background information and the actual document in different files. If you're writing an article, for example, you might have some notes in one file and the text of the article in another file. Because Works lets you have up to ten files open on the desktop at once, you can easily load all the files you need for a project and then switch among them quickly. For example, if you're preparing a grant request with the word processor, you might have a spreadsheet containing the projected expenses for the project in another window on the desktop so that you can easily copy some figures from the spreadsheet into the word-processor document. Multiple windows let you keep information stored logically in separate files, and yet refer to different files quickly when you need to pull information together. We'll look at some specific examples of multiple-window data transfer in Chapter 9.

WORD-PROCESSOR SPECIFICATIONS

Here are some specifications you may want to refer to as you use the word processor.

Maximum file size: Approximately 180 pages (512K) or 540 pages (1024K)

Maximum document width: 20 inches or 256 characters, whichever comes first

Maximum paper height: 300 inches (with the Custom Size Paper option in the Page Setup dialog box)

Maximum paper width: 15 inches

Minimum paper height: 1 inch

Minimum paper width: 1 inch

Default paper size: US Letter (8½ by 11 inches)

Default top, bottom, left, and right margins: 1 inch

Default line length: 6½ inches

Default tab settings: Every ½ inch

Default font: 10-point Boston

Maximum length of search/replace strings: 80 characters

Maximum length of headers or footers: 99 characters

Range of numbered pages in a document: 1–99,999

Maximum number of merged fields from a database: Unlimited (by merging from more than one file)

C H A P T E R

3

Word-processing Projects

In this chapter, we'll use the Works word processor to help Al Chroma, the owner of Al's Videorama, the video rental store of the future, with some word-processing projects in his business and personal life. Al, a retired film projectionist, wants to apply state-of-the-art retailing techniques to his new business enterprise, so he purchased a Mac Plus, an ImageWriter II, MacPaint, and Microsoft Works from his local Apple dealer. We'll help Al create a letterhead for the store's stationery, a personal letter to a relative, a sales flyer, a video club membership card, an organizational chart, and a form letter.

A LETTERHEAD

Al realizes that stationery is a high priority for a new business. So, although he could have opted for a drab, ordinary-looking letterhead available from a catalog at an instant print shop, he wants to design his own letterhead to reflect Videorama's unique identity. We can help him by creating a custom logo with MacPaint, and then copying it into the Works word processor to use as a template for future letters.

Creating a logo

We'll begin by using MacPaint to create the logo shown in Figure 3-1. This book isn't about MacPaint, so the directions that follow are somewhat general; for complete instructions about MacPaint, you may want to pick up *Inside MacPaint* (Microsoft Press, 1985) by Jeffrey S. Young.

We use MacPaint to enter the typewritten parts of the logo, as well as the drawing, because MacPaint features a wider selection of fonts and font sizes (up to 72-point) than Works. The font in Figure 3-1 is 48-point Athens, for example. And because a type font may distort slightly when made larger on a Mac, especially when it is enhanced

Figure 3-1. *You can design custom logos with MacPaint, and then transfer them into Works' word-processor documents.*

with italics, shadowing, or other styles, we can use MacPaint's FatBits option to clean up the letters a little bit. Once the logo is finished, we save the file, copy the logo to the Clipboard, and then quit MacPaint. We then load Microsoft Works and get ready to make a letterhead.

- ☐ Create a logo, such as the one shown in Figure 3-1, in MacPaint, save the file, copy the logo to the Clipboard, and then quit MacPaint.
- ☐ Choose the Eject command from the File menu in the Finder to eject the MacPaint disk.
- ☐ Insert the Works program disk.
- ☐ Open a new word-processor document by choosing the New... command from the File menu, and then double-clicking on the Word Processor icon. A new, blank document will appear on the screen, and the insertion point will be blinking at the top of the page.

□ Choose Paste from the Edit menu. The logo we copied from MacPaint to the Clipboard will appear at the insertion point position. The letterhead now looks as follows:

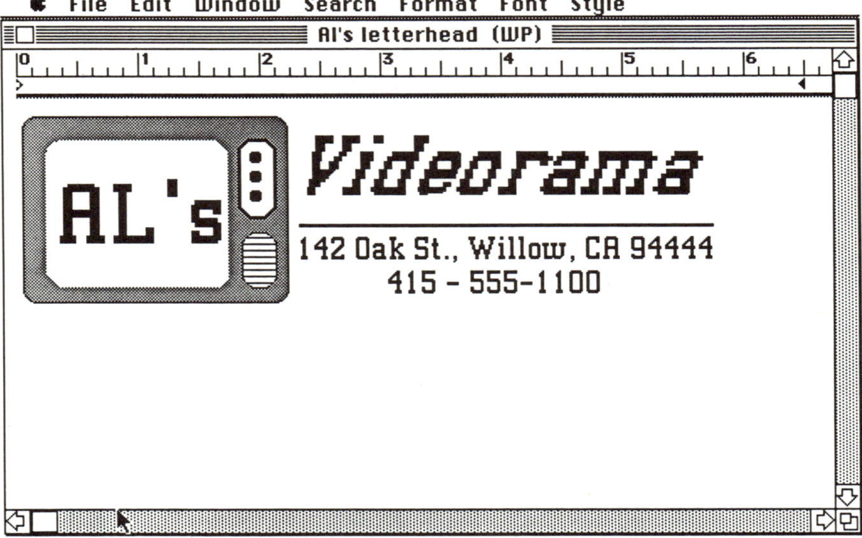

Positioning the logo

The problem now is that the logo is flush against the left margin, and we'd like it centered in the middle. We'll have to make a couple of changes. The logo is 6 inches wide. To roughly center it on a standard, 8½-inch wide page, we'll have to move it 1 inch to the right. First, we have to widen the line length from 6½ inches (the default) to 8 inches. Even though our logo is only 6 inches wide, we have to widen the line because we need to center the logo under the 1-inch and 7-inch marks on the ruler. With the right indent marker at 6½ inches, we can't put anything on this page to the right of the 6½-inch mark on the ruler. After increasing the line length, we'll move the logo so that it's centered on the page.

□ Point to the right indent marker (the left-pointing triangle located below the 6½-inch mark on the ruler).

- Drag the indent marker to the 8-inch mark on the ruler. (The document will scroll to the right as you move the triangle past the right edge of the window.) This sets a new line length of 8 inches for the document.

Now that we've widened the line, we can move the logo. When you want to move a picture in a Works word-processor document, you must first select it.

- Click on the logo to move the insertion point to the left margin next to the logo.
- Choose the Select Picture command from the Edit menu. (This command is available only when the current document contains a picture.) The logo darkens and its edges flash to indicate that it's selected.
- Move the pointer to the center of the logo. When you move the pointer on top of the selected picture, it changes from a blinking line to a hand.
- Hold down the mouse button, and drag the pointer to the right. The logo moves to the right. (You can move a selected picture anywhere on a page by dragging it this way.)
- Move the logo to the middle of the page by aligning its left edge with the 1-inch mark on the ruler, and then release the mouse button.

At this point, the logo is centered on the page. We could embellish it further by using the Draw... command on the Edit menu (perhaps by drawing a line under the entire logo, or putting a box around it), but we'll leave it as is for now. To de-select the logo, point to the blank area below it and click the mouse button.

The logo looks fine on the screen, but we must make sure that it prints properly on paper. To do this, we have to check the page setup.

☐ Choose the Page Setup… command from the File menu. The Page Setup dialog box appears.

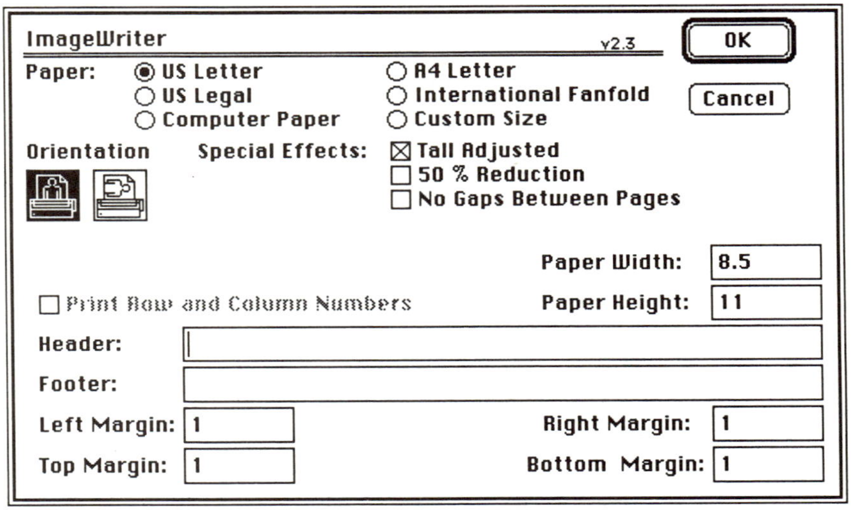

ImageWriter v2.3 OK
Paper: ◉ US Letter ○ A4 Letter
○ US Legal ○ International Fanfold Cancel
○ Computer Paper ○ Custom Size
Orientation Special Effects: ☒ Tall Adjusted
☐ 50 % Reduction
☐ No Gaps Between Pages
Paper Width: 8.5
☐ Print Row and Column Numbers Paper Height: 11
Header:
Footer:
Left Margin: 1 Right Margin: 1
Top Margin: 1 Bottom Margin: 1

☐ Look at the page setup options, to make sure they will accommodate the position of the logo.

Remember, we changed the line-width setting for the logo portion of the letterhead document to 8 inches. We are printing on standard-width paper (8½ inches wide), so our lines will fit on the page. But the left and right margins are set for 1 inch each, so there are only 6½ inches of printing width available on the page. Although we've set the line width in the document for 8 inches, the logo itself is just under 6 inches wide, so it should fit within the page's current margins when we print it. We don't have to make any changes to the Page Setup dialog box, so we can click the Cancel button to return to our document.

Saving the logo as a letterhead

We'll save the finished logo to disk as Al's letterhead.

☐ Select the Save command from the File menu. Because this is a new file that doesn't yet have a name, a dialog box appears.

☐ Type the new file name, *Al's letterhead*, into the space in the dialog box.

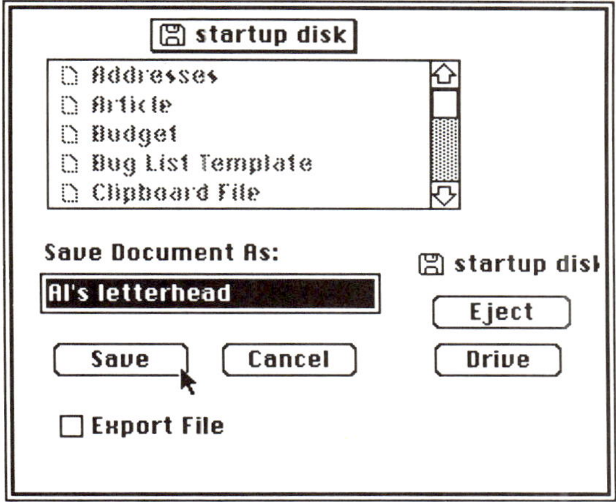

- ☐ Check the drive indicator to make sure the file will be saved to the proper disk. If you want to save the file to a different disk, click the Drive button to change drives, or click the Eject button and insert a different disk.
- ☐ Click the Save button to save the file to the current disk.

New files don't have names until you save them. If you use the Save command with a file that has already been named, Works will save the file to the current disk automatically, and the most recent version will replace the previous version. If you want to determine which drive is the current one and have Works warn you if you're about to overwrite an existing file, use the Save As... command. Save As... produces the dialog box we saw when we used Save, letting you type a different name for your file or change drives before saving.

When the letterhead is complete, Al will print out one copy to take to the instant print shop for reproduction in a different color of ink on deluxe paper and envelopes. But he'll keep this file on disk so that whenever he wants to write a quick memo, he can load the letterhead file instead of starting with a new file.

A PERSONAL LETTER

The next day, Al wants to dash off a note to his cousin Lou, explaining about the new store.

Entering the text of the letter

To help him do this, we first have to load the file called Al's letterhead.

- ☐ With Works' word processor active, choose the Open... command from the File menu.
- ☐ Works displays a list of all Works files available on the current disk drive. If the letterhead file is on a different disk drive, either click the Eject button and insert the correct disk or click the Drive button to change drives.
- ☐ Double-click on the name *Al's letterhead.* The file will open.
- ☐ Move the insertion point to a line or two below the logo.
- ☐ Enter the text of the letter shown in Figure 3-2.

February 24, 1986

Lou Buscaglia
4404 Provimi Ct.
Antioch, CA 99999

Dear Lou:

Well, Al's Videorama is now a reality. The store is just off Highway 101 in Willow. Oak street has good foot traffic, and there's plenty of free parking in the shopping center where the Videorama is located, so I'm looking to do a good business.

You should see the place: I got this great sign made up by Leo the Brush, and Cousin Lucille's brother-in-law Bernie threw in a bunch of orange indoor-outdoor carpeting for the floor. My old pal Willard Birch helped me build some shelves and a counter and a workbench for the back room--that's where we do the VCR servicing and check-outs. Here's a layout of the store:

Figure 3-2. *The text of a letter to Al's cousin Lou.*

Drawing a floor plan

After describing the Videorama and inviting Cousin Lou to see it, Al wants to draw a simple store layout. This is a perfect time to use the Draw... command.

☐ Choose the Draw... command from the Edit menu. A dialog box will appear, offering several drawing shapes from which to choose.

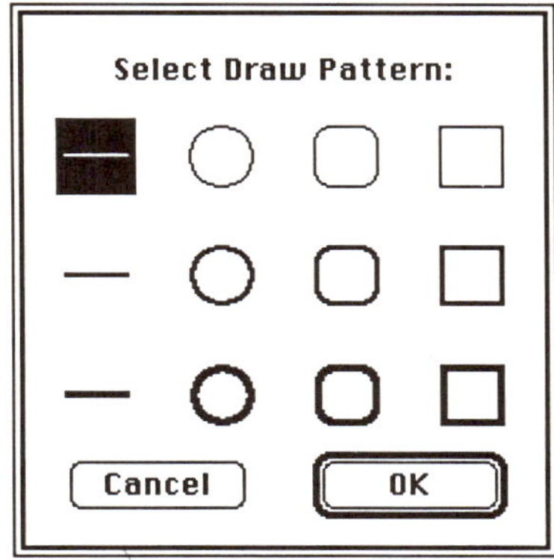

☐ Select a drawing shape (a medium square, in this case) by clicking on the correct shape and then clicking the OK button. The dialog box vanishes, and the pointer changes to a cross in the document window.

We want to draw a rectangle in the middle of the document to represent the outer walls of the Videorama. To do this:

☐ Move the pointer to the place where you want the upper-left corner of the rectangle to appear (two lines below the bottom of the text, and half an inch from the left margin).

☐ Hold down the mouse button, and drag the pointer down and to the right until the rectangle is about five inches wide and two inches high.

- When the rectangle is the size you want, release the mouse button to fix the rectangle on the screen.

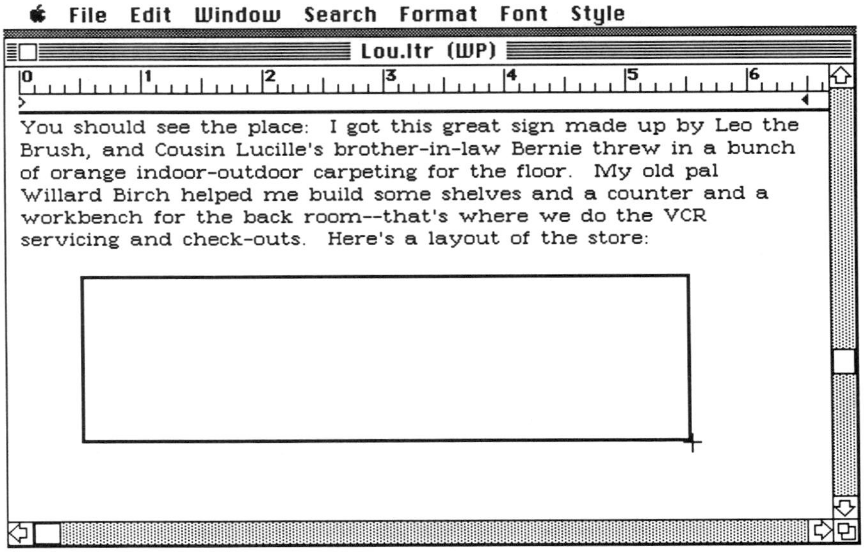

File Edit Window Search Format Font Style

Lou.ltr (WP)

You should see the place: I got this great sign made up by Leo the Brush, and Cousin Lucille's brother-in-law Bernie threw in a bunch of orange indoor-outdoor carpeting for the floor. My old pal Willard Birch helped me build some shelves and a counter and a workbench for the back room--that's where we do the VCR servicing and check-outs. Here's a layout of the store:

Now, we want to draw the inside walls of the Videorama. To do this, we need to change to a line shape:

- Choose the Draw Off command from the Edit menu.
- Choose the Draw... command from the Edit menu again, and click on the thin line option when the dialog box appears.
- Click the OK button to return to the document.
- Position the pointer on the top line where you want the new line to start. To make sure this new line begins on the line representing the outer wall of the store, line up the pointer so the crossbar is on the existing wall.
- Hold down the mouse button, and drag the pointer directly down to the opposite outside wall. Make sure the crossbar of the pointer is on the line representing the existing wall before releasing the mouse button. Notice that lines are drawn straight if you move the mouse in a straight vertical or horizontal line, and that they're drawn at a diagonal angle if you move the mouse diagonally.

□ Release the mouse button to fix the line on the screen. The wall now appears.

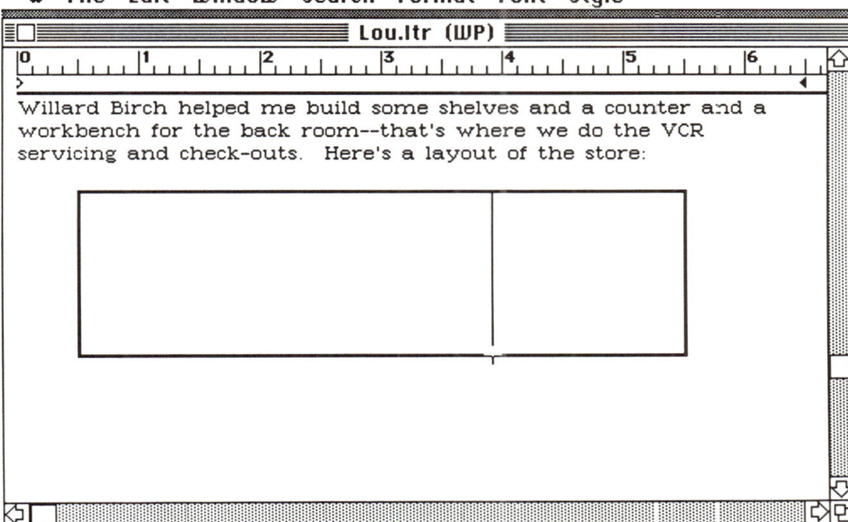

Correcting mistakes in drawings

If you make a mistake when drawing, you can do one of four things to remedy the situation. The easiest remedy is to use the Undo command. If you choose the Undo command from the Edit menu immediately after you draw a line, that line will disappear and your drawing will be "undone." You must use Undo immediately after you draw, however. For example, if you make a drawing, choose the Draw Off command, and then try to undo the drawing by using Undo, Undo will cancel your choosing Draw Off, because that was the last action you took.

If you want to delete a drawing you did some time ago, you can use the Select Picture command to select it, and then choose either the Clear or Cut command from the Edit menu to erase it. Clear simply deletes the drawing; Cut clears it from the screen and copies it to the Clipboard. You can also delete a selected picture by pressing the Delete key when the picture is selected.

The third way to fix a drawing problem is to resize or move the part of the drawing that is the wrong size or in the wrong place. If our line representing the inner wall turned out to be too far toward the right side of the rectangle, for example, we could move it to the left. This is easier than erasing the line and drawing a new one. Since we are using Select Picture in a part of the screen that contains more than one drawing on the line where the insertion point is located (the rectangle is one drawing and the new line is another), the drawings on the line indicated by the insertion point will be selected one at a time, in the order in which they were drawn. In this case, choosing Select Picture once will select the first drawing (the rectangle), and choosing Select Picture a second time will select the second drawing (the line). To select a drawing in an area that doesn't contain another drawing (even though the file contains one), just place the insertion point on the line containing the drawing you want to select before you choose Select Picture. To move a drawing:

- Choose the Select Picture command.
- Choose Select Picture a second time to select the next drawing (the line).
- Once the drawing is selected, move the pointer on top of it. (You can tell the drawing is selected because it is flashing, or there is a flashing border around it, depending on whether the drawing is a single line or a shape.)
- When the pointer changes shape to become a hand, move the misplaced line to where you want it by holding down the mouse button and dragging the line.

The fourth way to fix a mistake in a picture you've drawn is by resizing the entire drawing. For example, if you draw a rectangle and you discover it isn't big enough, you can resize it. If you hold down the mouse button and move the cross-shaped pointer toward the inside of the rectangle, you'll make the rectangle smaller. If you move the pointer toward the outside of the rectangle, you'll make it bigger. To resize a drawing:

- Choose Select Picture to select the drawing you want to change.

- Move the pointer until it is at the edge of the line or shape. The pointer will change to a cross.
- Hold down the mouse button and drag the line to resize the drawing.

You can use this resizing technique to widen or narrow rectangles or lines you've drawn, or you can make circles larger or smaller. However, resizing drawings can distort the original image, as you will see when we make the video club membership card.

We continue drawing lines on the store layout until we've finished.

- Complete the layout so that it looks like the drawing in Figure 3-3, on the next page.

Now, we can put some numbers on the layout and type in a legend below it, so Cousin Lou knows which part of the store is which. The nice thing about the Draw... command in Works is that you can place text on top of drawings you've done. You can't do this with drawings you've copied from another program, however.

- Choose the Draw Off command from the Edit menu to return to text-entry mode.
- Move the insertion point to the area in the layout that represents shelves and type the number *1* and a period.
- Move the insertion point and number the other areas in the layout.
- Move the insertion point to the first line below the drawing.
- Press the Tab key twice to indent the first line of the legend, and then type it.
- Press Tab twice before typing each subsequent item in the legend.

The final drawing and legend are shown in Figure 3-3.

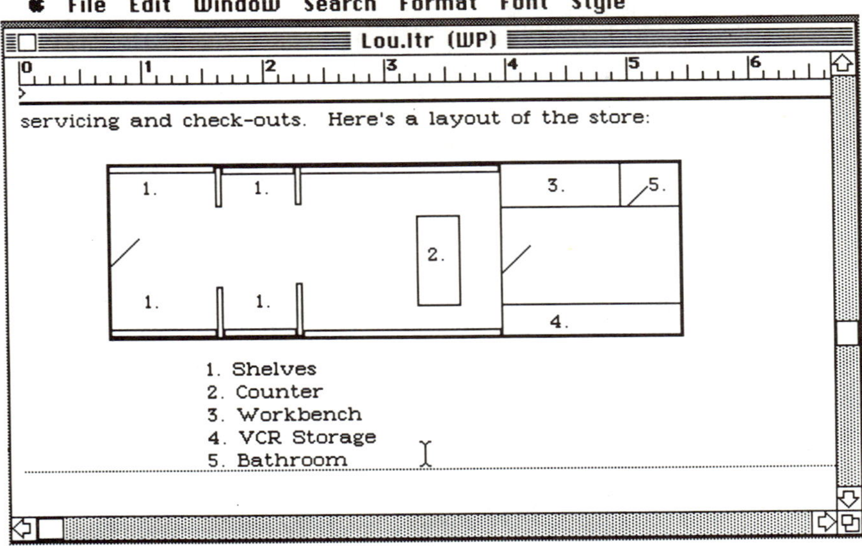

Figure 3-3. *You can type text directly on top of drawings you make with the Draw feature.*

Formatting the letter

Now, it's time to put the finishing touches on the letter with Works' format options. First, let's indent the first line of each paragraph. We want to indent every paragraph in the letter, so we can select the whole document.

- ☐ Choose the Select All command from the Edit menu.
- ☐ Point to the left indent marker (the right-pointing triangle) in the ruler.
- ☐ Hold down the mouse button and drag to the half-inch mark on the ruler. Notice that when you drag, the left indent marker remains in position, and a small square "pulls out" of the marker. This small square is the first-line indent marker—it tells Works to indent the first line of every paragraph that is currently selected.
- ☐ With the first-line indent marker placed under the half-inch mark, release the mouse button. Works reformats the text of

the letter, and now the first line of every paragraph is indented half an inch.

The problem with having every first line indented is that the lines in the drawing's legend are indented as well. We want them to remain where they originally were, so we'll have to reformat these few lines independently.

- ☐ Move the insertion point to the space just before the first character in the first line of the legend.
- ☐ Hold down the mouse button and move the pointer to the space just past the last character in the last line of the legend. All the text in the legend should now be highlighted.
- ☐ Release the mouse button to select this section of text.
- ☐ Point to the first-line indent marker (the small square in the ruler) and drag it back to the 0-inch mark on the ruler. The selected lines automatically move back to their original positions.

Saving and printing the letter

This letter is almost ready to be printed. But first, we need to save it by some name other than Al's letterhead. We want to keep the file named Al's letterhead as the letterhead only.

- ☐ Choose Save As… from the File menu.
- ☐ Type a new file name (such as *Lou Letter*) in the Save Document As box and click Save.

Now we're ready to print. To print the letter:

- ☐ Press Command-P from the keyboard (or choose the Print… command from the File menu).
- ☐ Check the paper size and type settings in the dialog box that appears.
- ☐ Make sure the printer is turned on and the Select light is on.
- ☐ Click the OK button in the Print dialog box to begin printing.

A SALES FLYER

As part of his promotional effort, Al will print handbills announcing the Videorama's grand opening and distribute them in supermarket parking lots. Since we already have that nice letterhead in a disk file, we can use it as the basic form for the flyer, and then build on it. Let's load the letterhead file and then get to work.

☐ Load the letterhead file.

The basic letterhead is fine for written correspondence, but a flyer being handed out to shoppers headed to or from their cars needs to be more of a grabber. We need to jazz up the format a little with some additional graphics and eye-catching copy. Following the practice of "Edit first, format later," let's begin by entering the copy that will go on the flyer. Once we've said all we want to say, we can worry about how to format it for maximum effect.

Entering the text

The main message, of course, is that Al's Videorama is open for business. The grand opening will last for one week, and the flyer can be used for a 50-percent discount on a Videorama Video Club membership. We want to mention the store's hours, and give readers a sense of the selection of video tapes that are available. Once all the text is entered, we can format the text to look better by changing some fonts and type styles. The finished flyer is shown in Figure 3-4. Type in the text you see, but don't worry about positioning the text or specifying different fonts and styles yet. We'll do that next.

Formatting the text

Since we want to draw some boxes around areas of text in this document, we should make the font and style changes first. Changing fonts will make text larger or smaller, and we'll need to see the exact size before knowing how large our outline boxes should be.

The text *Grand Opening,* for example, is 20-point bold shadowed Geneva. The *Bring This Flyer* message is 14-point bold Geneva. Sometimes, making text boldface or changing its font size will change the amount of text that will fit on one line. The line that begins *Hundreds of Titles,* for example, will wrap around and become two lines when we

Bring This Flyer For Discount Membership and Free TV Dustcloth

GRAND OPENING!!!
March 7 - 16 - All Titles $2.00 a day!
Hours: 9:00 a.m. - 12:00 midnight DAILY

Hundreds of Titles - VCR Rentals (VHS & BETA) - Blank Tapes - Video Supplies

Here's a sample of the outstanding video selections at Al's...

Adventure
Six Gun City
Two Guys In Trouble
Blazing Bullets

Comedy
Stale Crackers
Morris Goes Hollywood
The Mother-In-Law

Children's
Rampaging Prams
The Oatmeal Rebellion
Son of Colic

Aerobics
Tip O'Neill's Workout
George Will's Yoga Fun
Wimpy's Roll-a-thon

History
The Depression Tango
Three Nights In Detroit
Oswald The Obnoxious

Musical
Oh, Mexicali!
The Prunes Live
Vince Throat in Concert

Science Fiction
Star Crunchers
Galaxy Zappers
Planet Worms

Classics
Bonzo Gets Long Pants
Those Seattle Days
Forgotten Dreams

Horror
Blood Freeway II
Closet Noises
Subway Vigilante

Figure 3-4. *You can add a lot of visual impact to your text with the Works word processor's format options.*

change the text to 12-point bold Geneva. We could deal with these problems as they arise by selecting just the lines affected and then changing the right indent mark on the ruler to widen the line. But since we don't care about margins on this flyer, we'll take care of the problem once and for all by widening all the flyer's lines to 8 inches:

- ☐ Choose the Select All command from the Edit menu.
- ☐ Drag the right indent marker (the left-pointing triangle on the ruler) to the 8-inch mark. You'll see that the *Hundreds of Titles* message now fits on one line.

Besides changing the fonts and styles, we want to format the text so it appears in the right places. For the *Grand Opening* message, we'll use the Tab key to move the text so it lines up below the logo:

- ☐ Place the insertion point just before the G in *Grand.*
- ☐ Press the Tab key. The text moves over five spaces.
- ☐ Press the Tab key two or three times until the text is lined up under the logo. To fine-tune the alignment, you may have to use the spacebar instead of the Tab key.

The columns listing the video selections are separated by tabs. The columns happen to use the Works default tab settings (every half inch), but we can always insert new tabs by moving the pointer to the appropriate place just below the ruler mark (in the blank bar where the line length and indent markers are), and clicking the mouse button. A tab mark appears. To remove extra tab stops, point to the tab mark, hold down the mouse button, and drag the mark down below the ruler's edge.

Drawing boxes around text

The boxes around the logo and the *Grand Opening* message are done with the word processor's Draw... command. Since the box around the logo is quite large and since the box around the message surrounds text, some techniques beyond the basic ones we have already seen are involved.

- ☐ For the logo, choose the Draw... command and select a square-cornered box shape with the thickest line.

- Position the cross pointer just above the top-left corner of the logo, and then hold down the mouse button as you drag the pointer down and to the right. As you drag, the box appears.

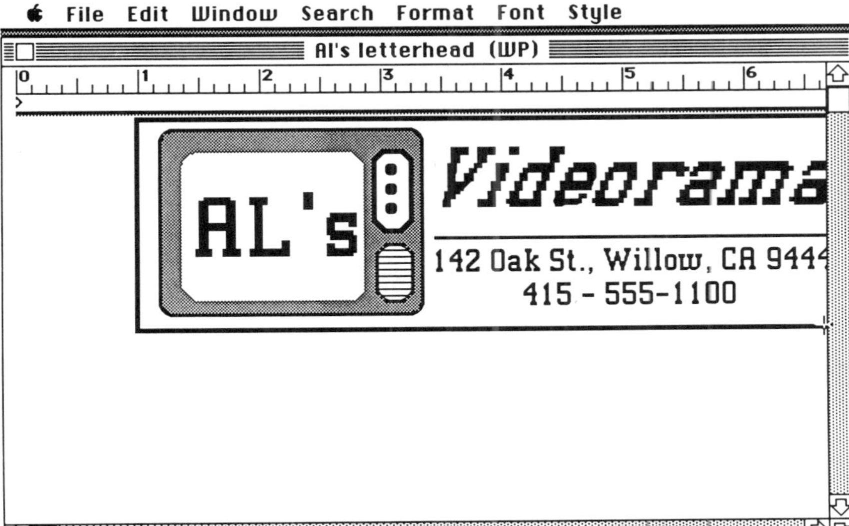

We can't see all of the logo on the screen at this point, so we can't extend the box to surrround the entire logo. We can drag the box only out to the edge of the screen. We need to take a few extra steps to stretch our box so that it surrounds the entire logo:

- Click the right arrow in the bottom scroll bar to shift the page so you can see the right side of the logo and the right side of the box on the screen.
- Choose the Select Picture command from the Edit menu to select the logo.
- Choose Select Picture again to select the box.

With the box highlighted, the pointer changes to a hand, and we can move the box around on the screen.

- Place the pointer exactly on the right edge of the highlighted box as follows:

The pointer changes back to a cross.

- Hold down the mouse button and move the pointer to the right. When the edge of the box is past the edge of the logo, release the mouse button.

So, by aligning the pointer with the edge of the box and then dragging to the right until the outline of the box is past the edge of the logo, we can stretch the box to surround the entire logo.

Remember, when you've made something with Draw... and then you select it with Select Picture, you have two ways of altering the drawing: When the pointer is a hand, you can *move* the drawing around the screen; and when the pointer is a cross, you can *resize* the drawing. Because you can resize a box this way, you don't have to worry whether a box is just the right size when you make it.

The box that surrounds the *Grand Opening* message is easier to do, since all the text appears on the screen at once:

- Choose the Draw... command again, and pick a shape with rounded corners. Click the OK button to return to the chart.

- ☐ Move the cross pointer to the upper-left corner of the text, hold down the mouse button, and then drag the pointer down and to the right to draw a box around the text. If the box isn't aligned evenly around the text, you can either move the box (using the Select Picture command) or move the text by deleting or adding spaces in front of each line.

Checking the page setup and printing

When the boxes and text look the way we want them, we only have to check the page setup before printing the flyer. Remember, we changed the line widths in the document to 8 inches, so we should reset the left and right margins to a quarter-inch each:

- ☐ Choose the Page Setup... command from the File menu.
- ☐ Double-click on the Left Margin box and type *.25*.
- ☐ Double-click on the Right Margin box and type *.25*.
- ☐ Check that the type of paper (US Letter) and orientation (tall) are correct, and then click the OK button.

Now, we're ready to print the flyer using the Print... command from the File menu or by pressing Command-P. We want this flyer to print as nicely as possible so that we can make dozens of photocopies. So before printing, we choose Best from the Quality options in the Print dialog box.

A VIDEO CLUB MEMBERSHIP CARD

The Videorama will have a video club that entitles members to discounts on tape and VCR rentals, so we need a membership card. Fortunately, we can reuse some of the work we've already done.

Creating the card

The membership card will contain some blanks for information about members, but it will use the same logo we created for the letterhead. The only thing we have to do is reduce the size of the logo so it fits on a wallet-sized card.

- ☐ Open the letterhead file by choosing the Open… command from the File menu and then double-clicking on the name of the letterhead file in the list. If the file is on a different disk, click Drive to display the contents of that disk, or click Eject and insert the correct disk.
- ☐ Once the file is on the screen, select the logo by choosing the Select Picture command from the Edit menu.
- ☐ With the logo selected, move the pointer until it's lined up with the right edge of the flashing border around the logo. The pointer becomes a cross.
- ☐ Hold down the mouse button and drag the pointer to the left to resize the logo. By dragging the pointer to the left, the logo becomes narrower. When the logo is 3½ inches wide, release the mouse button.
- ☐ Move the pointer to the bottom edge of the logo, and then drag it toward the top of the page. The picture becomes shorter. Make the logo's height proportionate to its new width.

After the logo is the right size, we can add the labels and blanks for the member data below it. We want blanks for the member name, address, card number, expiration date, and videotape format. All this data should fit on three lines. To make sure we don't create a card that's higher than normal walllet size, we can hold a wallet-sized card against the screen to match (remember, the text and pictures on the screen will print out exactly the same size on paper).

To make labeled blanks for the member information, such as Name and Address, we can use either the underline key in the top row of the keyboard (the shifted position of the dash, which is between the number 0 and the equal sign key), or we can use the Draw… command to draw the lines. The advantage to using the Draw… command is that we can make the lines end evenly at the right of the card. Using the underline key, the lines won't end evenly, because they don't begin in exactly the same position at the left (most Macintosh fonts, including the one we're using, are proportionally spaced—that is, the widths of different characters vary). Try the two methods and see for yourself. The finished card is shown in Figure 3-5.

Figure 3-5. *The video club membership card*

Making copies of the card

Once we have one card looking the way we want it, the only thing left to do is to make some copies of it on the same page. We plan to have a commercial printer produce the cards, so we'll save paper (and printing costs) by having several copies on each sheet of paper, instead of having only one card per page.

To make copies of this card, we have to remember that part of the card contains text (the names for the blanks) and part contains pictures (the logo and the blank lines). We have to copy these portions of the card separately. First, let's copy the logo.

- ☐ Move the insertion point to the left margin next to the logo.
- ☐ Choose the Select Picture command from the Edit menu to select the logo, and then press Command-C (a shortcut for choosing the Copy command from the Edit menu). This copies the logo to the Clipboard. Now, we can paste the logo from the Clipboard to the other places on the page where we want it.
- ☐ Move the insertion point to the bottom of the document (below the bottom data line in the card), and then press the

Return key a couple of times to add a few blank spaces below the first card.

- Press Command-V (a shortcut for choosing Paste from the Edit menu). A copy of the logo appears at the insertion point position.

We don't have to copy the logo each time we paste it—a copy of the logo remains on the Clipboard until we copy something else there or turn off the Macintosh. Instead, we can continue moving the insertion point to new locations and then using the Paste command from the Edit menu (or pressing Command-V). We can't copy the blank lines from the original card at this point, because we have to align them with the text and we haven't moved the text to the new positions yet.

So, let's copy the text. Just as in copying the logo, we can copy the text to the Clipboard only once and then paste it repeatedly. In some cases, the logos we copied might not be quite far enough apart for us to fit all of the text between them. This is no problem. Even though we might not be able to see all the text we've copied (because part of it is covered by a logo), all the text is there. We need only to move the logo or the text a little to make things right. For example, this is how our screen would look if part of the text were obscured by a logo:

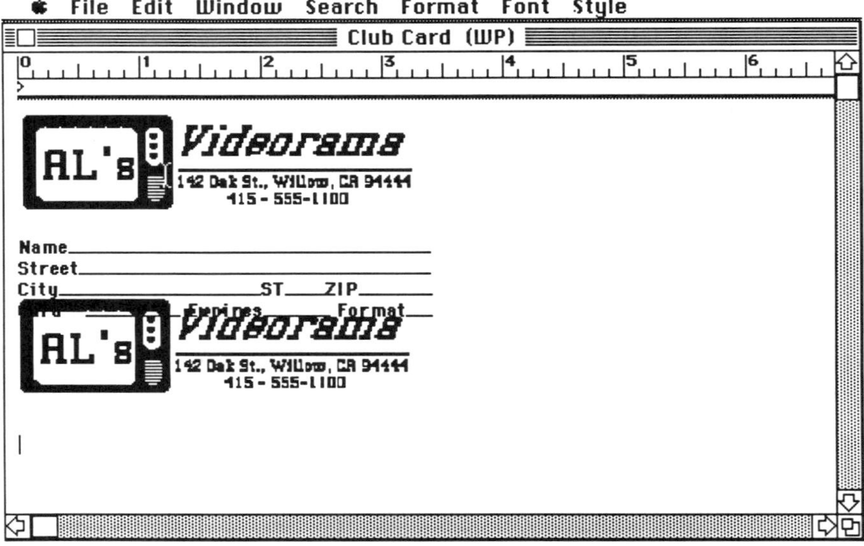

To fix this, we can move the pointer to the space below the upper logo, press Return a couple of times to move the next logo down a little, and then move the text into the new space we've created:

- ☐ Move the pointer to the blank space below the upper logo.
- ☐ Press the Return key three times to create some extra space.
- ☐ Select the text by dragging the pointer over it while holding down the mouse button. (You can't select a picture this way, so you don't have to worry about selecting the logo at the same time.)
- ☐ Cut the text to the Clipboard by pressing Command-X or choosing the Cut command from the Edit menu.
- ☐ Move the pointer to the first blank line below the top logo.
- ☐ Paste the text from the Clipboard by pressing Command-V or choosing the Paste command from the Edit menu.

Now, we need the lines that follow the text. Remember, the lines we drew didn't move when we cut and pasted the text, because the lines are pictures, not text. (Of course, if we had used the underline key to make the blank lines, then the lines would have been copied along with the labels.) To move them, we could use the Select Picture command, copy them, and then paste them into position. But it's probably just as easy to draw new lines after our new text.

An alternate method for creating the card

One problem with shrinking and stretching artwork on the Macintosh is that it sometimes becomes distorted. The letters in the logo shown in Figure 3-5, for example, are a little hard to read. If this happens to you during a project, you might consider an alternative way of creating small versions of artwork you've done: "the 50-percent solution." Instead of shrinking the logo down to size by dragging it, we could have created the video club card in a size twice as large as we really wanted it, and then we could have printed it at a 50-percent reduction.

To print items at half the size they appear on the screen, use the 50% Reduction option in the Special Effects area of the Page Setup dialog box (the box appears when you choose the Page Setup... command from the File menu). With our video club card, for example, we could have used the regular-sized logo in the letterhead file and then typed in some 20-point text and added some blank lines, creating a giant membership card. Printed at a 50-percent reduction, the logo, text, and lines would be about the right size, as shown in Figure 3-6.

If you know in advance that you're going to use a letterhead logo or other large text in a reduced version, you can think about how large the small version has to be, and then plan the large version accordingly. In our letterhead, for example, we made the logo about 6 inches wide, and when we reduced it, we ended up with a logo 3 inches wide. Ideally, we should have had a reduced logo 3½ inches wide. Had we planned for that in advance, our original logo would have been 7 inches wide instead of 6. As it is, we were thinking only about the proper logo size for the letterhead when we created the original logo. Whether you plan or not, however, the 50% Reduction option usually produces text and graphics of better quality than you can get by shrinking a larger image down to size with the Select Picture command. The images aren't distorted, and the printing is usually darker.

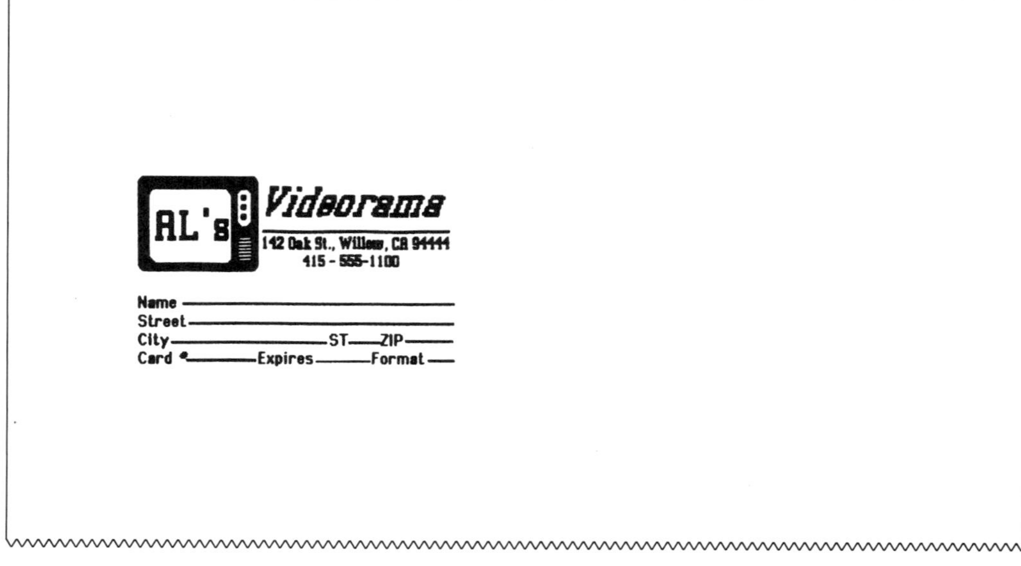

Figure 3-6. *You can usually produce crisper printouts with less distortion by printing big images at a 50-percent reduction.*

AN ORGANIZATIONAL CHART

Once Al has hired his employees, he wants to make an organizational chart showing where everyone falls in the Videorama hierarchy. This is an ideal application for the word processor and its Draw... command. The chart we'll end up with looks like the one in Figure 3-7, on the next page.

Entering employee names and titles

We'll begin by opening a new word-processor document and switching to 14-point bold Geneva type.

- ☐ Choose New... from the File menu and click the Word Processor icon.
- ☐ Choose 14 Point from the Style menu.
- ☐ Choose Bold from the Style menu.

Next, we'll insert two blank lines, and then type a title for the organizational chart.

- ☐ Press Return twice and then type *AL'S VIDEORAMA* as the first line, press Return and type *ORGANIZATIONAL CHART* as the second line.

After the title, we'll switch to 12-point normal Geneva type, and enter the names and titles of the top three management levels.

- ☐ Type in Al's name and title at the top, then the store manager's name and title, and then the two assistant managers' names and titles, as shown in Figure 3-7.

To type the names with the spacing shown in the example, use the spacebar and Tab key to separate the names. In the third row of the chart, for example, type Bud Flamer's name, and then press the Tab key a few times to leave some space between his name and Hanna Borisova's. Repeat this procedure with each name and title on the chart in Figure 3-7.

In the fourth row of the chart, we run into a little trouble: The store has six workers at the clerk level. In the 12-point type we're using, six entries won't fit in one row within our standard 6½-inch line.

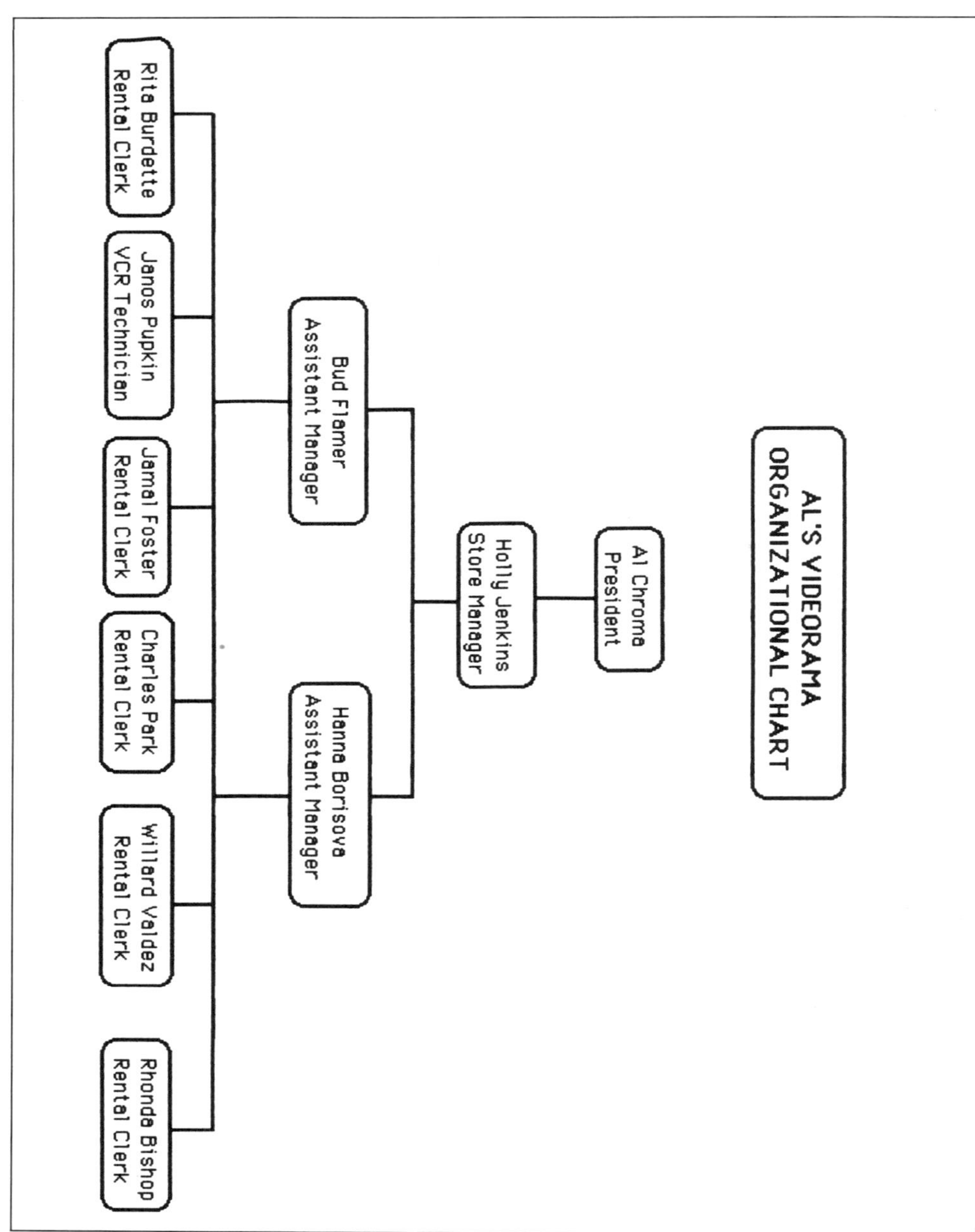

Figure 3-7. *You can create an organizational chart with the Works word processor, and print it sideways so that it fits on an 8½-by-11 page.*

There are two solutions to this problem. We could choose a smaller font size for the text in this row, or we could make the margins wider. Smaller letters would take up less room and would fit within our margins. But we don't want to make the type smaller in this case, so we'll make the page wider.

- ☐ Point to the right indent marker in the ruler (the left-pointing triangle), hold down the mouse button, and drag the right indent mark to the 11-inch mark on the ruler.

Now, our line is 11 inches wide, instead of 6½, and all the names will fit on it nicely (we'll print it so that the long dimension of the paper is the width).

Drawing boxes and lines

Next, we'll use the Draw... command to make boxes around each name and title and to connect the boxes with lines.

- ☐ Choose Draw... from the Edit menu, and the Draw dialog box will appear.
- ☐ Click on the round-cornered box with the medium-width lines.
- ☐ Click the OK button to select this shape. The Draw dialog box disappears and you're returned to the word-processor screen. Because you're using the Draw... command, the pointer is a cross.
- ☐ Position the cross pointer slightly above and to the left of Al's name and title.
- ☐ Hold down the mouse button and drag the cross down and to the right. As you do this, the box appears. When the box is the right size, release the mouse button to fix the box on the screen.
- ☐ Draw boxes around all the other names on the chart.

If for some reason the box isn't large enough, we can choose the Undo command from the Edit menu to make the box disappear. Remember, though, you have to choose Undo immediately after making your drawing. If you've done something else since making the drawing, you have to select the drawing with the Select Picture command and then use either the Clear command or the Backspace key to delete the drawing.

Remember, too, that you move boxes created with Draw... independently of the text inside them. If a box isn't quite centered around some text, move it:

- Move the insertion point to the box you want to move, and then choose Select Picture to select it. Remember, you may have to choose Select Picture more than once if there is more than one picture side by side on the screen.
- Move the pointer on top of the selected picture. The pointer changes to a hand.
- Hold down the mouse button and drag the pointer to reposition the picture.

Once all the boxes are drawn around the names, we need to draw connecting lines. We'll use the medium-width line for the job.

- To change drawing shapes, choose Draw... from the Edit menu again to re-display the Draw dialog box.
- Choose the medium line shape and click the OK button to select it and return to the chart.
- Place the cross pointer on the bottom edge of the box around Al's name, so that the horizontal bar is even with the edge of the box.
- Hold down the mouse button and drag straight down. As long as you hold down the mouse button, you can adjust the length and angle of the line.
- When the horizontal bar in the pointer is on top of the upper edge of the manager's box, release the mouse button to fix the position of the line.

To draw a horizontal connecting line between the assistant managers' boxes:

- Place the cross pointer so the vertical line in it is on top of the right edge of the left-hand assistant manager's box.
- Hold down the mouse button and drag to the right until the vertical line in the cross pointer is directly on top of the left edge of the right-hand assistant manager's box.
- Release the mouse button to fix the line on the screen.

Using these techniques, we create connecting lines between all the boxes, until the chart looks like the one shown in Figure 3-7.

Changing the page setup and printing

We are almost ready to print the chart. The only problem is that our chart is now nearly 11 inches wide, and the paper we're using is only 8½ inches wide. We can resolve this problem by using the Wide orientation option in the Page Setup dialog box:

- Choose the Page Setup... command from the File menu to display the Page Setup dialog box.
- Click the Wide icon in the Orientation options. This tells Works to rotate our text and drawings 90 degrees, so they'll print across the long dimension of our paper, instead of across the short dimension of the paper.
- Double-click on the Left Margin box, and enter the number *0*.
- Repeat the previous step for the Right Margin, Top Margin, and Bottom Margin boxes.
- Click the OK button to save these changes to the Page Setup dialog box and return to the organizational chart.
- To print the chart, select the Print... command from the File menu or press Command-P from the keyboard. Check the Quality option and the number of copies in the Print dialog box to make sure the settings are the ones you want, and then click the OK button to print the chart.

A FORM LETTER

In addition to distributing flyers in parking lots, Al wants to do some direct-mail advertising. So, he has acquired a mailing list from the Couch Potato Society of America (a group of devoted television viewers), and he wants to send each local member a letter announcing a special pre-opening preview at the Videorama. This is a great application for the form-letter capability in the Works word processor.

To create a form letter, Al must make two files: a word-processor file containing the text of his message, and a database file containing the names and addresses of the people to whom he'll send the letter. Let's assume Al has created the database file and saved it with the name Potatoes. For our purposes, we'll use the Addresses sample file on the Works startup disk. (See chapters 6 and 7 for information about making and using database files.)

Entering the text and saving

Now we can begin typing the sales letter shown in Figure 3-8 in the Format document. As we type, we need to leave a blank space wherever some merged data will appear. When the sales letter is done, we'll use the Save As... command from the File menu to save the letter on our data disk with the name Sales Letter:

- ☐ Choose the Save As... command from the File menu.
- ☐ Type the new file name, *Sales Letter*, in the entry line.
- ☐ Click the Save button in the dialog box to save the file with this new name onto the current disk.

Preparing the document for merge printing

The merging of database data takes place when we print the document, but we first have to set up the document to receive merged data.

- ☐ Load the Addresses sample file on the program disk onto the desktop. When you load the file, it becomes the active window. You still want to work with the sales letter file, though.
- ☐ Choose the Sales Letter file from the Window menu to make it the active window.

March 3, 1986

Dear :

You're invited to attend a special, pre-opening preview of Al's Videorama, the video store of the future. The preview is scheduled for Wednesday, March 5, 1986. Al's Videorama is located at 142 Oak Street in nearby Willow, freeway-close to virtually everywhere in the Bay Area, so why not pry yourself loose from that couch and come on down? Beginning Thursday, March 6, we'll be open daily from 9 a.m. to midnight, and we'll feature all the latest video releases as well as popular favorites from every genre. Each month, we'll be featuring a different type of film: Sci-Fi, Foreign, Adventure, Historical, you name it. But during our grand opening extravaganza, anything goes!

See you there...

Al Chroma

Figure 3-8. *You can use Works' word processor to create the text for a form sales letter.*

Each letter will have a name, address, and greeting made up of merged data from the database file. To set up Works so it will merge data, we must indicate where in the letter the data goes, and specify which database fields are to be merged at which locations.

- ☐ Move the insertion point to the first place in the letter (the first line of the address block, below the date) where merged data will be inserted. In this first location, we want to insert the name of the addressee.
- ☐ Choose the Prepare to Merge... command from the Edit menu (or press Command-M from the keyboard). The following dialog box appears:

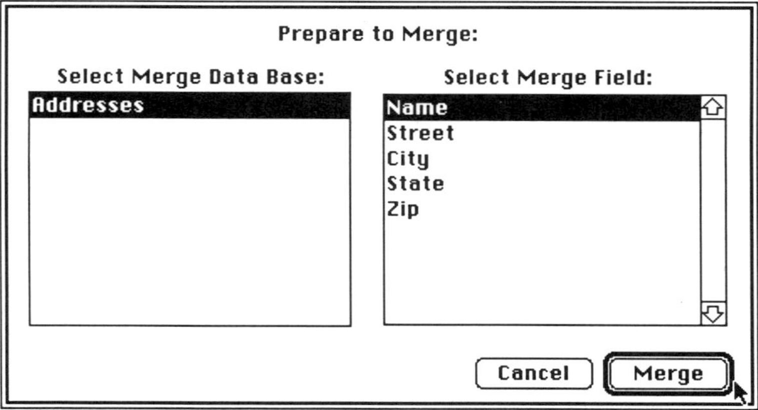

The dialog box shows all the database files currently on the desktop in its left-hand window. Normally, the uppermost file name in the file window is highlighted automatically, and the fields in that file are shown in the right-hand window. The Addresses file is the only database file on the desktop in this case, so it is automatically selected and the data fields it contains are shown in the window at the right. The first field in the database is Name, so it happens to be highlighted.

- ☐ Click the Merge button to inform Works that the Name data should be merged at this point. (Since the Merge button has a double line around it, you can select it by pressing Return instead of clicking on it—on the Mac, any screen button with a double line around it can be selected by pressing Return.)

You can select only one merge field at a time with the Prepare to Merge... command, so once we tell Works to merge the Name field, the Prepare to Merge dialog box disappears, and the field name and file name appear in a box at the insertion point's position in the letter.

- Move the pointer down to the next line in the letter's address block by pressing Return.
- Choose Prepare to Merge... again, and click on the Street field in the dialog box to merge the Street data at the insertion point.

We complete the form letter by merging the City, State, and Zip fields on the third address line, and then merging the Name field after *Dear* in the greeting. The letter is now ready to print, and the screen looks like this:

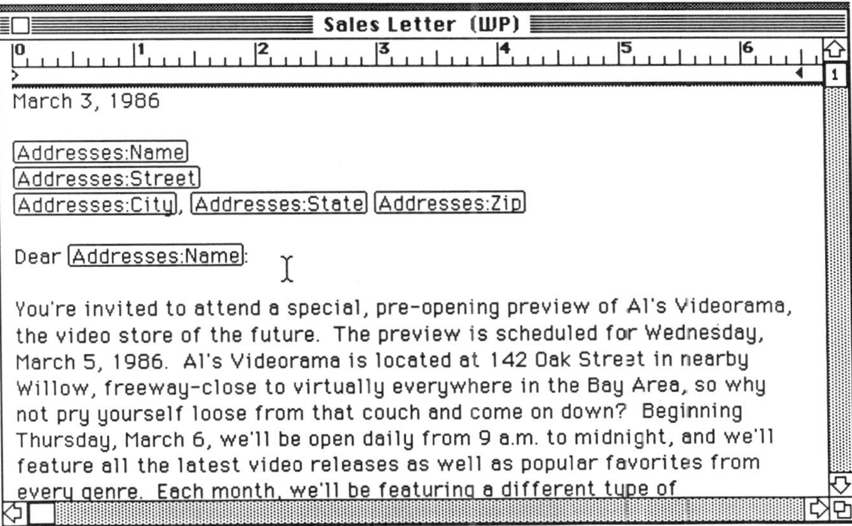

Notice that the name of the field and the name of the database file appear in the box at each merge location. If we want to preview how our data will look, we can choose the Show Field Data command from the Edit menu, and instead of the names of the data fields and file, the letter will show the actual data from the first record in the merged database file.

Printing with Print Merge...

When we're ready to print the letter, we use the Print Merge... command from the File menu, instead of the Print... command. Print Merge... tells Works that merged data will be included in the file, and commands it to get that data from the appropriate database file. Works checks to see that the database from which the merged data will be taken is on the desktop. If the proper database file isn't on the desktop, Works will warn you.

If we were to use Print... (instead of Print Merge...) to print this letter, the letter would be printed with the database file and field data boxes, instead of the actual data, at the insert locations.

Although merge-data boxes create links to a database file on the desktop, they can be edited in the word processor just like other text elements. You can delete them by using the Delete key or by cutting them with the Cut command. You can copy them or paste them with the Copy and Paste commands, and you can move them around by inserting or deleting letter spaces, carriage returns, or tab stops in front of them.

If you're merging the same field into more than one place in a document, as we did with the Name field, it's probably a little faster to copy the data box from one place to another than it is to re-select the same field with the Prepare to Merge... command. But if you do, make sure the location where you're pasting has the same formatting as the location from which you're copying: Although the Prepare to Merge... command assigns the same formatting as surrounding text, the Copy command doesn't.

ADDRESSING ENVELOPES

Al has fifty promotional letters printed and ready to go out to the local Couch Potatoes, and now it's time to address the envelopes. The fastest way to get this done is to print the names and addresses onto peel-off labels, and then stick the labels onto envelopes.

Creating a mailing-label file

To print mailing labels easily with the existing Addresses sample file data, we can create a new word-processor document and merge the data with it. Just as the form letter was a document, mailing labels are also documents. The difference is that they're very small documents—instead of having an 8½-by-11 format, they're only 3 by 1.

Let's begin by opening a new word-processor document and a database file with names and addresses.

☐ Choose New… from the File menu and click on the Word Processor icon.

This document will contain no typed text—only merged data from the database. The first line will be the Name data from the Potatoes file. The second line will be the Street data, and the third will contain City, State, and Zip data. We can insert these merge fields by using Prepare to Merge…, just as we did for the address block in the form letter. But we need to be sure to insert spaces between the City, State, and Zip field marker boxes, so the data won't run together when it is printed.

☐ Choose Prepare to Merge… from the Edit menu, select Addresses from the Select Merge Data Base box, select Name from the Select Merge Field box, and click the Merge button.

☐ Press Return to move to the second line.

☐ Choose Prepare to Merge…, select the Addresses file and the Street field, then click Merge.

☐ Press Return, then use Prepare to Merge… to insert the City, State, and Zip fields, separated by spaces.

Changing the page setup

Once the merge-data boxes are in place, we have to adjust the page format of this document so Works knows that it's printing on small labels. This is done with the Page Setup… command:

☐ Choose the Page Setup… command from the File menu.

☐ Click the Custom Size button in the Paper options at the top of the dialog box. The standard option is US Letter paper (8½ by 11 inches).

☐ Double-click on the Paper Width box, and type *3*.

☐ Double-click on the Paper Height box, and type *1*.

Now that we've changed the paper size, we also have to change the margins. The default margins in the Page Setup dialog box are 1 inch for the top, bottom, left, and right sides of the page. Obviously, we can't have margins like this on our labels, so we need to change the margins to 0 inches all around.

- ☐ Double-click on the Left Margin box, and type *0*.
- ☐ Repeat the previous step for the Right Margin, Top Margin, and Bottom Margin boxes.
- ☐ Click the OK button to save these changes to the Page Setup dialog box for this document.

Printing the labels

Now, we can feed continuous form labels into the ImageWriter (we'll have to adjust the paper tractors to accommodate the narrower paper), and then use the Print Merge... command to print our labels. Be sure to buy one-across label stock for your printer when doing labels with Microsoft Works. You can also find three-across label stock for the ImageWriter, but since you can't set Works up to print three-across labels, you'll be wasting a lot of labels.

Now that you know the basics of using the Works word processor, let's turn to the spreadsheet.

C H A P T E R 4

Using the Spreadsheet

In this chapter, we'll look at the Works spreadsheet—how it works, what makes it special, and how you can use it to work with numbers. Spreadsheets (or worksheets, as they're sometimes called) are very familiar tools to anyone who works regularly with numbers in business. Before we look at the specifics of the Works spreadsheet, we'll begin with a brief explanation of how these number-crunching tools work.

SPREADSHEET BASICS

Paper spreadsheets have been around for decades, but electronic spreadsheets such as the one in Works didn't appear until 1977, when VisiCalc was introduced. Electronic spreadsheets perform the same basic function as paper spreadsheets, but they use the computer's power to make working with numbers much easier.

A spreadsheet is a matrix of numbers in intersecting rows and columns. By presenting the numbers in rows and columns, spreadsheets let you see the relationships between the individual numbers. A common example is a personal expense budget, such as the one in Figure 4-1, which contains several rows, each of which shows different kinds of expenses (food, rent, and so on), and columns, which show how each type of expense varies monthly.

As you can see by the sample spreadsheet in Figure 4-1, the spreadsheet shows the results of mathematical calculations (the expenses for each month are totaled in the bottom row, and the quarter's totals for each expense appear in the right-hand column). But it also shows how each expense contributes to the totals. If you were to use a calculator to add all the expenses for March, for example, you'd end up with just a total, rather than a detailed listing of how each expense contributed to the total.

By showing you the relationship between the numbers and the totals, spreadsheets tell you more about these numbers than you would know if you looked at the totals alone. The budget total in April is

BUDGET

EXPENSE	MARCH	APRIL	MAY	QTR. TOTAL
FOOD	200 00	210 00	205 00	615 00
RENT	500 00	500 00	500 00	1500 00
UTILITIES	35 00	31 00	30 00	96 00
PHONE	25 00	50 00	30 00	105 00
TOTAL	760 00	791 00	765 00	2316 00

Figure 4-1. *The most common type of spreadsheet is a budget.*

higher than in March, for example, and you can see that the higher food and phone costs account for the difference. Knowing this, you know that the food and telephone costs are a good place to cut back if you want to lower your expenses.

Both handwritten and electronic spreadsheets show these relationships between numbers in the same way, but electronic spreadsheets make the calculations much easier. Instead of doing each calculation by hand, you can store formulas in an electronic spreadsheet that make calculations automatically. Also, once you've entered a formula, you can copy it to other places where you want to perform essentially the same calculation, thereby saving yourself the trouble of entering a formula over and over. (In our sample budget, the same basic addition formula is used to sum each month's expenses.)

Although you can write down numbers anywhere on a paper spreadsheet, electronic spreadsheets are divided into specific cells, which are laid out in rows and columns. Each cell is an area where you can store text labels (row or column titles, for example), numbers, or formulas. The Works spreadsheet contains 9,999 rows (which are numbered 1 through 9999) and 256 columns (which are labeled A through Z, then AA through AZ, then BA through BZ, then CA through CZ, and so on through IA through IV), for a total of over 2.5 million cells. This is a far larger matrix of cells than you will probably ever need (most electronic spreadsheets use fewer than 1,000 cells).

As you can see in Figure 4-2, each cell is identified by the intersection of a row and column. The first cell in the top-left corner of a spreadsheet is in column A and row 1, so it is known as cell A1.

While this arrangement takes a little getting used to, it allows the electronic spreadsheet user much more power to build relationships between cells (and thus between the numbers or formulas contained in the cells), as we'll see later in this chapter. But first, let's take a look at Works' spreadsheet menus and commands.

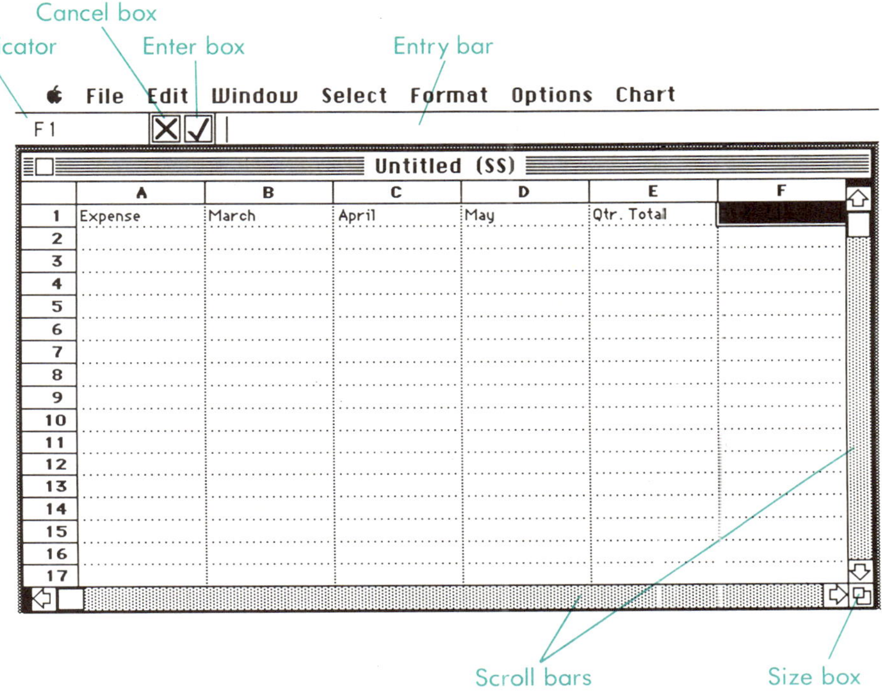

Figure 4-2. *The Works spreadsheet is a matrix of cells surrounded by a cell indicator, an entry bar, an enter box, and a cancel box for displaying the selected cell's contents and entering data; scroll bars for moving around the spreadsheet; and a size box for resizing the window in which a file is displayed.*

A QUICK TOUR OF THE SPREADSHEET MENUS

As mentioned in the tour of the word-processor menus in Chapter 2, the first four menus from the left side of the screen are essentially the same in all the Works applications. However, the Edit menu in the spreadsheet has a number of different commands. Also, some commands that have the same names as in the word processor work differently.

The Edit menu

The Cut, Copy, and Paste commands have some special features in the spreadsheet, although their basic functions are the same in every Works application. You can use the Cut command to remove data from a cell or group of cells and place it on the Clipboard. The Paste command takes whatever is on the Clipboard and places it in the cell or group of cells beginning at the insertion point or selection. Once you cut or copy data to the Clipboard, it stays there until you either cut or copy something else there, or until you quit Works. Because of this, you can paste the same Clipboard data into several different places in succession:

- ☐ Select the data you want to cut by highlighting it with the mouse. (Click on a cell to highlight one cell, or hold down the mouse button and drag the pointer if you want to highlight a group of cells).
- ☐ Choose the Cut or Copy command from the Edit menu.
- ☐ Click on the first cell where you want the data to appear.
- ☐ Choose the Paste command to copy the data from the Clipboard to the new location. The data will be pasted from the Clipboard.
- ☐ Click on the second cell where you want the data to appear, and choose the Paste command again. The data will be pasted from the Clipboard.

When you paste more than one cell's data from the Clipboard, the data is placed in the same order as it was when you cut it. If you cut five cells from a row, for example, and then select one cell as the place to paste the data, the five cells will appear in the same order, beginning at the cell you selected and extending four more cells to the right.

One last thing about the Cut command: When you cut an entire row or column from the spreadsheet, both the data and the row or column itself are removed from the spreadsheet. If you cut row 3 from a spreadsheet, for example, that row will be removed to the Clipboard, and the rows beneath it will move up and will be renumbered.

Remember that when you paste from the Clipboard, you are only pasting a copy of the Clipboard's data. The Clipboard retains a copy of the data until you copy new data there or quit the program. It's especially important to remember this when you have more than one file on the desktop, because Works retains the Clipboard's contents when you switch from one file to another. Thus, if you cut some data to the Clipboard from a spreadsheet file and then move to a word-processor file, the spreadsheet data is still on the Clipboard and will be inserted into your word-processor file at the insertion point if you choose the Paste command.

The Copy command works the same way as the Cut command, except that instead of removing selected data from the spreadsheet, Copy leaves the data where it is, placing a copy of it on the Clipboard.

The Clear command removes selected data completely from a spreadsheet. When you clear a selected cell or cells, the data is deleted. Unlike the Cut command, however, you can't remove rows or columns from the screen when you clear them—you can only remove the data inside those rows or columns.

The Move... command is a shortcut for cutting and pasting data, allowing you to move cells or groups of cells by selecting them and then choosing the Move... command. When you do, you see a dialog box that prompts you to enter the address of the cell to which you want to move the selected data.

There's also a keyboard shortcut for moving data within the spreadsheet:

- Select the data you want to move.
- Hold down the Command and Option keys together, and then click on the cell where you want to move the data.

The Paste With Options... command allows you to paste formulas and data or only data from cells you have copied or cut to the Clipboard (rather than always pasting data and formulas, which is the normal procedure). Paste With Options... also lets you transpose data, so that rows become columns and vice versa.

The Insert command is used to insert rows or columns into a spreadsheet. When you build a budget spreadsheet, for example, you may find that you forgot to include rows for certain expense items.

The Insert command automatically inserts one row or column at the insertion point, depending on whether you have selected a row, a column, or a cell. If you select a row (by clicking on the row number) or a cell, the Insert command inserts an empty row above the selected row or cell. If you select a column (by clicking on the column label), the command inserts an empty column to the left of the selected column. When you insert a row or a column, all the rows below or columns to the right of it are moved and renumbered. If the rows or columns contain formulas, the formulas adjust themselves to their new locations. We'll learn how they adjust later in this chapter.

The Paste Function... command lets you build formulas by selecting spreadsheet functions from a menu. Once you have pasted a function with this command, all you have to do to complete the formula is type in or click on the cells upon which you want the function to operate.

The Absolute Cell Ref command changes cell references in formulas from relative to absolute, or from absolute to relative. An absolute cell reference designates a specific cell. When a formula containing absolute references is copied, it still refers to those same cells in its new location. Absolute references are distinguished from relative references by dollar signs in front of their row and column designations (as in $A$1). A relative cell reference refers to cells by their location relative to the position of the cell containing the formula. When a formula using relative references is copied (or moved because you have inserted rows or columns), the cell references change to reflect the new location of the formula. The Absolute Cell Ref command is usually dimmed on the Edit menu (which means it isn't available). You can use this command only when you have selected a cell containing a formula and then clicked anywhere in the formula itself in the entry bar. To use the command:

- Select the cell containing the formula for which you want to change the references.
- Point to the formula in the entry bar and select the cell references you want to make absolute by holding down the mouse button and dragging across them.
- Choose the Absolute Cell Ref command from the Edit menu.

When you choose this command, the relative cell references you have selected in a formula become absolute references or absolute references become relative. The name of the command, however, is always Absolute Cell Ref.

Be aware that the Absolute Cell Ref command affects all the selected cell references in a formula, making all relative references absolute, or absolute references relative. The way to make some of a formula's references absolute but leave others relative is to type a dollar sign before the row designation, column designation, or both, in the references you want to be absolute.

The Fill Right and Fill Down commands let you quickly copy data from one cell into one or more adjacent cells directly beneath or to the right of the selected cell.

The Sort... command lets you rearrange the rows in a spreadsheet, based on the contents of up to three columns, or sort keys. The Sort... command works only on highlighted rows or cells in rows, so you can sort some of the rows in a spreadsheet and leave others unsorted. When you use the Sort... command, you must select from one to three columns on whose contents the sorting will be based. You can sort data in either ascending (0 to 9 or A to Z) or descending (9 to 0 or Z to A) order. Whether you sort in ascending or descending order, though, Works always places values before labels. If a column contains both values (or formulas) and labels and you sort it in ascending order, for example, Works will place the values and formulas (based on the ranking of the values they produce) in ascending order before placing the labels in ascending alphabetical order.

The last four menus are unique to the spreadsheet, so we'll look at them in detail.

The Select menu

The commands on the Select menu let you move the selection to specific cells quickly, or let you select either the entire spreadsheet or the last cell you worked with.

The All Cells command selects the entire spreadsheet. This is useful when you want to copy a whole spreadsheet to the Clipboard, widen all the spreadsheet's columns at once, or change a value or label format throughout the file.

The Last Cell command moves the selection to the bottom-right corner of the area of the file that contains data. If you have entered data into rows 1 through 4 and columns A through C, for example, the Last Cell command will move the insertion point to cell C4.

The Find Cell... and Go To Cell ... commands let you move the selection to a specific cell or spreadsheet area based on a cell's contents. The Find Cell... command lets you specify a label, cell reference, or value, and then moves the selection to that cell. The Go To Cell... command also locates labels, cell references, or values, but instead of selecting that cell, it scrolls the spreadsheet to the area containing that cell and leaves the selection where it was before.

The Show Active Cell command scrolls the spreadsheet to the area containing the currently active cell. This command is useful when you are viewing a distant area, and want to return quickly to the area of the spreadsheet containing the active cell.

The Format menu

The Format menu contains a number of spreadsheet-specific formatting commands. Except for the Column Width... command, all of these formatting commands affect the appearance of letters and numbers in the spreadsheet. To use any of these formats on a cell or group of cells, you must first select the cell or cells you want to work with, then choose the appropriate format command. A check mark will appear on the menu beside those formats you've chosen.

The six commands above the first dividing line on this menu affect the way numbers are represented in the spreadsheet.

The General command is the default format in the spreadsheet. When you enter numbers in this format, they appear just as you typed them, but without leading or trailing decimal zeroes. If you type either *0025* or *25.00*, for example, the spreadsheet will show *25*.

The Fixed command presents numbers with a fixed number of decimal places. The default number of decimals when you select this command is 2, but you can use the Number of Decimals... command to change this number. You can also use the Number of Decimals... command to specify the number of decimal places you want to appear with numbers formatted with the Dollar and Percent commands. If you use a smaller number of decimals in a long number, Works will round the number. For example, if you were to specify two decimal places for the number *1.1356* with the Number of Decimals... command, Works would display *1.14*.

The Dollar command causes numbers to be represented with dollar signs in front of them. Dollar values are shown with two decimal places after them, unless you use the Number of Decimals... command to change the display.

The Percent command displays numbers as percentages, dividing the contents of the affected cells by 100 and then putting a percent symbol (%) after them. You can use the Number of Decimals... command to set the number of decimal places in percent values.

The Scientific command shows numbers with exponential notation, and is useful when you're working with large numbers. When this command is in effect, numbers are represented as the smallest decimal number, along with an exponent. If you enter *1,000,000,* for example, Works will translate this to *1E+06,* which means 1 raised to the exponential power of 6.

The next three commands on the Format menu control the alignment of labels and values in the spreadsheet. Normally, labels are aligned along the left edge of cells and values are aligned along the right edge. You can change the alignment with the Align Left, Align Center, and Align Right commands.

The Normal Text, Bold, and Underline commands let you emphasize labels or values with these stylistic enhancements. Unless you specify otherwise, all characters are shown in the Normal Text format.

The Commas and No Commas commands let you choose whether numbers larger than 999 are displayed with commas. The default setting is No Commas, so that the number *1,000* appears as *1000.*

The Column Width... command lets you set a column width (expressed in the number of characters) for a selected column or columns. When you choose this command, you see a dialog box into which you can enter the desired column width, in characters. The default column width is 12 characters, but you can specify a column width of anywhere from 1 through 40 characters. The alternative to using the Column Width... command is dragging a column divider, which we'll see how to do later in this chapter.

The Options menu

The Options menu contains various spreadsheet commands that let you control the way data appears or the way it is calculated.

The first three commands on this menu (Calculate Now, Manual Calculation, and Automatic Calculation) control the frequency with which the Works spreadsheet recalculates formulas. In its default mode, the spreadsheet recalculates all its formulas automatically whenever you add or change data. After you make a change in a large spreadsheet, however, there is a slight delay in processing while Works recalculates the entire spreadsheet. If you're entering a lot of numbers at once, you may prefer not to have Works recalculate (thereby forcing you to pause) after each entry. If so, choose the Manual Calculation command from the Options menu so that the spreadsheet recalculates formulas only when you tell it to. The Calculate Now command tells Works to calculate the spreadsheet immediately. You usually use this command when you have Works set to Manual Calculation.

The Show Formulas and Show Values commands let you view either formulas or the values the formulas produce in the cells. The Works spreadsheet normally shows values rather than formulas. Sometimes, you may want to see all the underlying formulas in a worksheet, however. For example, some values may appear inconsistent, and you may want to check a series of formulas to make sure they're correct. You can display a single cell's formula in the entry bar by selecting that cell, but if you want to display all the formulas in a worksheet at once, choose the Show Formulas command. When you want to hide the formulas again and look at values, choose the Show Values command. The Show Formulas command is also handy when you want to print a spreadsheet with its formulas showing, for reference.

The Protected and Not Protected commands let you fix the contents of selected cells so they can't be changed. In its default mode, the spreadsheet contains no protected cells. You can enter data or change data in any cell you want. Sometimes, though, you may want to prevent anyone from entering data into cells or changing their contents. If so, select the cell or cells and then choose the Protected command. Once a cell or group of cells is protected, no one can enter data into them. Existing data in those cells can't be changed and blank cells can't be filled with data. The Not Protected command removes protection from cells that have been protected.

The Set Page Break command tells Works when to advance paper to a new page when printing a spreadsheet file. This command is useful in forcing the beginnings of new pages when you want to keep certain rows of a spreadsheet together. Normal page breaks appear in Works as dashed vertical and horizontal lines, like this:

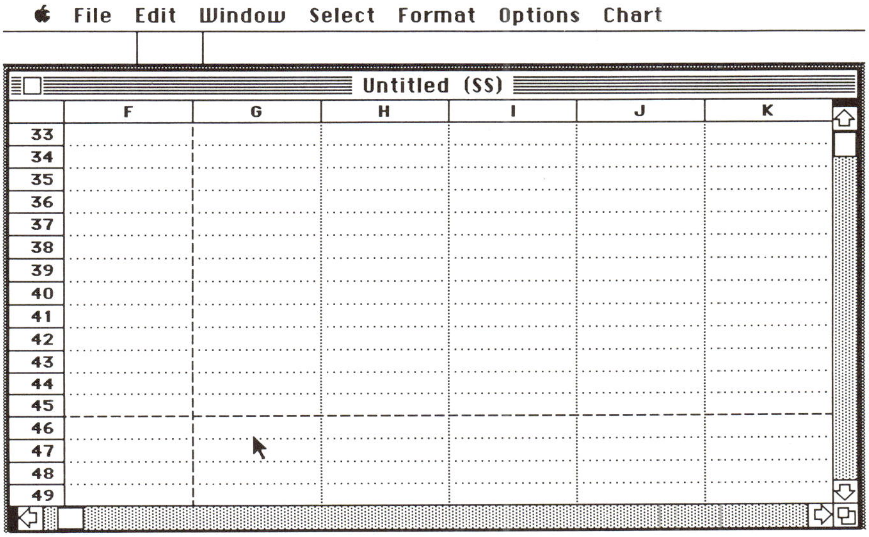

Works determines how many columns and rows of data will fit on a page, based on the settings in the Page Setup dialog box. To force a page break, select the cell at the upper-left corner of the area you want to begin a new page, and choose the Set Page Break command. To remove a page break you have set, select the cell at the upper-left corner of the page (just inside that page's horizontal and vertical dashed lines) and choose the Remove Page Break command.

The Show Grid and No Grid commands let you display or hide the matrix of lines dividing rows and columns. The grid helps you determine the specific addresses of cells a little more quickly, but often you may want the grid hidden when you print your spreadsheet data.

The Chart menu

The Chart menu is the gateway to making charts from spreadsheet data. When you want to draw a new chart or recall a chart you have defined and stored with a spreadsheet, you use the Chart menu.

You can create charts only from the data in the spreadsheet you are currently working with. To define a chart, you must indicate the cells containing the data you want to chart, select the type of chart you want Works to draw, and, optionally, enter chart titles. You can choose from among line, pie, bar, stacked bar, or combination line and bar chart formats to represent your data. (We'll explore these various types of charts in Chapter 5.)

Once you define a chart, Works automatically stores it with the spreadsheet you're currently working on. You can store up to eight chart definitions with each spreadsheet file. If you don't give a chart a name, it is stored with the same name as your spreadsheet. If a spreadsheet is called Budget, for example, the first chart you design will be called Budget Chart 1 unless you specify a different name.

The Draw Chart... command produces a dialog box containing a list of previously defined charts you have created for the spreadsheet you are working with. When you select one of the names in the list, that chart is automatically drawn on the screen. If your spreadsheet has no chart definitions, this command is unavailable.

The New Series Chart... and New Pie Chart ... commands produce the dialog boxes in which you define the data sources and chart types and enter the titles for new charts. To define a chart, you choose either the New Series Chart ... or New Pie Chart... command from the Chart menu to display a chart-definition dialog box.

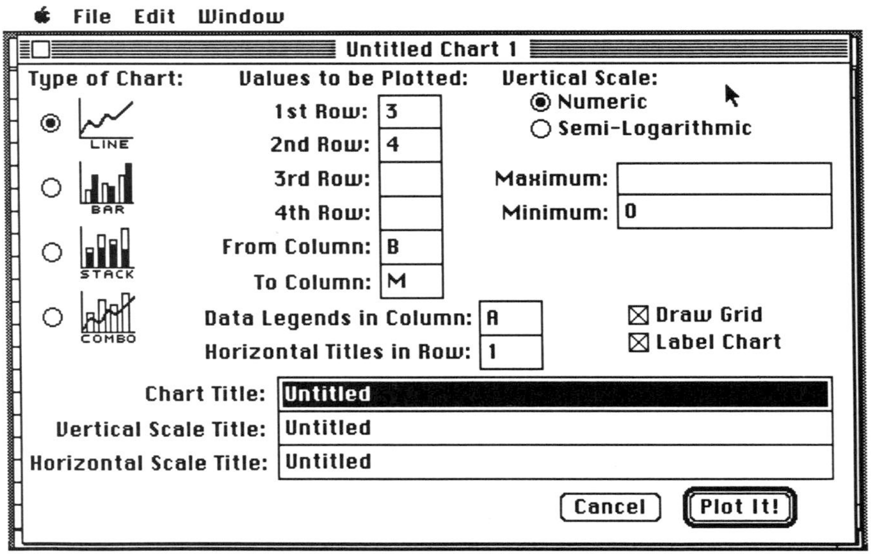

The chart-definition dialog box lets you select the type of chart, the locations of the data you want to represent (by row and column), and the row and column locations of the titles you want assigned to the data representations in the chart. Also, you can specify vertical and horizontal axis titles (in series charts), and a main chart title at the top of the chart. You'll get more specific information about how to use chart-definition dialog boxes in Chapter 5.

Before you have defined a chart for a spreadsheet, the only commands available are New Series Chart... and New Pie Chart..., because all other commands on the Chart menu affect existing charts.

The Select Definition... command, like the Draw Chart... command, produces a list of previously defined charts. When you select a chart name from the list in the dialog box produced by this command, however, Works displays the chart-definition dialog box, instead of drawing the chart itself.

The Duplicate Chart... and Erase Chart... commands let you duplicate chart definitions and erase chart definitions you have previously created.

Keyboard shortcuts

Many of the menu commands in the spreadsheet have keyboard equivalents, and it may be faster to type these commands than it is to choose them from a menu. A list of the keyboard command equivalents is shown in Figure 4-3, on the next page.

The best way to learn how Works' spreadsheet commands work is to see them in use. So let's look at an example.

A SAMPLE SPREADSHEET

Let's use Microsoft Works to build an electronic version of the budget worksheet in Figure 4-1:

- ☐ Load Microsoft Works.
- ☐ Select the New... command from the File menu.
- ☐ Double-click on the spreadsheet icon. A new, blank spreadsheet is displayed.
- ☐ Point to cell A1 and click the mouse button.

Action	Command	Menu	Keyboard Equivalent
Open a file	Open...	File	Command-O
Save a file	Save	File	Command-S
Print a file	Print...	File	Command-P
Quit Works	Quit	File	Command-Q
Undo a command	Undo	Edit	Command-Z
Cut text	Cut	Edit	Command-X
Copy text	Copy	Edit	Command-C
Paste text	Paste	Edit	Command-V
Insert a row or column	Insert	Edit	Command-I
Change relative references to absolute or absolute to relative	Absolute Cell Ref	Edit	Command-A
Fill a range to the right	Fill Right	Edit	Command-R
Fill a range below	Fill Down	Edit	Command-D
Change the size of a window	Full Window/ Small Window	Window	Command-W
Find a cell	Find Cell...	Select	Command-F
Go to a cell	Go To Cell...	Select	Command-G
Apply normal text style	Normal Text	Format	Command-N
Boldface text	Bold	Format	Command-B
Underline text	Underline	Format	Command-U
Calculate immediately	Calculate Now	Options	Command-=

Figure 4-3. *Works offers keyboard equivalents for 19 spreadsheet commands.*

Whenever you click the mouse button with the pointer on a cell, that cell becomes the active cell, and you can then enter a label, number, or formula into it.

☐ Type the label *Expenses*.

Since this label begins with a letter, the spreadsheet automatically knows that you are entering a label, rather than a value (or number). The spreadsheet stores labels as text—you can't perform calculations on them. If you make a typing mistake at this point, just use the Backspace key to erase the error and then re-type the label.

☐ Press the Tab key to enter the label and select cell B1.

When you press the Tab key, Works stores the label or value you've just entered, and moves the selection one cell to the right. If, on the other hand, you press the Return key to enter a label or value, the label or value is entered, and the selection moves down to the cell directly underneath. A third way to enter labels or values is to point to the enter box (the box with the check mark, next to the entry bar) and click the mouse button—this enters the label or value and leaves the selection on that cell. To correct a mistake in a cell where you've already entered a label or value, click on the cell to select it, and then edit the entry (using the Backspace key, spacebar, and other keys) in the entry bar.

- ☐ Type the label *March* and press the Tab key. Enter the labels *April, May,* and *Qtr. Total* in this row.
- ☐ Move the selection back to column A by pointing to cell A3 and clicking the mouse button.
- ☐ Type the label *Food* and press the Return key. Notice that when you press the Return key, the selection moves down to cell A4, instead of to the cell at the right.
- ☐ Refer to Figure 4-1 to fill in the rest of the labels.
- ☐ Point to cell B3 and click to make that cell active. Type the number *200*, and press the Tab key. Since the first character in this entry is a number, Works knows that it should treat the entry as a value, instead of a label.
- ☐ Enter food expenses shown in Figure 4-1 for April and May.

Entering formulas

Now we're ready to enter the first formula on this sample spreadsheet.

- ☐ Move the selection to cell E3 (if it isn't there already), and then type this formula:

  =Sum(B3:D3)

☐ Click the enter box (the box with the check mark, next to the entry bar) when you're done. Notice that the sum of the numbers in cells B3, C3, and D3 appears in cell E3.

File Edit Window Select Format Options Chart

E3 =Sum(B3:D3)

Budget (SS)

	A	B	C	D	E	F
1	Expense	March	April	May	Qtr. Total	
2						
3	Food	200	210	205	615	
4	Rent	500	500	500		
5	Utilities	35	31	30		
6	Phone	25	50	30		
7						
8	Total					
9						
10						
11						
12						
13						
14						
15						
16						
17						

Let's look at how this formula was entered. The first character you typed was the equal sign. This tells the Works spreadsheet you're about to enter a formula, instead of a label or a value. Works treats formulas differently from labels and values, but since all formulas begin with either a number or a letter, you have to type the equal sign to let Works know that you're entering a formula instead of a value.

Following the equal sign, you typed the word *Sum*. Sum is a spreadsheet function that tells Works to add the values that follow. The Works spreadsheet has 56 built-in functions that do everything from addition to financial calculations. There's an alternate way to enter a function into a formula: Instead of typing the function, you can choose the Paste Function... command from the Edit menu and then select a function from a list. As described earlier in this chapter, the Paste Function... command inserts the function that you have selected into your formula.

Once you enter the function, you must enter the argument—the cell location, value, or range of cell locations to be acted upon (summed, in this case) by the function. Arguments are always enclosed in parentheses. In our example, the argument is B3:D3, which indicates the range of cells B3, C3, and D3. In this example, you could have typed the actual numbers you wanted to sum (200, 210, and 205), but you entered the locations of these numbers instead. This allows you to take advantage of the spreadsheet's matrix structure to build a formula that can easily recalculate if you change the values in those cells.

By using cell locations (or references) you're telling Works to sum the contents of the cells B3, C3, and D3. Those cells in our example just happen to contain the values 200, 210, and 205. You could change the values in those cells, and the spreadsheet would automatically recalculate the Sum formula to present the new total. If you had used specific numbers instead of cell references in the formula, changing the cell contents would have no effect. To change the result of the formula, you would have to change the formula itself because it is adding specific values.

The argument in this particular formula is a range (a continuous group of cells in the same row or column), so Works adds all the numbers in cells B3 through D3. You indicate a range of cells by typing a colon between two numbers.

Once you type the entire formula and click the enter box (or press the Return or Enter key), the spreadsheet automatically calculates the formula and presents the result of the formula in the cell. (Recall that you can display formulas in their cells by choosing the Show Formulas command from the Options menu.)

For now, let's finish entering the expense numbers in the spreadsheet, following the steps outlined above: Point to the cell where a value belongs, and then type the number.

☐ Enter the rest of the expense numbers shown in Figure 4-1.

When you're through, you're ready to enter the rest of the formulas.

☐ Select cell B8.

☐ Type an equal sign, followed by the formula:

Sum(B3:B6)

☐ Click the enter box, or press Return or Tab.

The sum of the expense values for March appears in cell B8.

Copying formulas

Now, you can take advantage of having used cell references instead of specific values in the two formulas you copied.

☐ Point to cell E3 and hold down the mouse button.

☐ Drag the mouse down to cell E6. All the cells in this range are now highlighted.

☐ Release the mouse button, and select the Fill Down command from the Edit menu. Totals appear in cells E4, E5, and E6.

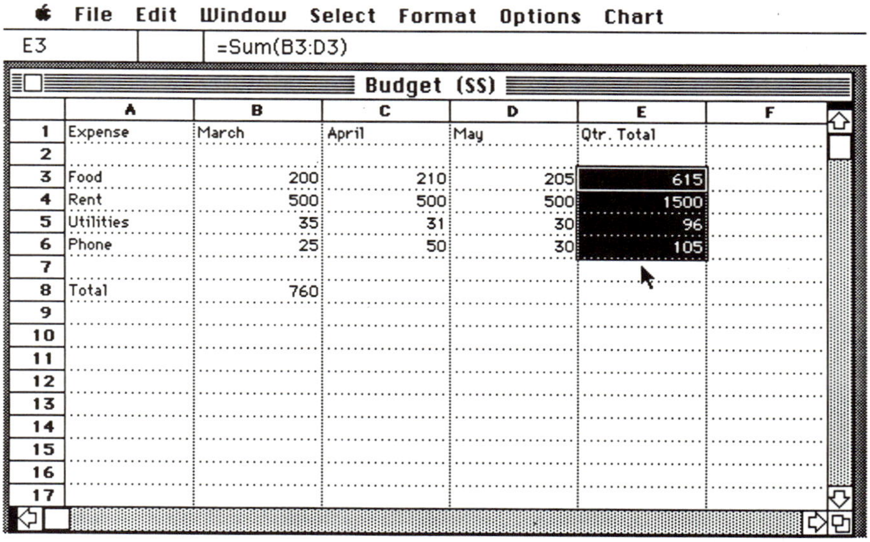

File Edit Window Select Format Options Chart

E3 =Sum(B3:D3)

Budget (SS)

	A	B	C	D	E	F
1	Expense	March	April	May	Qtr. Total	
2						
3	Food	200	210	205	615	
4	Rent	500	500	500	1500	
5	Utilities	35	31	30	96	
6	Phone	25	50	30	105	
7						
8	Total	760				
9						
10						
11						
12						
13						
14						
15						
16						
17						

As mentioned earlier in this chapter, the Fill Down command tells Works to copy the contents of a cell into the highlighted range of cells below it. In our sample spreadsheet, cell E3 contains the formula Sum(B3:D3), so that formula was copied into the cells in E4, E5, and E6. Notice, however, that the totals in these cells reflect the contents of rows 4, 5, and 6, not the contents of row 3. This is because the formula in E3 contained relative cell references, rather than absolute cell references. Unless you specifically tell Works otherwise (by putting dollar signs in front of cell references in a formula to make them absolute), Works uses relative references when you copy formulas and the references are adjusted according to the new position of the formula. If we had used absolute references in the sample formula we copied, Works would have summed the specific values in cells B3, C3, and D3, even if we copied that formula to another location. Because the formula in cell E3 contains relative references, it tells Works to sum the three cells to the left of the formula's location. So, the copy of the formula in cell E4 has summed the contents of cells B4, C4, and D4; the copy of the formula in cell E5 has summed the contents of cells B5, C5, and D5; and so on. Figure 4-4, on the next page, shows the results of both relative and absolute references. (The columns in these spreadsheets have been widened to show the complete formulas.)

To finish our sample budget worksheet, we could re-enter what is essentially the same Sum formula in cells C6, D6, and E6. But because we've used relative references in the formula, it's much simpler to copy it, and have the references adjust themselves automatically.

- ☐ Point to cell B8 and hold down the mouse button.
- ☐ Drag the pointer across to cell E8 and release the button.
- ☐ Choose the Fill Right command from the Edit menu. The formula in cell B8 is automatically copied into cells C8, D8, and E8, and the results of the formulas are shown in these cells.

Entering new values

Now that this simple spreadsheet is complete, you can see the other major advantage of electronic spreadsheets in action. We've entered the formulas, rather than specific numbers, so we can change the

Budget (SS)

	A	B	C	D	E
1	Expense	March	April	May	Qtr. Totals
2					
3	Food	200	210	205	=Sum(B3:D3)
4	Rent	500	500	500	=Sum(B4:D4)
5	Utilities	35	31	30	=Sum(B5:D5)
6	Phone	25	50	30	=Sum(B6:D6)
7					
8	Total	=Sum($B$3:$B$6)	=Sum($B$3:$B$6)	=Sum($B$3:$B$6)	

Budget (SS)

	A	B	C	D	E	F
1	Expense	March	April	May	Qtr. Totals	
2						
3	Food	200	210	205	615	
4	Rent	500	500	500	1500	
5	Utilities	35	31	30	96	
6	Phone	25	50	30	105	
7						
8	Total	760	760	760		

Figure 4-4. *By displaying absolute and relative formulas (top) and then the values they produce (bottom), you can see that the absolute Sum formula in cell B8, when copied to cells C8 and D8, always produces the same result. But the relative Sum formula in cell E3, when copied to cells E4, E5, and E6, produces varying results because it refers to different cells, depending on its new location.*

values in the locations referred to in the formulas, and the formulas themselves will recalculate automatically.

- ☐ Click on cell B3, and enter the number *220*.
- ☐ Press the Return key. The Sum formula at the bottom of this column automatically recalculates the total in cell B8.

By using cell references, rather than specific numbers to make up formulas, you can take advantage of the fixed relationships between various locations in this spreadsheet. You can change the numbers in the expense rows as you please, and Works will immediately recalculate the formulas that are affected.

ADVANTAGES OF THE WORKS SPREADSHEET ON THE MAC

The basic spreadsheet features of recalculation, stored formulas, and calculating the contents of cells by their locations are common to every spreadsheet program on any computer. Microsoft Works and the Macintosh make using them a lot easier.

You can use the mouse

The Works spreadsheet is a lot easier to learn than spreadsheets on most other computers because you can select commands and cells and enter formulas by pointing with the mouse, rather than having to remember keyboard commands for everything. If you want to widen a column, for example, you can simply point to that column's right divider and drag the divider over. If you want to enter a formula, you can choose Paste Function... from the Edit menu and then click on the cells you want included in the formula. If you forget how to do something, you can choose Help from the Window menu and then simply point to the menu command you want to learn about.

You can move around quickly

Spreadsheets often become quite large, with more filled cells than you can see on the screen at once. When you want to move around a large conventional spreadsheet, you must use cursor keys to scroll a screen at a time, or indicate a specific cell to which you want to move. In Works, you can drag the scroll boxes in the scroll bars at the right and bottom of the spreadsheet window, which allows you to move quickly to distant parts of a file. If you know exactly where you want to go, on the other hand, you can use the Find Cell... or Go To Cell... commands on the Select menu to find formulas, values, text, or cell numbers in a spreadsheet.

You can easily move data from one location to another

Using the Clipboard, you can use the Cut or Copy commands from the Edit menu to move spreadsheet text, values, or formulas from one place in a spreadsheet to another, or from one spreadsheet to another.

You can even move spreadsheet data into word-processor documents or database files the same way, as we'll see in Chapter 9. Formulas transfer as easily as values and labels, and you can copy only the values produced by a spreadsheet's formulas if you like.

You can have different views of your spreadsheet at your fingertips

You can split one spreadsheet window into as many as four different views, each of which can be scrolled independently. To divide the spreadsheet into more than one window, you use the pane markers. Pane markers are the black bars located at the left edge of the bottom scroll bar and the top edge of the right scroll bar. To view two sections of a spreadsheet side by side, point to the pane marker at the left of the bottom scroll bar, hold down the mouse button, and drag the marker to the right. As you do this, a vertical dividing line appears on the spreadsheet. When you release the mouse button, the line stops at its current position, and the bottom scroll bar is divided into two separate scroll bars (one for each half of the viewing window), like this:

File Edit Window Select Format Options Chart

Budget (SS)

	A	B	C	D	E	F
1	Expense	March	April	May	Qtr. Total	
2						
3	Food	200	210	205	615	20
4	Rent	500	500	500	1500	50
5	Utilities	35	31	30	96	3
6	Phone	25	50	30	105	3
7						
8	Total	760	791	765	2316	77
9						
10						
11						
12						
13						
14						
15						
16						
17						

You can then click in either of these scroll bars to scroll the two parts of the spreadsheet independently. This means you can display row titles in the left half of the screen, and scroll the part of the spreadsheet in the right half of the screen by using the right-hand portion of the bottom scroll bar.

You can do the same thing with the pane marker at the top of the right-hand scroll bar, to split the view of the spreadsheet horizontally. This lets you display column titles in the top window, and then scroll down to distant rows in the bottom window. If you want, you can use both pane markers at once to display four different windows for the same spreadsheet, and scroll each independently of the others.

You can also have as many as ten spreadsheet files open on the desktop at once. So, between multiple windows on one spreadsheet and the multiple-file capability of the desktop, you can have lots of different spreadsheet views on hand at once.

You can graph spreadsheet data

By using commands on the Chart menu of the spreadsheet, you can create up to eight bar charts, pie charts, or line graphs for each spreadsheet file, and store them so you can instantly visualize your data. You can resize charts, so they occupy only a portion of the screen, allowing you to consult your data on the spreadsheet while looking at a chart of it at the same time. You can also print charts by themselves on paper, or copy them into word-processor documents for reports.

These are some of the advantages of the Works spreadsheet. Now, let's look at some specific features and how they work.

ENTERING AND CALCULATING DATA WITH THE WORKS SPREADSHEET

As with word processing, working with a spreadsheet can be logically divided into two activities: entering and calculating data, and formatting the data once you've entered it. Let's look at some data entry and calculating advantages of Works first.

Point-and-click data handling

Most spreadsheets require you to learn large numbers of keyboard commands to manipulate data. But with Works, you can do just about anything to your spreadsheet numbers by simply pointing and clicking with the mouse. There's still no substitute for the keyboard for actually entering labels and values, but once the raw numbers are entered, life is easier if you use the mouse.

You've already seen how the Fill Right and Fill Down commands let you copy a cell's contents using just the mouse. Now, let's build an entire formula without touching the keyboard. Suppose we've enhanced the spreadsheet so there's a new column that shows average monthly expenses, as follows:

File Edit Window Select Format Options Chart

F3

Budget (SS)

	A	B	C	D	E	F
1	Expense	March	April	May	Qtr. Total	Averages
2						
3	Food	200	210	205	615	
4	Rent	500	500	500	1500	
5	Utilities	35	31	30	96	
6	Phone	25	50	30	105	
7						
8	Total	760	791	765	2316	
9						
10						
11						
12						
13						
14						
15						
16						
17						

- ☐ Enter the label *Averages* in column F.

Now let's enter the formulas to calculate those averages:

- ☐ Point to cell F3 and click the mouse button to make it active.

- ☐ Select the Paste Function... command from the Edit menu. A dialog box appears, containing a list of functions from which to choose.

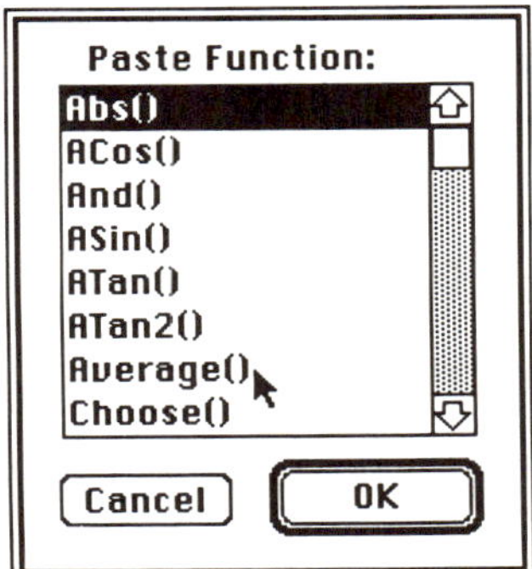

- ☐ Double-click on the Average function. The function is entered as the beginning of a formula in the entry bar at the top of the spreadsheet window. Notice that a set of parentheses (to contain the argument, or cell references) is automatically entered following the function. All you have to do now is specify the cells you want to include in the argument.
- ☐ Point to cell B3 and hold down the mouse button.
- ☐ Drag the pointer across to cell D3, and release the mouse button. The range B3:D3 is automatically entered inside the parentheses in the entry bar.
- ☐ Click the enter box to enter the formula. The average of cells B3, C3, and D3 is calculated and appears in cell B7.

Paste Function... is a handy command, because the Works spreadsheet has 56 functions available, and it would be very difficult to remember all of them well enough to enter them quickly from the keyboard. If you do remember how to spell a function name, however, it is usually faster to type the function's name from the keyboard, as we did with the Sum formulas in our original budget spreadsheet.

You can copy data selectively

You've already seen how easy it is to copy relative formulas from one cell into a series of adjacent cells. But often, you'll want to copy data to a cell that isn't adjacent to the original cell's location. To do this, you'll have to use Copy and Paste.

Let's assume we want to expand our budget spreadsheet to examine our expenses more closely. Suppose, for example, that we want to use the total figures in a more comprehensive budget in another file:

- ☐ Point to the number 6 in row 6 and click the mouse button. The entire row is highlighted. (Pointing to a row or column label and clicking highlights the entire row or column.)
- ☐ Select the Copy command from the Edit menu. The contents of row 6 are copied to the Clipboard.
- ☐ Select the New... command from the File menu, and double-click the spreadsheet icon in the dialog box that appears. A new, blank spreadsheet file is displayed.
- ☐ Select cell A2, and then choose Paste With Options... from the Edit menu. A dialog box appears.

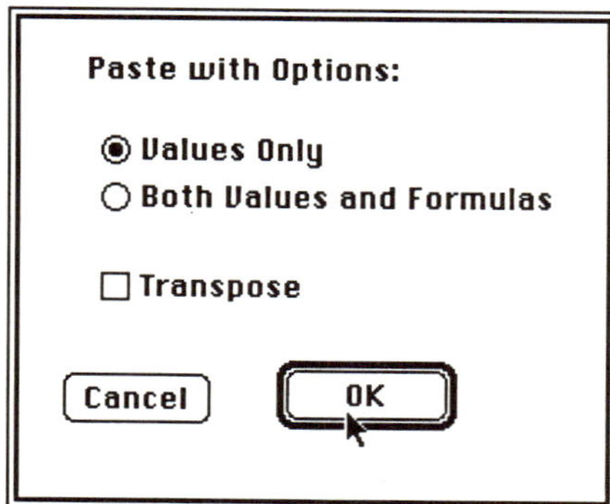

- The Paste With Options dialog box appears with the option to paste only values (Values Only) selected. This is the option you want, so click the OK button. The values from row 6 in the original spreadsheet are pasted into row 2 in the new spreadsheet.

When you copy data with the Paste command, Works always copies both the values and the formulas that produce them. Since we need only the total values in this row in our new spreadsheet, we chose the Paste With Options... command so we could paste only the values.

You can transpose numbers

Some people find spreadsheets simpler to work with when they contain more rows than columns, and other people like spreadsheets that contain more columns than rows. But it isn't always easy to tell when you begin building a spreadsheet whether the finished product will be short and wide or long and narrow. If you find yourself wishing that the data in a spreadsheet's rows was in columns and the data in columns was in rows, you can transpose them with Works:

- Select the data you want to transpose.
- Cut or copy the data to the Clipboard.
- Move the selection to the new location of the data.
- Choose the Paste With Options... command from the Edit menu.
- Click the Transpose box in the dialog box.
- Click the OK button in the dialog box or press the Return key. The data you copied to the Clipboard will be pasted into the worksheet, beginning at the new selection location. If you copied data in a row, it will appear in a column, and vice versa.

You can sort data selectively

Looking at the budget worksheet, we may decide that it would look better if the expense items were in alphabetical order. This is easy to do with the Sort... command:

- ☐ Point to the label *Food* in row 3 and click the mouse button.
- ☐ Drag the pointer down through row 6. All four expense labels in column A are now highlighted.
- ☐ Select the Sort... command from the Edit menu. The Sort dialog box appears.

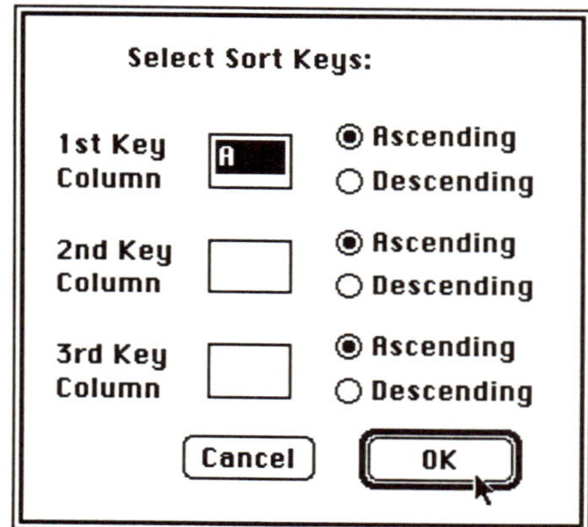

Since we selected labels in column A before choosing Sort..., the dialog box already shows column A as the first sort key. We could choose two other columns as sort keys now, but we only want to sort the rows based on the labels in column A. The Ascending button is selected, so our labels will be sorted from A to Z, which is the order we want them in.

- ☐ Click the OK button. The dialog box disappears, and the rows are rearranged so the labels are now in alphabetical order. Notice that even though you rearranged the rows, the Sum formulas in row 8 still show the same totals as before. This is because the Works spreadsheet is smart enough to adjust formulas whenever you sort rows that contain cells those formulas use.

It's hard to get lost

When you're working with a very large spreadsheet, you may leave the area where you're currently making changes to look at some numbers in a distant part of the spreadsheet. Once you have looked at those numbers, you have to find your way back to where you were. In those cases, use the Show Active Cell command to return to the active cell in your spreadsheet from wherever you were.

Suppose your budget worksheet had gotten quite large, for example. You were entering your food expenses for May in cell D3, when you decided to scroll to cell B32 to look at your child-care expenses for March. If you want to return quickly to cell D3 after your side trip to cell B32:

- ☐ Choose the Show Active Cell command from the Select menu. The portion of your spreadsheet containing the active cell (D3) will instantly be displayed.

FORMATTING WITH THE WORKS SPREADSHEET

We've seen some of the features that make it easier to calculate numbers with the Works spreadsheet. Now, let's look at what Works offers for formatting.

It's easy to change column widths

Non-Macintosh spreadsheets make you remember specific commands to change column widths. With Works, you just have to point and drag with the mouse. Suppose we want to widen column A in our budget spreadsheet.

☐ Point to the dividing line between column A and column B in the column heading area above row 1. The pointer becomes a double arrow.

File Edit Window Select Format Options Chart

A8 | Total

Budget (SS)

	A	B	C	D	E	F
1	Expense	March	April	May	Qtr. Total	Averages
2						
3	Food	200	210	205	615	
4	Rent	500	500	500	1500	
5	Utilities	35	31	30	96	
6	Phone	25	50	30	105	
7						
8	Total	760	791	765	2316	
9						
10						
11						
12						
13						
14						
15						
16						
17						

☐ Hold down the mouse button, and drag the pointer to the right. The dividing line between columns A and B moves right as you drag the pointer.

☐ When the dividing line is where you want it (column A seems wide enough), release the mouse button to fix the dividing line in its new position.

If you want to specify a particular width, in characters, for the column or columns you currently have selected, you can use the Column Width… command on the spreadsheet's Format menu, as mentioned earlier in this chapter.

You can display a grid

The spreadsheets on most other computers show numbers in rows or columns, but no actual matrix of lines dividing the spreadsheet into individual cells. Seeing the matrix that divides rows and columns is a considerable help when you're trying to locate a specific spreadsheet value. With Works, all new spreadsheets are displayed with a grid. If you would prefer not to see the grid, you can hide it by choosing the No Grid command from the Options menu.

You have many paper sizes to choose from

The Works spreadsheet is one of the few spreadsheets that let you print your work on custom-sized paper. If you want, you can print on a page as small as 1 inch by 1 inch, or one as large as 15 inches wide and 300 inches long. You can set custom paper sizes by selecting Custom Size from the Paper options in the Page Setup dialog box.

You can print sideways

The eternal problem with spreadsheets is that they're usually wider than they are long, and you must usually try to print them on paper that is longer than it is wide. With the wide Orientation icon in the Page Setup dialog box, however, you can print your spreadsheets sideways, so that the rows run down the length of your paper instead of across its width. In such cases, a spreadsheet with particularly wide rows can extend onto the next sheet of paper (if you're using continuous paper) so spreadsheets can be as wide as you like.

You can reduce your print

If you want to cram more spreadsheet data on one standard-sized piece of paper, you can choose the 50% Reduction option from the Page Setup dialog box. That way, spreadsheet data will be printed at half its normal size, allowing you to fit twice as much onto each sheet of paper.

You can stylize your data

Although you don't have a choice of fonts for printing or displaying spreadsheet data, you can apply boldfacing or underlining to any one cell or larger portion of a spreadsheet. This comes in handy, in particular, when you're setting off worksheet titles, or emphasizing your bottom-line conclusions.

WHAT THE SPREADSHEET WON'T DO—AND WHAT TO DO ABOUT IT

Despite the spreadsheet's power and ease of use, there are some things it won't do. If you're new to spreadsheets, you may never miss the features we're going to look at. But if you are an old hand at electronic spreadsheets, you should be aware that the Works spreadsheet can't do everything.

You can't name cells

Some spreadsheets let you refer to cells or groups of cells by name, which you can use to locate a particular cell quickly. You can't do this with Works. But you can search for labels in the Works spreadsheet. Or, you can use the scroll boxes to move quickly through a spreadsheet.

You can't link separate worksheets

When you work on a large, complex spreadsheet project, you might want to create separate worksheet files for different aspects of the job. In a corporate budget, for example, you might have individual budget files for each department. Works doesn't allow you to link worksheets. But there is an alternative when you're working on complex tasks. The Works matrix contains over 2.5 million cells, so one spreadsheet file could contain several spreadsheets in different areas of the available grid. Each departmental budget might be in a different part of the matrix for one file, for example, and the consolidated corporate budget could be yet another part of the same file. By putting all of the data in one file, you can use cell references to transfer data automatically from one cell to another.

Let's look at the budget worksheet as an example. Suppose food, rent, utilities, and phone expenses are only the household part of a larger personal budget. We might, for example, have other line items that have to do with long-term debts and short-term debts, as follows:

 File Edit Window Select Format Options Chart

B20

Budget (SS)

	A	B	C	D	E	F
7						
8	Total House Exp.	760	791	765	2316	7
9						
10	Mortgage	750	750	750	2250	
11	Car Loan	185	185	185	555	
12	Personal Loan	103	103	103	309	
13						
14	Total Long-Term	1038	1038	1038	3114	
15						
16	Visa	50	50	50	150	
17	Mastercard	25	25	25	75	
18						
19	Total Short-Term	75	75	75	225	
20	Total Long-Term					
21	Total House Exp.					
22	Total Expenses					
23						

In such a spreadsheet, we might want to duplicate the contents of the household and long-term debt total rows in a summary portion farther down the spreadsheet. We could simply type in the same numbers from these other total rows, or copy them with the Clipboard, but let's duplicate the values in these upper rows by using cell references:

- ☐ Enter the additional labels, values, and Sum formulas.
- ☐ Click on cell B20 to select it.
- ☐ Type the equal sign, followed by the cell designation B14. Press the Return key when you're done. The value *1038* appears in cell B20.

By using a cell reference, we have told Works to take whatever value is in cell B14, and duplicate it in cell B20. This way, we can change the value in cell B14 (or change the values above it, which affect the total amount that appears in B14), and the value in B20 will change automatically. This is the advantage of using a cell reference to duplicate a value from elsewhere in a spreadsheet, instead of re-entering the value or copying it.

Using this technique, we could transfer totals from departmental budgets to rows in a consolidated budget, as long as all the budgets we were working with were in the same spreadsheet file. This is a good substitute for spreadsheet linking. Now let's look at some tips that will help you while you work with the spreadsheet.

BASIC SPREADSHEET TIPS

We'll see how the different spreadsheet features work as we perform various types of tasks in Chapter 5, but there are some fundamentals that apply to every type of spreadsheet, no matter what its purpose.

Plan first, execute later

Instead of jumping right into new spreadsheets by entering labels and values, take a few moments to plan what you'll be doing so you have a reasonable mental picture of how your spreadsheet will look. If you're new to spreadsheets, you may want to draw a rough plan of a spreadsheet on paper before you begin making it with Works. Once you gain some experience, you can keep a plan in your head fairly easily. By planning ahead, you can avoid having to rearrange several rows or columns and having to re-enter a number of formulas when you're halfway through a project.

Take a budget, for example. Before you begin, you should have some idea of the kinds of expense items you will be listing and how you will group those items. You may lump household expenses in one set of rows, long-term debt in another set of rows, discretionary income in another set of rows, and so on.

Of course, the general structure of your spreadsheets will depend on what you're trying to accomplish. A budget spreadsheet, for example, will look different from an investment analysis or an amortization table. Whatever the task, though, think before you leap. Consider what you're trying to do, what types of calculations will be necessary, and how best to organize your data so you can enter formulas easily and make sense out of the results with a minmum of effort.

Format last

As with word processing, you should concentrate on entering the data, labels, and formulas into your spreadsheet first. The usual order of tasks in building a spreadsheet is:

- ☐ Enter row and column labels.
- ☐ Enter values.
- ☐ Enter formulas.
- ☐ Format the spreadsheet.

A classic result of formatting too soon is ruined spreadsheet titles. You might begin a new spreadsheet with a nice, multiple-column title in row 1. But as you enter row and column labels, numbers, and formulas, you may find it necessary to make columns wider or narrower, or to insert, delete, or rearrange columns. Of course, when you do, that lovely title at the top of the spreadsheet is rearranged as well.

Point with the mouse to indicate cell references

Use the mouse whenever possible to indicate the specific cells being entered into formulas or as references elsewhere. When you type, you are far more likely to make a mistake that may mean an improper reference that doesn't show up until much later; but when you point, you are fairly sure of indicating the correct cell. Works makes it simple to indicate the cells you want to include in a formula by simply pointing to them.

Check all formulas and results

There's a false legitimacy about spreadsheets that makes us trust them too easily. Somehow, we get the idea that an electronic spreadsheet can't be wrong. But remember, a spreadsheet's results are only as good as the formulas and data make them, and the formulas and data entered by a human are subject to errors. It's true that the spreadsheet won't produce an incorrect calculation, but it's quite possible that you could inadvertently specify the wrong cell references or even the wrong functions in a formula.

It's particularly tempting to take a spreadsheet at its word when you've entered and tested one formula and then copied it to a number of other locations. Whether you enter all your formulas by hand or copy them, though, you should check every formula in the file before you sit back and begin relying on the calculations the spreadsheet is producing. Individuals and even large corporations have made serious financial blunders because somebody didn't check every formula in a spreadsheet. Remember, the numbers are only as good as the formulas, and formulas can be wrong.

SPREADSHEET SPECIFICATIONS

Here are some specifications you may want to refer to as you use the spreadsheet.

Maximum worksheet size (rows by columns): 9,999 by 256

Total number of built-in functions: 56

Maximum file size: Approximately 7,500 filled cells with a 512K Mac; 22,500 filled cells with a Mac Plus (actual limit depends on specific spreadsheet contents)

Maximum number of decimal places in a value: 15

Calculating precision: 15 decimal places

Maximum column width: 40 characters

Maximum length of a value or formula: 256 characters

Maximum number of chart definitions per spreadsheet: 8

Number of chart types available: 5

Maximum paper length: 300 inches (with Custom Size selected in the Paper options of the Page Setup dialog box)

Maximum paper width: 15 inches (with Custom Size selected in the Paper options of the Page Setup dialog box)

Minimum paper length: 1 inch (with Custom Size selected in the Paper options of the Page Setup dialog box)

Minimum paper width: 1 inch (with Custom Size selected in the Paper options of the Page Setup dialog box)

Default paper size: US Letter (8½ by 11 inches)

Default Top, Bottom, Left, and Right Margins: 1 inch

Default Font: 9-point Geneva

Number of fonts available: 1

Maximum length of search/replace strings: 80 characters

Maximum length of headers or footers: 99 characters

Range of numbered pages in a document: 1 through 9,999

C H A P T E R 5

Spreadsheet Projects

In this chapter, we'll see several of the spreadsheet's features in action as we help Al Chroma, proprietor of Al's Videorama, do a variety of business and personal projects. To begin, we'll work on a long inventory project that shows how you can enter, copy, sort, and format data in the spreadsheet. Also, we will help Al develop a loan-amortization table and a customer-volume report that includes a chart. And finally, we'll pull all of Al's personal and business finances together on a single, consolidated spreadsheet.

AN INVENTORY

In an effort to offer his customers the very best selection of VCR programming, Al has been stocking videotapes like a madman for a couple of months now. But, for his records, Al has only a stack of videotape order receipts. He wants to set up a worksheet that will let him know exactly how much capital he has tied up in his inventory. This worksheet will quickly calculate the value of all the tapes in stock. For the purposes of this exercise, we'll work with a small sample worksheet that contains only two categories of Al's videotapes. The finished sample worksheet is shown in Figure 5-1.

Entering inventory items and category titles

Let's begin by opening a new spreadsheet file and entering the names of all the videotapes in stock:

- ☐ Click the spreadsheet icon on the Works opening screen, and then click the New button. A new spreadsheet appears.
- ☐ Click on cell A1 to select it, and then type the column label *Title*.
- ☐ Press Command-B to make the column title boldface and enter it at the same time.

All of the style commands, such as Underline or Bold, work this way, whether you choose them from the Format menu or use the keyboard: Applying the stylistic enhancement enters the value at the same time.

	Videotape Inventory		
Title	**Quantity**	**Cost**	**Total Value**
Adventure			
Blazing Bullets	1	$34.95	$34.95
Jungle Fever	2	$32.95	$65.90
Six Gun City	1	$22.95	$22.95
The One-Eyed Assassin	3	$34.96	$104.88
The Spy Who Said No	3	$28.95	$86.85
Two Guys In Trouble	2	$34.95	$69.90
Subtotal Adventure	12		$385.43
Aerobics			
Aerobic Profit-Taking	4	$34.95	$139.80
George Will's Yoga Fun	1	$22.95	$22.95
Tip O'Neill's Workout	2	$19.95	$39.90
Wimpy's Roll-a-thon	1	$22.95	$22.95
Subtotal Aerobics	8		$225.60
Grand Totals	20		$611.03

Figure 5-1. *An inventory spreadsheet for Al's Videorama might look like this.*

- ☐ Press the Tab key to move the selection to cell B1, and type the column label *Quantity*.
- ☐ Press Command-B to make this title boldface and enter it at the same time.
- ☐ Enter the title *Cost* into column C and the title *Total Value* into column D, using the procedures you used for the first two labels.

Now, we're ready to enter the two category titles for the tapes in the sample inventory. Instead of just entering tape titles willy-nilly, we'll organize them by subject. The videotapes in this example are divided into two subject areas: Adventure and Aerobics. Let's assume we don't know at this point exactly how many titles we have in each category. We'll just skip five rows between each category name for now.

- ☐ Select cell A3 and type the category name *Adventure*. Press Command-B to boldface this category name and enter it at the same time.
- ☐ Press the Return key five times to skip four rows.
- ☐ Enter the category name *Aerobics*, and make it boldface, as you did with the first title.

The spreadsheet now looks like this:

File Edit Window Select Format Options Chart

Untitled (SS)

	A	B	C	D	E	F
1	Title	Quantity	Cost	Total Value		
2						
3	**Adventure**					
4						
5						
6						
7						
8	**Aerobics**					
9						
10						
11						
12						
13						
14						
15						
16						
17						

Now, we're ready to enter some tape titles.

- ☐ Select cell A4 and type the first tape title, *Six Gun City*.
- ☐ Click on cell A5 or press Return. The label you just typed is automatically entered in cell A4, and cell A5 is selected. Type the second tape title, *Two Guys In Trouble*, and then click on cell A6 or press Return to select the next cell in the column and enter the second label.

Notice at this point that the label *Two Guys In Trouble* is wider than the current column width, and that it has extended into column B at the right. When you type a long label into a Works spreadsheet, if there isn't enough room for the whole label in the current column, it automatically extends into columns to the right. In this case, we will want to use column B to enter Quantity numbers later, so we want all of the labels we enter in column A to stay inside that column. To do that, we'll have to widen column A so there's enough room in it for *Two Guys In Trouble* and other long labels we'll enter.

The easiest way to widen a column in the Works spreadsheet is to drag the column divider.

- Move the pointer to the dividing line between the labels for columns A and B at the top of the screen. When the pointer is exactly on top of the dividing line, it becomes a double arrow.
- Hold down the mouse button and drag the dividing line to the right about one inch.
- Release the mouse button to fix the dividing line in its new location. Column A is now wide enough to hold *Two Guys In Trouble* and other long labels.
- Repeat the label-entering process for the titles *Blazing Bullets* and *The Spy Who Said No.*

Once you've typed the second of these titles into cell A7, you're out of room for entering tape titles because the category title for the Aerobics section is in the next row. You need to insert some rows so you can add two more titles and a blank row in this category:

- Click on cell A8 and press Command-I, the keyboard equivalent for the Insert command. A blank row appears above row 8, and what was row 8 becomes row 9.
- Press Command-I two more times. The Insert command inserts only one row at a time, but if you want to add several rows, just use the Insert command repeatedly.
- Type in the final two titles, *Jungle Fever* and *The One-Eyed Assassin.*

We notice after we type these two labels that they appear in boldface, rather than normal text. This is because we inserted rows at the position where a boldfaced label formerly appeared (cell A8). To display these two labels in normal text, like the other tape titles:

- ☐ Click on the cell containing *Jungle Fever* and hold down the mouse button.
- ☐ Drag the pointer down to the cell containing *The One-Eyed Assassin* and release the mouse button. Both A8 and A9 should now be selected.
- ☐ Press Command-N to specify the normal text style for these two cells.
- ☐ Click on cell A10 to remove the selection from the labels in A8 and A9. You can see these labels are now displayed in normal text, like this:

File Edit Window Select Format Options Chart

A10

Untitled (SS)

	A	B	C	D	E
1	**Title**	**Quantity**	**Cost**	**Total Value**	
2					
3	**Adventure**				
4	Six Gun City				
5	Two Guys In Trouble				
6	Blazing Bullets				
7	The Spy Who Said No				
8	Jungle Fever				
9	The One-Eyed Assassin				
10					
11	**Aerobics**				
12					
13					
14					
15					
16					
17					

We now have one blank row between the Adventure and the Aerobics categories. Let's insert two more rows at this point so we can add a row to subtotal the tapes by category.

- ☐ Select cell A10, if it isn't already selected.
- ☐ Press Command-I twice to insert two blank rows.
- ☐ Click on cell A11 and type the title *Subtotal Adventure.* Press the Return key to enter it. (Notice that the label appears in bold, because you inserted a row at a location where the existing label had been boldfaced.)

Sorting inventory items

Now we have entered one complete category of tapes. Looking at the order in which the titles were entered, however, we decide the inventory sheet would be easier to use if the list were in alphabetical order (that's the way the tapes are stocked). We can use the spreadsheet's Sort... command to rearrange the titles in this section quickly:

- ☐ Select cell A4.
- ☐ Hold down the mouse button, drag the pointer down to cell A9, and then release the mouse button. All the tape titles in this category are now selected.
- ☐ Choose the Sort... command from the Edit menu. The Sort dialog box appears. Since the data you selected is in column A, this column is automatically shown as the first sort key. The default sort order is ascending order (A to Z), and that's what you want.
- ☐ Click the OK button in the Sort dialog box. The titles in rows 4 through 9 are rearranged alphabetically.
- ☐ Using the graphic of the finished worksheet as a guide, enter the Aerobics tape titles, along with a label for Aerobics subtotals. Don't forget to make the subtotals label boldface. In row 21 at the bottom, enter the title *Grand Totals* in column A, and make it boldface.

Now, we can enter the values for the Quantity and Cost columns. This is just a matter of selecting each cell and typing the appropriate number—either the number of tapes in stock or the tape's price—into each cell.

- ☐ Enter the rest of the labels and values shown in Figure 5-1.

Entering formulas

Now that we have entered all the video titles, quantities, and costs in the sample inventory, we're ready to enter some formulas. The first formula we'll enter calculates the total value of the tapes by title. That means we'll need a formula for each row that contains a tape title: We'll want to multiply the Quantity value found in column B by the Cost value in column C and place the result in the Total Value cell in column D. Let's do the formulas for the Adventure category at the top of the spreadsheet:

- ☐ Select cell D4.
- ☐ Type an equal sign to tell Works that you're beginning a formula.
- ☐ Click on cell B4. Notice that the reference B4 appears in the entry bar at the top of the worksheet. (If you prefer, you can type the cell references from the keyboard instead of pointing to cells to enter them into formulas.)
- ☐ Type an asterisk (*) to indicate multiplication. This appears after the B4 reference in the entry bar.
- ☐ Click on cell C4. This reference appears in the entry bar. The formula (cell B4 multiplied by cell C4) is complete, so click the

enter box (the box with the check mark in it next to the entry bar). The result of the multiplication appears in cell D4.

File Edit Window Select Format Options Chart

D4 =B4*C4

Untitled (SS)

	A	B	C	D	E
1	**Title**	**Quantity**	**Cost**	**Total Value**	
2					
3	**Adventure**				
4	Blazing Bullets	1	34.95	34.95	
5	Jungle Fever	2	32.95		
6	Six Gun City	1	22.95		
7	The One-Eyed Assassin	3	34.96		
8	The Spy Who Said No	3	28.95		
9	Two Guys In Trouble	2	34.95		
10					
11	**Subtotal Adventure**				
12					
13	**Aerobics**				
14	Aerobic Profit-Taking	4	34.95		
15	George Will's Yoga Fun	1	22.95		
16	Tip O'Neill's Workout	2	19.95		
17	Wimpy's Roll-a-thon	1	22.95		
18					

Copying formulas

Now, we want to copy this formula to all of the other rows containing film title, price, and quantity information in this category. Since all the cells where we want to copy this formula are directly below the formula's original location, we'll use the Fill Down command:

- Point to cell D4 and hold down the mouse button.
- Drag the pointer down to cell D9 and release it to select this block of cells.
- Press Command-D (the keyboard equivalent for Fill Down). The formula in D4 is copied into all the cells between D5 and D9, and the total values appear in these cells. Since the original formula contained relative cell references, the cell references in the copied formulas have adjusted themselves to reflect the new formula locations. If you click on cell D8, for example, you'll see that the cell references in the formula shown in the entry bar are B8 and C8, instead of B4 and C4.

The film-title rows in the Aerobics category need similar formulas. But we can't use the Fill Down command at this point, because the rows we want to fill aren't adjacent to the cells containing the formula. (There are Subtotal and blank rows between the Adventure and Aerobics categories.) Instead, we'll have to copy a formula with the Copy command, and then paste it into its new location:

- ☐ Select cell D9.
- ☐ Copy the formula in D9 to the Clipboard by pressing Command-C.
- ☐ Select cell D14 (the row containing the title, *Aerobic Profit-Taking*).
- ☐ Press Command-V (the keyboard equivalent for the Paste command). The formula (B14*C14) appears in the entry bar, and the references have adjusted themselves to match the formula's new location. The calculated value from the formula appears in cell D14.

Now, we can use Fill Down.

- ☐ Select cells D14 through D17 by dragging and use the Fill Down command to copy the formula.

Entering subtotal and total formulas

Row 21 at the bottom of the spreadsheet is called *Grand Totals* and will contain totals of the *Quantity* and *Total Value* columns, B and D. We also have category-subtotal rows at the bottom of each category. Let's enter the subtotal formulas for the first category, Adventure. First, we want to sum all the Quantity values in cells B4 through B9, and place the result in cell B11:

- ☐ Select cell B11.
- ☐ Choose the Paste Function… command from the Edit menu.
- ☐ Scroll down the list of functions to the Sum function (be sure to choose Sum, not SSum), then double-click on it. The Sum function appears in the entry bar, followed by the two parentheses that will enclose the argument (the cells or values on which the function will operate).

☐ To enter the range of cells from B4 through B9, position the pointer on cell B4, press and hold down the mouse button, drag the pointer down through cell B9, and release the mouse button. Notice that the range B4:B9 now appears in the entry bar, and that the range itself is outlined on the spreadsheet.

File Edit Window Select Format Options Chart

B11 =Sum(B4:B9)

Untitled (SS)

	A	B	C	D	E
1	**Title**	**Quantity**	**Cost**	**Total Value**	
2					
3	**Adventure**				
4	Blazing Bullets	1	34.95	34.95	
5	Jungle Fever	2	32.95	65.9	
6	Six Gun City	1	22.95	22.95	
7	The One-Eyed Assassin	3	34.96	104.88	
8	The Spy Who Said No	3	28.95	86.85	
9	Two Guys In Trouble	2	34.95	69.9	
10					
11	**Subtotal Adventure**				
12					
13	**Aerobics**				
14	Aerobic Profit-Taking	4	34.95	139.8	
15	George Will's Yoga Fun	1	22.95	22.95	
16	Tip O'Neill's Workout	2	19.95	39.9	
17	Wimpy's Roll-a-thon	1	22.95	22.95	
18					

☐ Click the enter box. The formula is entered, and its result appears in cell B11.

This Sum formula is the same basic formula we need to produce a subtotal for the Total Value column in cell D11. We could enter the formula again, but it's simpler to copy it:

☐ Select cell B11.

☐ Press Command-C, the keyboard equivalent for the Copy command.

☐ Select cell D11.

☐ Press Command-V, the keyboard equivalent for the Paste command. The formula is copied into cell D11, and, since the formula contains relative cell references, the references adjust themselves to the new location of the formula. The subtotaled value now appears in cell D11.

The relative formulas in cells B11 and D11 tell Works to add the contents of the six rows above them. Wherever we copy this formula, Works will adjust the cell references, and add the six rows above the formula's location. It would be nice if we could just copy this same formula into the subtotals row in the Aerobics category, but the Aerobics category doesn't contain six titles—it has four. For this reason, a formula that sums six rows won't work. So, we need to re-enter the Sum formula in column B for the Aerobics category subtotal and then copy that formula to column D. We know that the formula, except for the cell references, will be the same in both columns of the Aerobics category, because both formulas will sum the same number of rows. So, once we've entered the revised formula in column B, we can copy it to column C. To complete the subtotal formulas for the Aerobics category, then:

- ☐ Select cell B19.
- ☐ Choose the Paste Function... command from the Edit menu, and double-click on the Sum function.
- ☐ Select cell B14, hold down the mouse button, and drag the pointer down to cell B17.
- ☐ Release the mouse button to enter this range of cells into the Sum formula's argument in the entry bar, and then click the enter box to enter the formula.
- ☐ Cell B19 should be selected at this point, but if it isn't, select it.
- ☐ Press Command-C to copy the formula to the Clipboard.
- ☐ Select cell D19.
- ☐ Press Command-V to paste the formula from the Clipboard. The references in the formula adjust, and the correct sum appears in cell D19.

Once the category subtotals are completed, we can enter two formulas to produce the grand totals. We can't drag the mouse over a range of cells to sum them, because we want to sum the subtotal cells and they're not in a continuous group. Instead, we'll point to the cells individually to add them together:

- Select cell B21.
- Choose the Paste Function... command from the Edit menu, then select Sum from the list of functions.
- Click on cell B11 (the subtotal of quantities from the Adventure category). This reference is automatically entered into the Sum formula's argument in the entry bar.
- Click on cell B19 to enter this reference into the formula. Works automatically adds a plus sign in front of the second cell reference as you click on it.

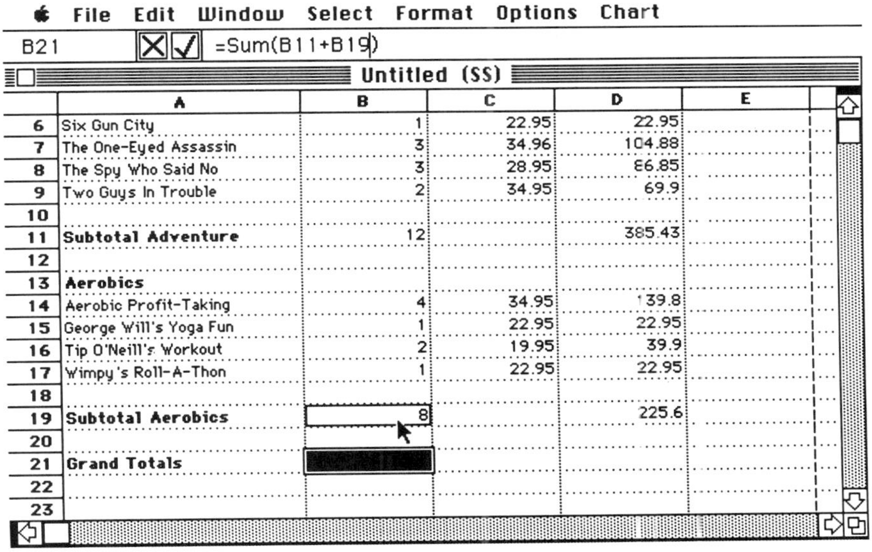

File Edit Window Select Format Options Chart

B21 =Sum(B11+B19)

Untitled (SS)

	A	B	C	D	E
6	Six Gun City	1	22.95	22.95	
7	The One-Eyed Assassin	3	34.96	104.88	
8	The Spy Who Said No	3	28.95	86.85	
9	Two Guys In Trouble	2	34.95	69.9	
10					
11	**Subtotal Adventure**	12		385.43	
12					
13	**Aerobics**				
14	Aerobic Profit-Taking	4	34.95	139.8	
15	George Will's Yoga Fun	1	22.95	22.95	
16	Tip O'Neill's Workout	2	19.95	39.9	
17	Wimpy's Roll-A-Thon	1	22.95	22.95	
18					
19	**Subtotal Aerobics**	8		225.6	
20					
21	**Grand Totals**				
22					
23					

- Click the enter box to enter the formula, and the result appears in cell B21.

Now, all we have to do is copy this formula to cell D21 to get a grand total of the cost of the tapes. The formula in B21 uses relative references, so we can simply copy the formula from cell B21 and paste it into cell D21. The cell references will adjust automatically.

Formatting the spreadsheet

The final thing we want to do with this spreadsheet is apply a little formatting. First of all, we should give the spreadsheet a title. We'll insert two rows above the current top row (select a cell in the top row and use the Insert command from the Edit menu twice). Then select a cell in column B, and type the title, *Tape Inventory.* Notice that since column B isn't wide enough to display the whole title, the label automatically extends into columns C and D. As was mentioned earlier in this chapter, labels always extend into neighboring columns if they're too long to display, but values don't. (When you enter a value too long to display, the cell stores the number, but it displays the number in scientific notation.) Also, the label appears in bold type because the previous label in that row was bold. Now, we'll format the price and total value amounts as dollars:

- ☐ Point to the letter *C* at the top of column C, hold down the mouse button, and drag across to column D, so both columns are highlighted.
- ☐ Choose the Dollar command from the Format menu. The values in columns C and D are automatically formatted as dollars and cents.

The spreadsheet is done, for now. We'll save it with the name *Inventory*:

- ☐ Choose the Save command from the File menu. Since this is a new file, the Save As dialog box automatically appears, asking us to enter a name for the new file.
- ☐ Type the name *Inventory,* and then click the Save button to save the file to disk.

Adding items to the inventory

This spreadsheet now contains all the titles in Al's inventory, but as he acquires more videotapes, he'll have to expand it. When it's necessary to add new titles within each of these categories, he can simply insert new rows. The references in all the Sum formulas will adjust themselves to accommodate the new rows. Let's look at an example: Suppose we want to add the title *East Village Exercises* to the Aerobics section:

- ☐ Click on the title *George Will's Yoga Fun*. We want to add a row above this title.
- ☐ Press Command-I to insert the new row.
- ☐ Type the title *East Village Exercises,* and press the Tab key to enter the label and move the selection one cell to the right.
- ☐ Type *2* for the quantity, then press the Tab key.
- ☐ Type the amount, *28.95*, and press the Tab key to enter it.
- ☐ Select cell D16 and press Command-C to copy the Total Value formula from the row above.
- ☐ Click on cell D17 and use the Paste command (Command-V) to paste the formula into the new row. The formula calculates the new row's total value, and all of the affected Sum formulas in the subtotal and grand total rows change to reflect the new addition.

As you'll see when you check the formula in the Aerobics category's subtotal row (by selecting either cell B22 or cell D22), the cell references there have automatically changed to accommodate the new row we've inserted.

AN AMORTIZATION TABLE

Al is considering borrowing money to expand the Videorama, and he wants to know what the payments will be. This is a good opportunity to build an amortization table with the Works spreadsheet. If we build the table properly, we'll always be able to change the loan amount, interest rate, and term to determine what a loan will cost.

You can think of each spreadsheet you build as a calculating machine that uses formulas to process numbers in a specific way. As mentioned in Chapter 4, you can use cell references instead of actual values in formulas, and that way you can change the values whenever you want to calculate a different set of numbers. We'll use that technique here, to build an amortization table we can use over and over to calculate the costs of loans of various amounts, terms, and rates.

The amortization table consists of two distinct parts: the Loan Summary area, which spells out the loan amount, term, interest rate, and monthly payment, and the Loan Activity area, which shows how the loan is paid off over its life.

Creating the summary area

Let's begin with a new, blank spreadsheet, and enter the loan-summary information first. Before entering any data, let's double the width of column A, so there's plenty of room to enter row labels:

- ☐ Point to the divider between the A and B column designations at the top of the spreadsheet. The pointer turns into a double arrow.
- ☐ Hold down the mouse button, and drag the divider to the right until it's on top of the divider between columns B and C.
- ☐ Release the mouse button to fix the relocated column divider on the screen.

Now, we'll enter some summary information, and a formula to calculate the loan payment:

- ☐ Click on cell A1 and type the label *Loan Summary.*
- ☐ Press Command-B to boldface the label and enter it at the same time.
- ☐ In cells A3, A4, A5, and A6, respectively, enter the labels *Loan Amount, Interest Rate, Term,* and *Monthly Payment.*

Now, we'll complete this area by entering the values and formulas. Let's assume Al wants to borrow $10,000. So we'll enter that amount in cell B3, next to the Loan Amount label.

As for the interest rate in cell B4, we'll enter the monthly interest rate. We'll assume the annual interest rate is 12 percent, so the monthly rate is 1 percent. (We need to express the rate as a monthly figure, because we're calculating a monthly payment.) First, we'll enter this amount as .01, then we'll reformat this cell so the value is displayed as a percentage:

- ☐ Select cell B4, type *.01,* then click the enter box.
- ☐ Choose the Percent command from the Format menu. The value .01 is multiplied by 100 and a percent sign is placed after it, so the cell now displays *1.00%*.

Whenever you create a payment formula, both the interest rate and the term have to be monthly or both have to be yearly. You can't enter a monthly interest rate and then specify the term in years, for example. We specified a monthly interest rate for Al's three-year loan, so we need to enter the value 36 in cell B5 to indicate the number of months in the term.

Using the Pmt function to calculate the monthly payment

Now we come to the actual formula that will calculate the payment on this loan. The Works spreadsheet contains 12 built-in financial functions that make it much easier to analyze investments and debts. You can read more about each of these functions in the Works Reference Manual, but for now, we'll focus on the function called Pmt (short for "payment").

As it is structured in Microsoft Works, the Pmt function calculates payments of equal amounts resulting from investments. When you use Pmt to calculate a loan payment, it helps to look at the loan from the bank's point of view. As far as the bank is concerned, it is an investment: The bank spends a fixed amount of money at the beginning of the loan (the loan amount, also known as the investment's present value), and in return it gets back the loan plus interest (at a certain rate) in the form of regular cash flows (your payments) for a specified term (period of time) until the loan is paid off. When the loan is paid off, its value (or balance) is zero. This is the future value of the loan.

Present value, future value, rate, and term are all common financial terms, and these terms are the elements of the Pmt function in Works. To enter a Pmt formula, you must specify the loan's interest rate; the term (abbreviated as nper, which is short for "number of periods"); the loan amount, or present value (pv); and the future value (fv), which usually is zero, because you're paying off the loan completely. You must also specify whether each payment comes at the beginning of a period, or at the end (type), because the timing of the payment affects how the interest is calculated. If you don't specify a type in a Pmt formula, Works assumes the first payment comes at the end of the period.

With the abbreviated argument names instead of actual numbers, the Pmt formula in Works looks like this:

```
Pmt(rate,nper,pv,fv,type)
```

You must always format the Pmt formula this way, with the various values in exactly this order, and with commas separating them.

With this background in mind, then, let's enter the Pmt formula in cell B6:

- ☐ Select cell B6.
- ☐ Choose the Paste Function... command from the Edit menu, and scroll down the list of functions until you see *Pmt()*.
- ☐ Double-click on the Pmt function. The function is entered in the entry bar.
- ☐ Click on cell B4 to enter the rate value, then type a comma after it.
- ☐ Click on cell B5 to enter the term value, then type a comma after it.
- ☐ Click on cell B3 to enter the present value (the loan amount).

We could go ahead and enter the number 0 to indicate the future value and then another 0 to indicate the type of payment, but if we don't enter these amounts, Works automatically enters them for us. Instead:

- Click the enter box. Works adds the two zeroes as the last two arguments in the entry line, calculates the Pmt formula, and displays the payment amount in cell B6.

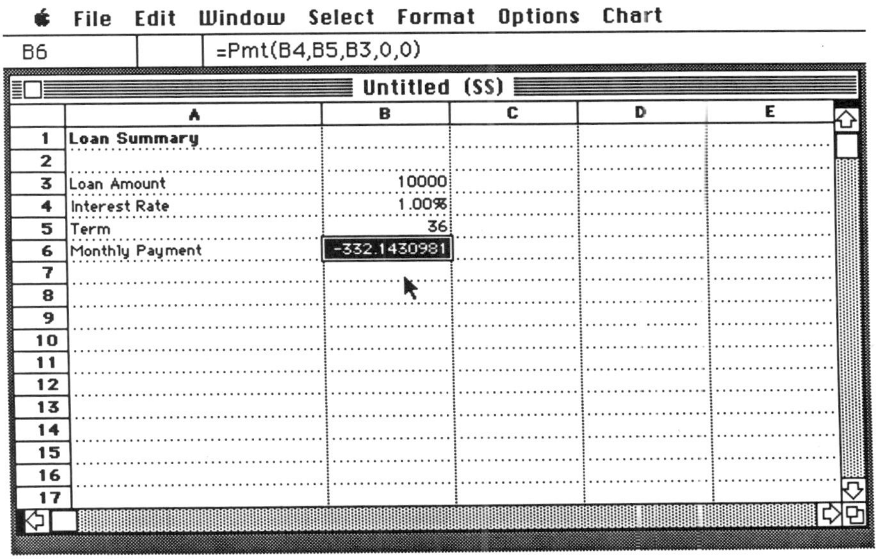

File Edit Window Select Format Options Chart

B6 =Pmt(B4,B5,B3,0,0)

Untitled (SS)

	A	B	C	D	E
1	**Loan Summary**				
2					
3	Loan Amount	10000			
4	Interest Rate	1.00%			
5	Term	36			
6	Monthly Payment	-332.1430981			
7					
8					
9					
10					
11					
12					
13					
14					
15					
16					
17					

You'll notice in this example that the payment amount appears as a long decimal number, and that it's a negative number. That's because the payments are considered outgoing cash flow, or debits. Of course, you probably will be well aware that loan payments are outgoing cash flow when you start making payments, so you won't need to be reminded by the minus sign. And you'd probably like the amount formatted as dollars and cents. Here's how to change the formats:

- Select cell B6 if it isn't already selected.
- Choose the Dollar command from the Format menu. The payment amount is reformatted as dollars and cents. but it appears in parentheses, because it's still considered a negative number.

To make a negative number positive, we must include the Abs (or absolute value) function in the formula. The Abs function will tell Works to present the positive value of the Pmt formula's results. Here's how:

- ☐ Select cell B6.
- ☐ Move the insertion point to the beginning of the Pmt formula in the entry bar by clicking in front of the *P* in *Pmt.*
- ☐ Choose the Paste Function... command from the Edit menu, and double-click on the Abs function (it's the first one on the list). The Abs function appears in the entry bar.

There's just one problem with the way Works has pasted the Abs function: A function can't act on anything that's outside the parentheses that follow it, and right now, the Pmt formula is outside the Abs parentheses. To move the Pmt formula:

- ☐ Position the pointer between the parentheses that follow Abs and the *P* of *Pmt,* hold down the mouse button, drag the pointer across the Pmt formula, and release the mouse button. Everything in the entry bar from the *P* in *Pmt* to the right should now be selected.
- ☐ Press Command-X to cut the formula from its place in the entry bar.
- ☐ Click in the space between the two parentheses that follow Abs to move the insertion point there.
- ☐ Press Command-V to paste the Pmt formula into position inside the parentheses.

- ☐ Click the enter box to enter the modified formula. The payment amount now appears without parentheses around it, indicating that it has been converted to a positive number.

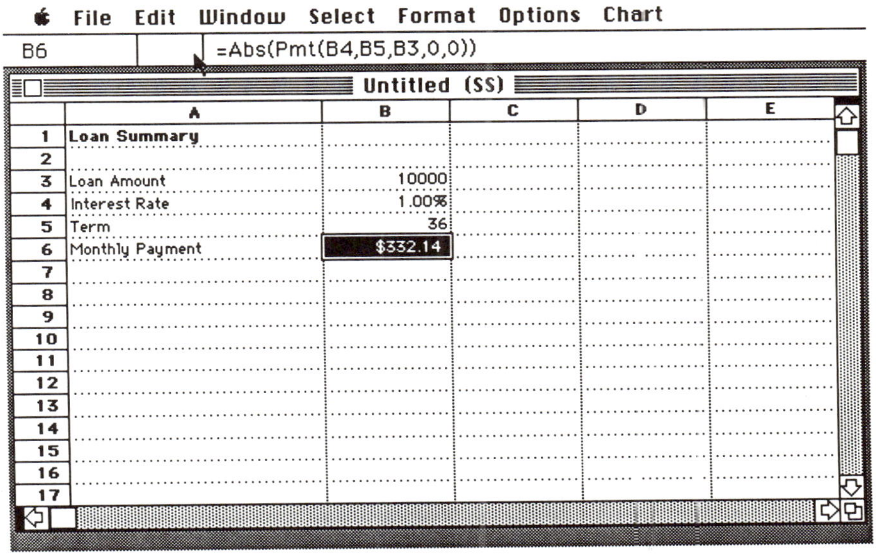

File Edit Window Select Format Options Chart

B6 =Abs(Pmt(B4,B5,B3,0,0))

Untitled (SS)

	A	B	C	D	E
1	**Loan Summary**				
2					
3	Loan Amount	10000			
4	Interest Rate	1.00%			
5	Term	36			
6	Monthly Payment	$332.14			
7					
8					
9					
10					
11					
12					
13					
14					
15					
16					
17					

Creating the loan-activity area

The loan-summary portion of the worksheet is all you may need, if you simply want to know how much the payment on a certain type of loan will be. But you might like to see the loan's activity as well. By including a loan-activity section in this amortization table, you'll be able to see how much principal and interest you're paying each month, and how the remaining balance of the loan is affected after each payment.

Now we'll create the loan-activity area of the spreadsheet. To begin, we'll separate the loan-summary portion of the spreadsheet from the loan-activity area with a double dashed line:

- ☐ Select cell A8.
- ☐ Type a quotation mark (") to indicate that you're about to enter a label.
- ☐ Hold down the equal-sign key until equal signs fill the entry bar, then press the Return key. The equal signs appear across row 8 as a divider.

We had to type the quotation mark first when entering this label, because the equal sign is normally the signal that you'll be entering a formula or value. The quotation mark tells Works that this time the equal sign is text, not part of a value or formula.

Now, we'll get on with the loan-activity area.

- ☐ Select cell A10 and type the label *Loan Activity.*
- ☐ Press Command-B to make the label boldface and enter it.
- ☐ Enter the labels *Interest, Principal,* and *Balance* in cells B11, C11, and D11 and make them boldface in the same manner.
- ☐ Select cell A12 and enter the boldface label *Loan Begins.* Press the Return key. The worksheet now looks like this:

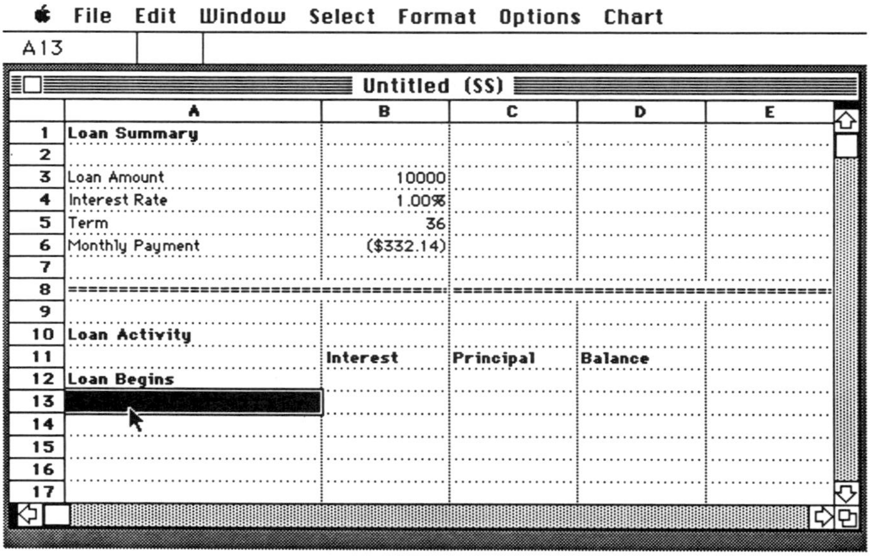

File Edit Window Select Format Options Chart

A13

Untitled (SS)

	A	B	C	D	E
1	**Loan Summary**				
2					
3	Loan Amount	10000			
4	Interest Rate	1.00%			
5	Term	36			
6	Monthly Payment	($332.14)			
7					
8	====================	====================	====================	====================	====================
9					
10	**Loan Activity**				
11		**Interest**	**Principal**	**Balance**	
12	**Loan Begins**				
13					
14					
15					
16					
17					

Now, we're ready to enter formulas and values by using references to the cells containing the rate, term, and loan amount values we've already entered in the Loan Summary area above. There are three formulas to enter this way, plus the beginning loan amount. We'll enter the beginning loan amount first:

- ☐ Select cell D12 and type an equal sign to begin the formula. We want to enter the beginning loan amount here, and we can do that by referring to the loan amount value in cell B3.

- ☐ Click on cell B3 to enter that reference into the formula in cell D12.
- ☐ Click the enter box in the entry bar to complete the formula. The value 10000 appears in cell D12.

Now, we'll calculate the amount of interest paid each month. This is simply the interest rate applied to the previous month's balance.

- ☐ Select cell B13, then type an equal sign to begin the formula.
- ☐ Click on cell B4 to enter the interest rate value.
- ☐ Type an asterisk (*) to indicate that B4 is to be multiplied by the next value.
- ☐ Click on cell D12 to enter the beginning loan amount value.
- ☐ Click the enter box to enter the formula. The result, 100, appears in cell B13.

The next formula shows us how much of each month's payment is principal. We already know how much the monthly payment is (it's in cell B6), and we just calculated how much interest we're paying each month (in cell B13), so we just have to subtract the interest from the payment amount to determine the principal each month:

- ☐ Select cell C13, and type an equal sign to begin the formula.
- ☐ Click on cell B6 to enter the value of the monthly payment.
- ☐ Type a minus sign to indicate subtraction.
- ☐ Click on cell B13 to enter that month's interest.
- ☐ Click the enter box to enter the formula. The amount of principal appears in cell C13.

Finally, we want to determine the first month's loan balance, after deducting the amount of principal paid. We simply subtract the current month's principal from the previous month's loan balance:

- ☐ Select cell D13.
- ☐ Type an equal sign to begin the formula.
- ☐ Click on cell D12 to enter the previous month's balance.

- Type a minus sign to indicate subtraction.
- Click on cell C13 to enter the current month's principal.
- Click the enter box to enter the formula. The current month's balance then appears in cell D13.

The spreadsheet now looks like this:

File Edit Window Select Format Options Chart

D13 =D12-C13

Untitled (SS)

	A	B	C	D	E
1	**Loan Summary**				
2					
3	Loan Amount	10000			
4	Interest Rate	1.00%			
5	Term	36			
6	Monthly Payment	$332.14			
7					
8	================================	================	================	================	================
9					
10	**Loan Activity**				
11		**Interest**	**Principal**	**Balance**	
12	**Loan Begins**			10000	
13		100	232.14309813	9767.8569019	
14					
15					
16					
17					

We've made all these calculations without typing one number from the keyboard.

So far, we've calculated one month's loan activity. However, we want to see the loan's activity over the entire 36 months. To see that, we'll have to copy the three formulas in row 13 down through row 48.

We've copied a lot of formulas before, but in this case, we need to take a different approach because we don't want all the cell references in the formulas to be relative. If you remember, we referred to cells in the Loan Summary area (B4 and B6) in our interest and principal formulas, and we want those references to be absolute—that is, we want every copy of these formulas to contain the same B4 and B6 references. If you remember, we entered the B4 and B6 references into cells B13 and C13 just by clicking on them, making the references relative. To make these references absolute, we'll have to change them slightly:

- ☐ Select cell B13. The existing formula from B13 appears in the entry bar.
- ☐ Click between the equal sign and the *B* to move the insertion point there.
- ☐ Type a dollar sign to indicate that the reference to column B is absolute.
- ☐ Click between the *B* and the *4* in the reference to move the insertion point there.
- ☐ Type another dollar sign to indicate that the reference to row 4 is absolute.
- ☐ Click the enter box to enter the modified formula.

As you can see, the results of the formula don't change. All we've done is tell Works that the references to column B and row 4 in the B4 part of this formula are absolute. Now whenever we make a copy of this formula, this reference will always remain the same.

You'll also notice that we put dollar signs in front of both the *B* and the *4* in the reference. This is to make both the row and column references absolute. If we had put a dollar sign only in front of the *B*, for example, then the reference to row 4 would have remained relative, and it would change to reflect the location of any copied formulas.

Now, we can repeat these same six steps to convert the formula in cell C13. We want to make the reference to cell B6 absolute, in the same way. Once we've done that, filling out the rest of the Loan Activity section is a simple matter of copying the formulas in row 13 down through row 48 (this is a 36-month loan, so we want it to contain 36 rows of calculations).

- ☐ Select cell B13 and hold down the mouse button.
- ☐ Drag the pointer down to cell B48, and release the mouse button.
- ☐ Press Command-D (the keyboard equivalent for the Fill Down command). The formula will be copied into all the selected cells.

- Repeat the previous three steps for cells C13 and D13 to complete the Loan Activity section of the spreadsheet. Figure 5-2 shows the completed spreadsheet.

Notice that the spreadsheet in Figure 5-2 shows formulas, instead of values. As you may recall from Chapter 4, you can display the formulas (rather than values) in a spreadsheet by choosing Show Formulas from the Options menu. This helps when you want to remember what formulas you used throughout a spreadsheet, or when you want to print out a spreadsheet's formulas so you can easily show somebody else how you built it.

Now that we've entered all the formulas and copied them, you can see why it was important to build the Loan Activity formulas from references to the Loan Summary area (rather than entering the loan amount, rate, term, and Pmt formula again): We can change any value in the Loan Summary area, and the Loan Activity area automatically recalculates to reflect the change. Since the formulas in row 13 use the cell references B4 and B6 instead of the values *1%* and *$332.14,* we can easily change the contents of these cells to see how a different loan stacks up. Now is a good time to format columns B, C, and D for dollars. We don't want to reformat the Loan Summary area, because we have one value formatted for percent there, so we'll just reformat these columns from row 12 down:

- Point to cell B12, hold down the mouse button, and drag the pointer across to cell D12, then down to cell D50.
- Choose the Dollar command from the Format menu. When you scroll back up to cell D12, you'll see that the value there is now shown as dollars and cents. Any other value you enter in this block of cells (B12 through D50) will also appear as dollars and cents.

Let's save this spreadsheet with the name *Amort.Table,* so that whenever we want to check the payments and activity of a loan, we can easily retrieve this file and enter the new figures.

- Choose Save As... from the File menu.
- When the dialog box appears, type *Amort.Table* in the text box and click the Save button.

Loan Summary			
Loan Amount	10000		
Interest Rate	.01		
Term	36		
Monthly Payment	=Abs(Pmt(B4,B!		
====================================	====================	====================	====================
Loan Activity			
	Interest	**Principal**	**Balance**
Loan Begins			=B3
	=$B$4*D12	=$B$6-B13	=D12-C13
	=$B$4*D13	=$B$6-B14	=D13-C14
	=$B$4*D14	=$B$6-B15	=D14-C15
	=$B$4*D15	=$B$6-B16	=D15-C16
	=$B$4*D16	=$B$6-B17	=D16-C17
	=$B$4*D17	=$B$6-B18	=D17-C18
	=$B$4*D18	=$B$6-B19	=D18-C19
	=$B$4*D19	=$B$6-B20	=D19-C20
	=$B$4*D20	=$B$6-B21	=D20-C21
	=$B$4*D21	=$B$6-B22	=D21-C22
	=$B$4*D22	=$B$6-B23	=D22-C23
	=$B$4*D23	=$B$6-B24	=D23-C24
	=$B$4*D24	=$B$6-B25	=D24-C25
	=$B$4*D25	=$B$6-B26	=D25-C26
	=$B$4*D26	=$B$6-B27	=D26-C27
	=$B$4*D27	=$B$6-B28	=D27-C28
	=$B$4*D28	=$B$6-B29	=D28-C29
	=$B$4*D29	=$B$6-B30	=D29-C30
	=$B$4*D30	=$B$6-B31	=D30-C31
	=$B$4*D31	=$B$6-B32	=D31-C32
	=$B$4*D32	=$B$6-B33	=D32-C33
	=$B$4*D33	=$B$6-B34	=D33-C34
	=$B$4*D34	=$B$6-B35	=D34-C35
	=$B$4*D35	=$B$6-B36	=D35-C36
	=$B$4*D36	=$B$6-B37	=D36-C37
	=$B$4*D37	=$B$6-B38	=D37-C38
	=$B$4*D38	=$B$6-B39	=D38-C39
	=$B$4*D39	=$B$6-B40	=D39-C40
	=$B$4*D40	=$B$6-B41	=D40-C41
	=$B$4*D41	=$B$6-B42	=D41-C42
	=$B$4*D42	=$B$6-B43	=D42-C43
	=$B$4*D43	=$B$6-B44	=D43-C44
	=$B$4*D44	=$B$6-B45	=D44-C45
	=$B$4*D45	=$B$6-B46	=D45-C46
	=$B$4*D46	=$B$6-B47	=D46-C47
	=$B$4*D47	=$B$6-B48	=D47-C48

Figure 5-2. *You can show formulas instead of values in a spreadsheet by using the Show Formulas command from the Options menu.*

CUSTOMER-VOLUME REPORT

Because he's an astute businessman, Al Chroma is monitoring the traffic in his store, and he's using the spreadsheet shown in Figure 5-3 to keep track of the results. The spreadsheet stores the weekly customer volumes and the number of new video club members. It also tracks the advertising source that brought each customer in. We'll use this spreadsheet and Works' charting feature to help Al visualize the data.

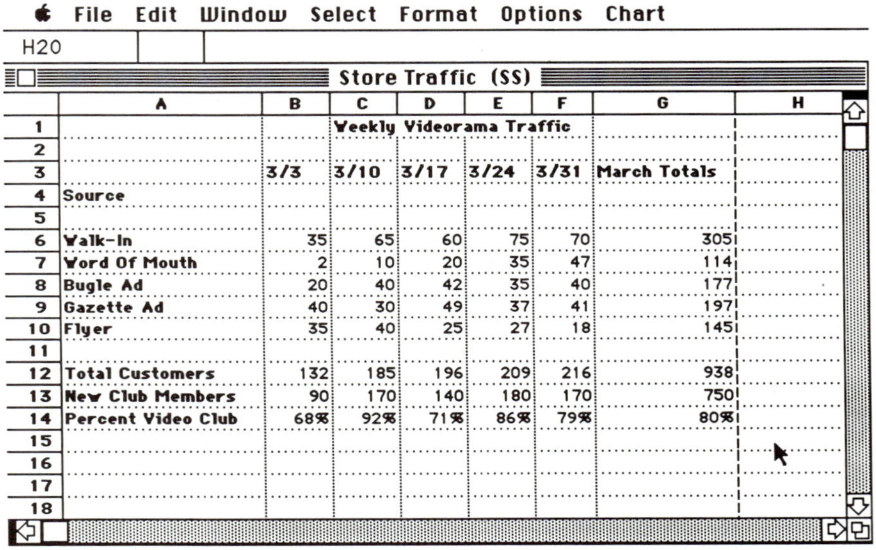

File Edit Window Select Format Options Chart

H20

Store Traffic (SS)

	A	B	C	D	E	F	G	H
1			Weekly Videorama Traffic					
2								
3		3/3	3/10	3/17	3/24	3/31	March Totals	
4	Source							
5								
6	Walk-In	35	65	60	75	70	305	
7	Word Of Mouth	2	10	20	35	47	114	
8	Bugle Ad	20	40	42	35	40	177	
9	Gazette Ad	40	30	49	37	41	197	
10	Flyer	35	40	25	27	18	145	
11								
12	Total Customers	132	185	196	209	216	938	
13	New Club Members	90	170	140	180	170	750	
14	Percent Video Club	68%	92%	71%	86%	79%	80%	
15								
16								
17								
18								

Figure 5-3. *Al uses this spreadsheet to keep track of the number of customers in his video store each week.*

In this exercise, we're mainly interested in the charting features of the spreadsheet. Before we can explore Works' chart functions, though, we need to create a spreadsheet like the one in Figure 5-3.

- ☐ Open a new spreadsheet file, and then, using Figure 5-3 as a guide, enter the labels and values to create this sample spreadsheet.

You can practice entering Sum formulas in column G and in row 12, if you like, but it isn't necessary to have actual formulas that produce the total values. If you prefer, just type the numbers you see in the spreadsheet here.

Creating a chart that tracks store traffic and new members

Suppose we first want to get a visual picture of how customer traffic fluctuates from week to week, and how the traffic total compares with the number of new video club members during March. We want to see how the numbers change over time (in this case, five weeks), so we want to make a series chart. (Figure 5-4 later in this chapter shows the completed chart, if you want to refer to it as we go along.)

☐ Choose the New Series Chart... command from the Chart menu. A new chart-definition window appears.

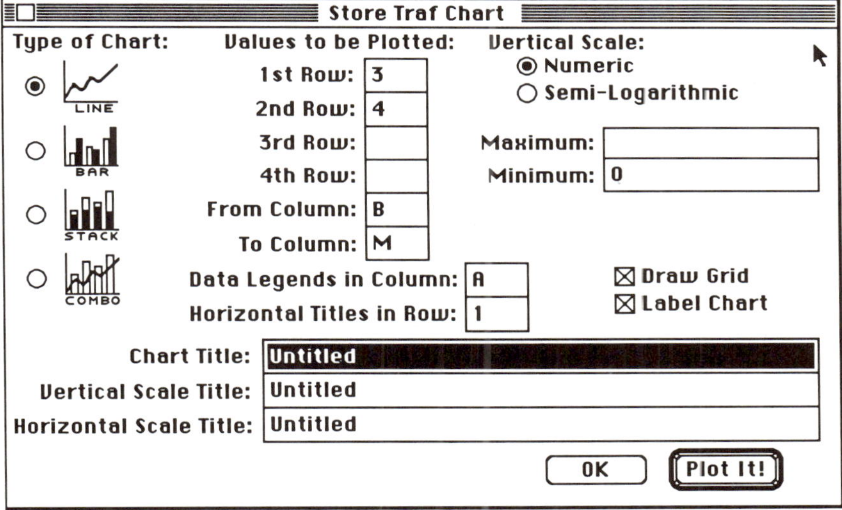

We want to represent not only the total number of customers each week, but also the number of new video club members, so that Al can see how these two values stack up against each other. The best way to show this is with a bar chart. If we select the two appropriate data rows (Total Customers and New Club Members), Works will draw a bar for each value.

☐ Click on the button next to the bar-chart icon in the chart-definition window.

Now, we have to specify the rows from which the charted data will be taken. Unfortunately, the chart-definition window is covering the Store Traffic spreadsheet at this point, and it's hard to remember the exact number of the rows containing the data we want to graph. Let's move the chart-definition window to uncover the spreadsheet:

- ☐ Point to the title bar at the top of the chart-definition window.
- ☐ Hold down the mouse button and drag the window toward the bottom of the screen, until rows 12 and 13 are revealed on the spreadsheet.

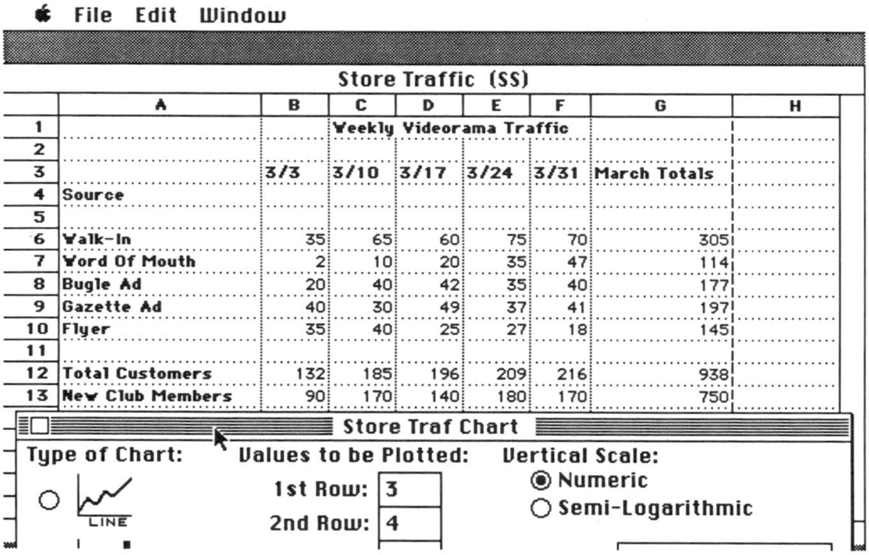

File Edit Window

Store Traffic (SS)

	A	B	C	D	E	F	G	H
1			Weekly Videorama Traffic					
2								
3		3/3	3/10	3/17	3/24	3/31	March Totals	
4	Source							
5								
6	Walk-In	35	65	60	75	70	305	
7	Word Of Mouth	2	10	20	35	47	114	
8	Bugle Ad	20	40	42	35	40	177	
9	Gazette Ad	40	30	49	37	41	197	
10	Flyer	35	40	25	27	18	145	
11								
12	Total Customers	132	185	196	209	216	938	
13	New Club Members	90	170	140	180	170	750	

Store Traf Chart

Type of Chart:
LINE
Values to be Plotted:
1st Row: 3
2nd Row: 4
Vertical Scale:
Numeric
Semi-Logarithmic

Now, we can enter the value locations for our chart in the chart-definition window:

- ☐ Double-click in the 1st Row box, and enter the number *12*. This tells Works to get the data for the first bar in the bar chart from row 12 of the spreadsheet. Do not press Return yet—pressing Return at any time while the chart-definition window is displayed tells Works to plot the chart according to the current definition.

- Double-click in the 2nd Row box and enter the number *13* to indicate the second row of data. Again, don't press the Return key yet.

If you press Return by mistake and the chart is plotted, you can display the chart-definition window again by closing the chart window and redisplaying the chart-definition window, like this:

- Click the close box in the upper-left corner of the chart window. The chart will disappear, and the spreadsheet from which you made the chart will be displayed again.
- Choose the Select Definition... command from the Chart menu. A list of currently defined charts will appear.
- Double-click on the name of the chart you want to redefine (or choose New Series Chart...), and that chart-definition window will open again (either the previously stored window you selected, or a new window).

Rows 12 and 13 contain all the data we want to chart, so now we must specify the range of cells in these rows that we want to chart. First, we need to make the appropriate portion of the chart-definition window visible.

- Drag the chart-definition window up toward the top of the screen until the From Column and To Column boxes are revealed. When you do this, you'll see that the default reference, column B, is already entered in the From Column box.

Since our weekly traffic data runs from column B through column F, we don't have to change the From Column value. We do, however, have to change the To Column value:

- Double-click in the To Column box, and enter the value *F*.

We have now defined two different bars—one representing data in row 12, and another representing data in row 13—for each of five weekly periods. The data is in columns B through F in those two rows. Next, we must tell Works which spreadsheet labels to use to identify the bars it will draw. Works will visually differentiate the two bars in each period by filling them with a different pattern, as you can see in Figure 5-4, but we need to tell Works how to label each pattern so we know which bar represents which data. The Data Legends In Column box lets us do this. As you can see, the box contains the default value *A*, which tells Works to use the labels found in column A of the spreadsheet to identify data legends. Since we're plotting rows 12 and 13, Works will use the labels *Total Customers* and *New Club Members* to identify the bars it draws. This is exactly what we want, so we don't have to change this value.

We also need to tell Works where to find the horizontal titles that will identify each set of bars on the chart. We are charting five weekly periods here, so we want to identify each group of bars by the week. These titles are located in row 3 of our spreadsheet, as you can see in Figure 5-3. Works' default value for the Horizontal Titles In Row box is row 1. But we want the horizontal titles taken from row 3.

☐ Double-click on the Horizontal Titles In Row box and change this value to *3*.

Now, we can adjust the formatting of this bar chart before we plot it. The Chart Title box allows us to enter a name that will appear at the top of the chart:

☐ Double-click in the Chart Title box and enter the name *March Traffic*. Remember, don't press Return after typing the name.

The Vertical Scale Title box lets us enter a title to identify the numbers on the chart's vertical scale (the scale running up and down the left side of the chart). Our numbers indicate the number of customers, so we'll enter the title Customers.

☐ Double-click in the Vertical Scale Title box and enter the name *Customers*.

Likewise, the Horizontal Scale Title box lets us identify the numbers on the chart's horizontal scale (the scale running across the bottom of the chart). In our case, the numbers are weekly periods, so we'll enter the title Week.

- ☐ Double-click on the Horizontal Scale Title box and enter the name *Week.*

Finally, we must decide which scaling method Works will use to increment the vertical scale, whether the chart should appear on a grid, and whether a chart label should be included. The Vertical Scale section in the upper-right corner of the chart-definition window lets us choose between straight numeric and semi-logarithmic scales. A numeric scale is divided into 10 regular increments, depending on the minimum and maximum values found in the data being graphed. If the minimum value is 0 and the maximum value is 200, for example, the scale would show 20, 40, 60, and so forth up to 200. In a semi-logarithmic scale, on the other hand, the distances between the increments decrease geometrically as the numbers get larger. For example, a data sample from 0 to 200 might be scaled as 0, 100, and 1000. Generally, you'll want to use the numeric scaling unless your data sample contains both very large and very small numbers.

The Maximum and Minimum boxes below the scaling options let you specify maximum and minimum scale values. The default setting in the Minimum box is 0, which means chart scales will begin with the value 0. If you're graphing values between 10,000 and 50,000, you would probably want to reset the minimum value to 10,000.

The Draw Grid box lets you choose to either display or not display a grid underneath the data you chart. Grids often help you determine exactly which values are being represented on a chart, and this option is selected automatically, which means a grid will be drawn. The Label Chart box lets you either display or not display all the text labels on a chart, including horizontal and vertical scale titles, data legends, and the chart title. Usually, you'll want to display titles, so this box should have an X in it.

The completed chart-definition window looks like this:

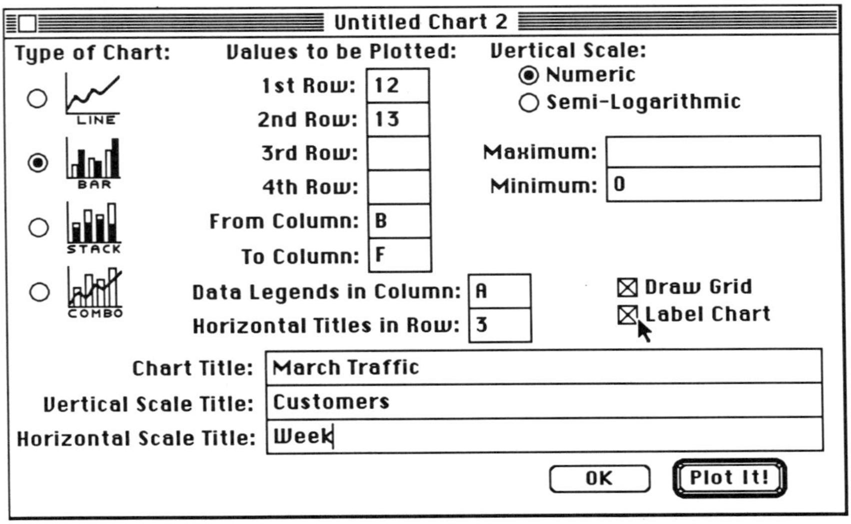

Untitled Chart 2

Type of Chart: LINE / BAR / STACK / COMBO

Values to be Plotted:
1st Row: 12
2nd Row: 13
3rd Row:
4th Row:
From Column: B
To Column: F
Data Legends in Column: A
Horizontal Titles in Row: 3

Vertical Scale:
Numeric
Semi-Logarithmic
Maximum:
Minimum: 0

Draw Grid
Label Chart

Chart Title: March Traffic
Vertical Scale Title: Customers
Horizontal Scale Title: Week

OK | Plot It!

To draw the chart we've just defined:

- Press the Return key or click the Plot It! button. The chart appears, as shown in Figure 5-4.

Now that we've defined this chart, it will be stored automatically with the Store Traffic spreadsheet. When we add or change the numbers in the spreadsheet, the chart will reflect the changes whenever we draw it. Although we had to make a chart definition to draw this chart originally, we can simply tell Works to draw the chart any time in the future. When we use the Draw Chart... command from the Chart menu, we can choose from a list of charts we've already defined, and then select a chart to be drawn. If, on the other hand, we want to modify a chart's definition, we can use the Select Definition... command to re-display any chart's original definition window.

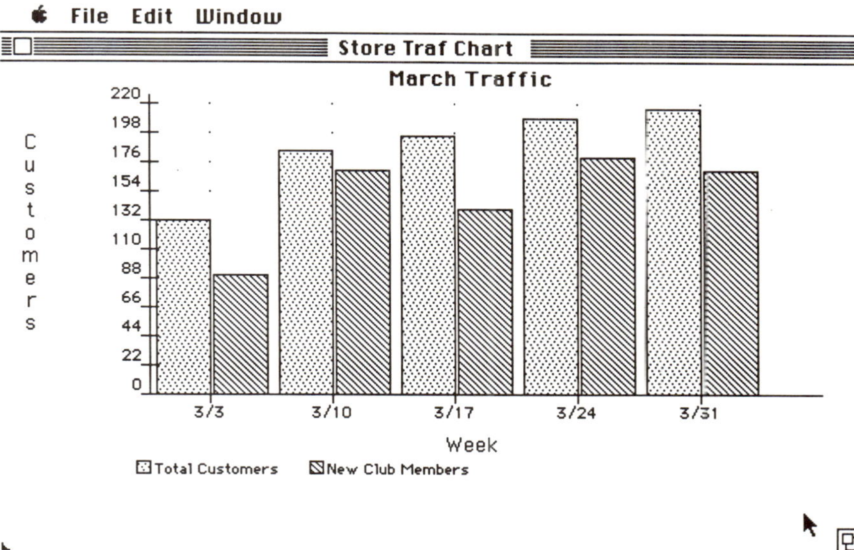

Figure 5-4. *It's easy to produce professional-looking charts with Works.*

Creating a chart that tracks traffic by advertising source

There's one other chart that might be useful for this spreadsheet. Since the number of customers visiting the store is broken down by advertising source, it might be useful to draw a pie chart that shows how each of these sources contributed to the total customer base during March. Each Works spreadsheet can store up to eight different chart definitions at once, so we can make this chart without losing the bar chart we've just drawn.

To begin a new chart, we'll click the close box at the upper-left corner of the bar-chart window we now have on the screen. This closes that chart window and returns us to the spreadsheet. Then, to make a pie chart:

□ Choose the New Pie Chart... command from the Chart menu. The Pie Chart Definition window appears.

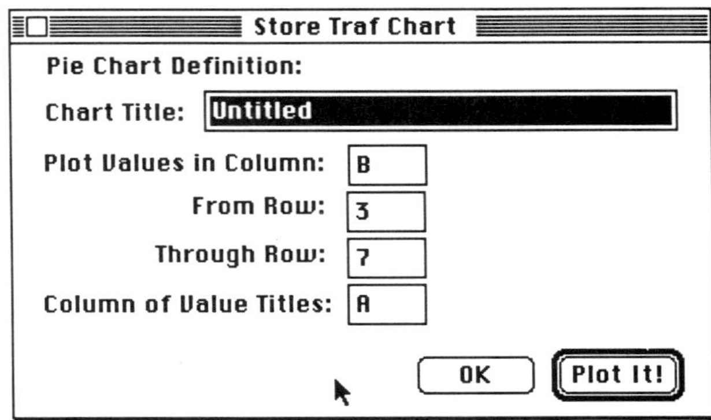

Pie charts represent the contents of only one column in a spreadsheet, and since there are no horizontal or vertical legends, the definition window is much simpler. First, we'll give the chart a title.

□ Enter the title *Traffic Sources* in the Chart Title box. Remember, don't press the Return key after typing the title.

Next, we have to identify the column from which the chart's values will be taken. We could chart any column from B through F to plot one week's traffic, but let's plot the entire month's traffic instead.

□ Double-click in the Plot Values In Column box, and enter the letter *G*. Column G contains the March totals.

□ Double-click in the From Row box, and enter the number *6*. Row 6 is the first row of traffic-source breakdown.

□ Double-click in the Through Row box, and enter the number *10*. Row 10 is the last row of the traffic-source data.

When the chart is plotted, each individual cell in column G from row 6 through row 10 will represent a slice of the pie. We want these slices identified by the row labels in column A. The Column Of Value Titles box already contains the letter A (this is the default), so we're now ready to plot the chart.

- Click the Plot It! button or press the Return key, and the chart is plotted.

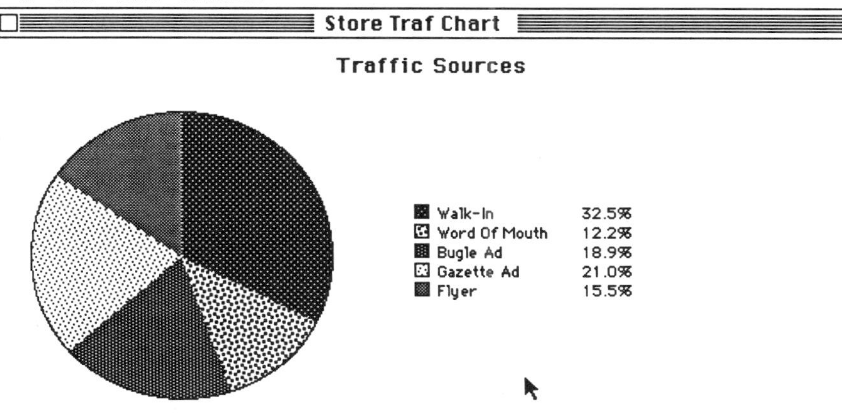

You can use the size box to resize charts on the screen, so that the spreadsheet underneath them is showing and you can refer to the original data while you look at the chart. For example, we might want to resize the pie chart, so we can consult the totals, change them, and then instantly see the results of those changes:

- Resize the pie-chart window by dragging the size box up and to the left.
- Click on the spreadsheet to activate the spreadsheet window, and change the Walk-In total in cell G6 from 305 to 935.

When you click on the spreadsheet to activate its window, the chart window disappears, but you can bring it back quickly by choosing it from the Window menu. To redisplay the chart:

- Select the chart's name from the Window menu. The chart

now appears on top of the spreadsheet again, and it has changed to reflect the changed value in cell F6.

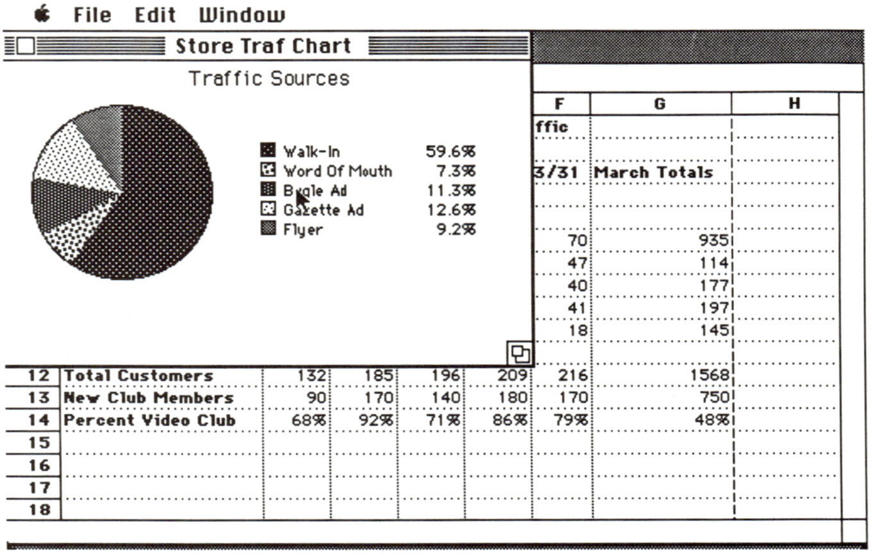

File Edit Window

Store Traf Chart

Traffic Sources

Walk-In	59.6%
Word Of Mouth	7.3%
Bugle Ad	11.3%
Gazette Ad	12.6%
Flyer	9.2%

						F	G	H
						ffic		
						3/31	March Totals	
						70	935	
						47	114	
						40	177	
						41	197	
						18	145	
12	Total Customers	132	185	196	209	216	1568	
13	New Club Members	90	170	140	180	170	750	
14	Percent Video Club	68%	92%	71%	86%	79%	48%	
15								
16								
17								
18								

A CONSOLIDATED SPREADSHEET

Suppose our friend Al wants to consolidate all of his personal and business financial information in one spreadsheet file. Having everything in one file will make it easier for Al to copy and compare data. He could put all of his data in one large matrix, but that would get pretty messy: Because Al has a number of income and expense items, both personal and business, the bottom line figures would be widely separated, making quick comparison difficult. So, instead of doing all these expense and income items in one big matrix, we'll divide the spreadsheet file into five different areas: Business Income, Personal Income, Business Expenses, Personal Expenses, and Summary, in the placement shown in Figure 5-5. Then, we'll copy the totals from each of these areas into one summary area.

Creating the summary area

To begin, we'll put the summary area of the worksheet at the top of a new spreadsheet file, beginning in column A and row 1. The summary is what we'll probably want to see most often, so it makes sense to place it here. Since this is a summary area for values that will come from other areas we'll create later, right now we'll enter only labels for the summarized expense or income items and the months of the year.

☐ Open a new spreadsheet and create a summary area that looks like this:

File Edit Window Select Format Options Chart

Income/Expense (SS)

	A	B	C	D	E	
1	**Income-Expense Summary**					
2						
3		Jan	Feb	Mar	Apr	May
4	**Income**					
5	Videorama					
6	Personal Income					
7						
8	**Total Income**					
9						
10	Expenses					
11	Videorama					
12	Personal-Fixed					
13	Personal-Discretionary					
14						
15	**Total Expenses**					
16	**Total Income**					
17	**Cash Flow**					
18						

Be sure to include columns for every month, not just through May as shown here.

Now, we want to create the detail areas that will contribute totals to the summary area. Instead of placing these areas underneath or to the right of the summary area, we'll place them below and to the right, on the diagonal, as shown in Figure 5-5 on the next page.

When you have more than one detail area in a spreadsheet file, it's best to place each area in a diagonal layout. A diagonal arrangement lets you add or delete rows or columns or make columns wider or narrower in one area without affecting the other areas. (If you had two areas, one underneath the other, adding or deleting columns in one of them would affect the other one as well.)

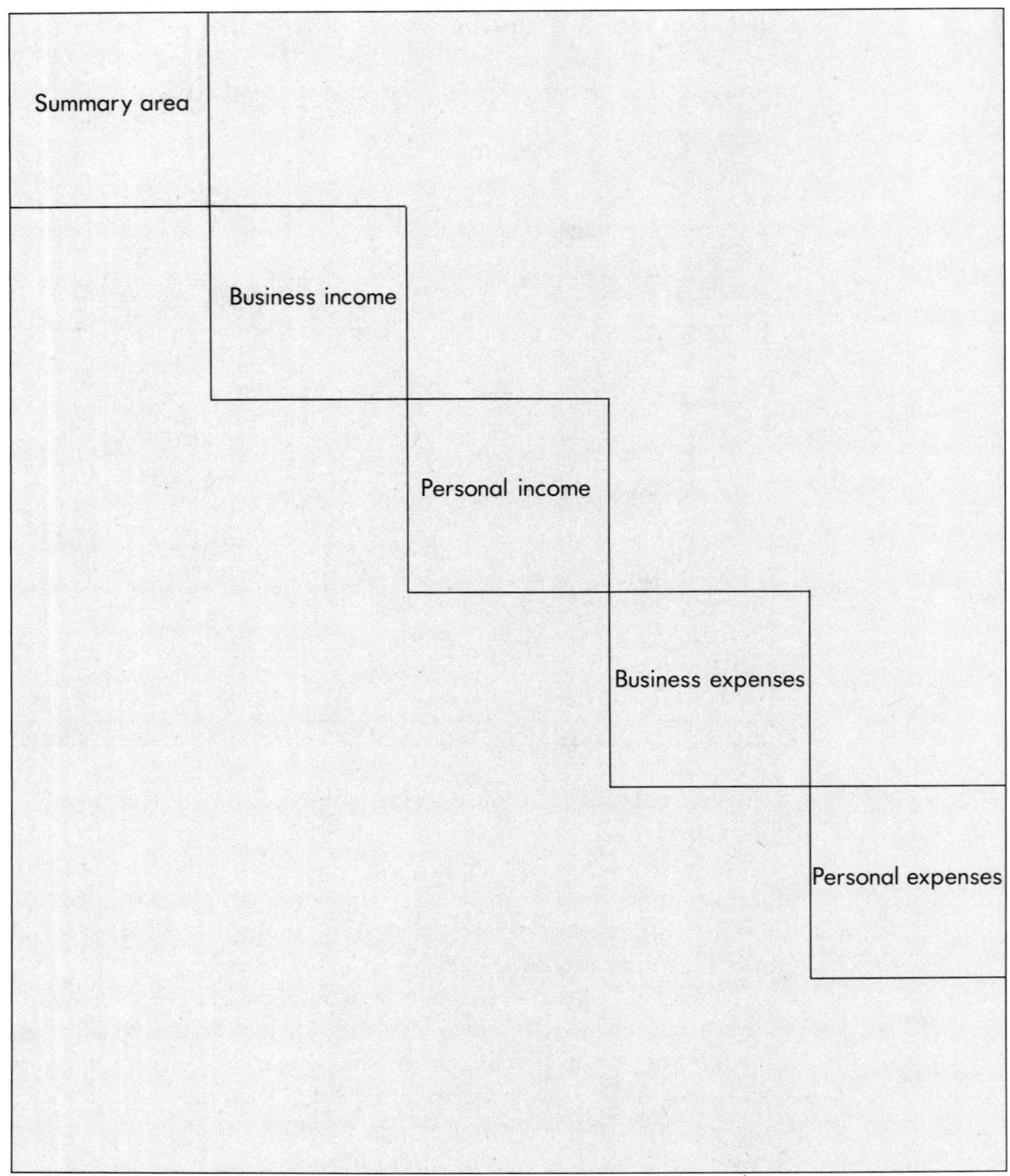

Figure 5-5. *A diagonal layout for a consolidated spreadsheet lets you add rows or columns to any area without affecting the others.*

Creating the first detail area

To place our first detail area on the diagonal with the summary area, we have to locate the last cell (the one in the lower-right corner) of the summary area. Whenever you build a spreadsheet, Works considers the last cell to be the filled cell that's farthest down and to the right. In our summary area, that cell is N17. If we want, we can scroll down to row 17 and column N manually, but Works has a command that finds this cell quickly:

- ☐ Select the Last Cell command from the Select menu. The spreadsheet scrolls and cell N17 is selected.

To begin a new area on the diagonal with the summary area, then, we want to select the next cell on the diagonal, which is cell O18. We'll consider that cell the upper-left corner of the first detail area.

First, we'll enter the label *Business Income* in the upper-right corner of this area (cell O18). (You'll have to widen column O about half an inch to make room for this label.) That way, we'll be able to use the Find Cell... command whenever we want to move quickly to this area. We'll simply ask Works to find the label *Business Income.* Then, working as we would with any new spreadsheet, we'll enter row labels for each expense item and column labels for each month. The column labels are the same as the ones we already entered in the summary area, so, to save time, we can copy them:

- ☐ Scroll up the spreadsheet until cell B3 is showing.
- ☐ Click on cell B3 and drag the pointer across row 3 to cell N3. All the month columns and the totals column are highlighted.
- ☐ Press Command-C to copy these labels to the Clipboard.
- ☐ Choose the Last Cell command from the Select menu. The spreadsheet scrolls down to cell O18 and that cell is highlighted.
- ☐ Click on cell P19 to select it. (We want the column labels to be in the row below the area label.)

☐ Press Command-V to paste the column labels into row 19, beginning at column P and extending to the right.

File Edit Window Select Format Options Chart

T27

Income/Expense (SS)

	N	O	P	Q	R	S
10						
11						
12						
13						
14						
15						
16						
17						
18		**Business Income**				
19			Jan	Feb	Mar	Apr
20						
21						
22						
23						
24						
25						
26						
27						

Now, we can enter the labels in column O, beginning in row 20.

☐ Complete the Business Income area to look like this:

File Edit Window Select Format Options Chart

O27

Income/Expense (SS)

	N	O	P	Q	R	S
14						
15						
16						
17						
18		**Business Income**				
19			Jan	Feb	Mar	Apr
20		Club Memberships				
21		Videotape Rentals				
22		Videotape Sales				
23		Accessory Sales				
24		VCR Rentals				
25						
26		Total Income	0	0	0	
27						
28						
29						
30						
31						

Adding a formula that transfers totals to the summary

This area is now ready to receive income totals as they come in each month. A Sum formula in the Total Income row (row 26) will calculate total business income, and we can enter cell references to transfer these totals to the appropriate row in the summary area:

- ☐ Scroll the spreadsheet back up to cell B5.
- ☐ Select cell B5, and type *=P26* (P26 is the cell that will contain the business income totals for January).
- ☐ Press the Tab key to enter this reference and move the insertion point to cell C5.
- ☐ Type *=Q26* (the cell that will contain the business income totals for February), and press the Tab key.
- ☐ Repeat the previous two steps to enter the corresponding cell references from the rest of row 5, so that the values from the Total Income row (26) are all transferred to row 5.

Now that the Business Income row (row 5) contains references to the Total Income row from the Business Income area (row 26), those totals will automatically transfer when the values are entered or changed. We can enter the membership sales, tape rental and sales, and other income values each month in the Business Income area, and the Sum formula will produce the total. Since the Business Income row in the summary area contains references to the row of totals in the Business Income area, the sums will automatically appear in both places. To see how this works, enter a value in cell P26, and then check cell B5—the value from P26 will also appear there.

Creating additional detail areas

By now, you probably get the idea of how to create a consolidated spreadsheet.

When you want to use separate detail areas and consolidate them in a summary, there are just a few major points to remember:

- Build the spreadsheets on the diagonal, so the insertion of rows or columns in one area doesn't affect other areas.

- Use the Last Cell command to find the lower-right corner of each area, so you know where to begin the next area below and to the right of it.
- Label each spreadsheet area, so you can jump there quickly using Works' Find Cell... command.
- Enter the cell references from the total rows of each detail area in the appropriate row in the summary area, so the total values from the detail areas automatically transfer to the summary area.

Using this simple approach, you can build extremely complex spreadsheets without using one huge matrix that is difficult to find your way around. And you can create charts of individual detail areas, or of the summary area.

Adjusting page breaks

The only consideration that remains is where the pages break. Unlike a word-processor document, in which page breaks occur horizontally between pages only, a spreadsheet's page breaks divide it up both horizontally and vertically. It's quite possible that you'll have more columns than can fit across one page of paper, and you may also have more rows than will fit on the length of one piece of paper. So page breaks for both width and height are necessary.

As mentioned in Chapter 4, in the Works spreadsheet, page breaks are indicated by horizontal and vertical dashed lines that take the place of the normal, solid row and column dividers. To get an idea of how these page breaks occur, you can scroll a blank spreadsheet to see the first default page breaks between columns F and G, and between rows 45 and 46. Every Works spreadsheet starts out with these default page breaks, but you can change them, using the Set Page Break command on the Options menu.

When you specify a new page break, Works inserts both horizontal and vertical page breaks directly above and to the left of the currently selected cell. Thus, if you were to select cell D29 and then use the Set Page Break command, a new horizontal break would appear dividing rows 28 and 29, and a new vertical break would appear between columns C and D. In other words, cell D29 would become the upper-left cell in a new spreadsheet page.

If we were to print our consolidated spreadsheet file, we would probably want each detail area printed on its own separate page. To ensure that, we'll have to adjust the page breaks. Whenever you adjust page breaks in a Works file, it's best to start from the top of the file and work your way down. Changing a page break near the top of a file can change the locations of the page breaks that follow it.

Unless you specify otherwise, each worksheet page contains the same number of rows and columns, as determined by the margins you set with the Page Setup... command. A blank spreadsheet with the default margin settings contains pages with 6 columns and 45 rows, for example. If you reset a page break on such a spreadsheet so that the first page contains only 20 rows, the next page will begin on row 21 (instead of row 46), and will end on row 66 (instead of row 90). Since you usually want to have specific information included on specific printed pages of a spreadsheet, you should check the contents of pages and adjust page breaks beginning at the top of the spreadsheet and working your way down. That way, any page breaks you adjust toward the bottom of the spreadsheet won't affect page breaks you've specified for areas closer to the top of the spreadsheet.

- ☐ Scroll to the top of the spreadsheet file, so that cell A1 is showing.

A page will hold about 45 rows and the summary area is only 17 rows deep, so we know that it will print easily on one page. When we scroll to the right, however, we see that a page break (the vertical dashed line) occurs after column E (April). We'd rather that all the months in this area were printed on one page, if possible. To do that, we will have to adjust the page setup and change the way the spreadsheet is printed.

☐ Choose the Page Setup... command from the File menu. The Page Setup dialog box appears.

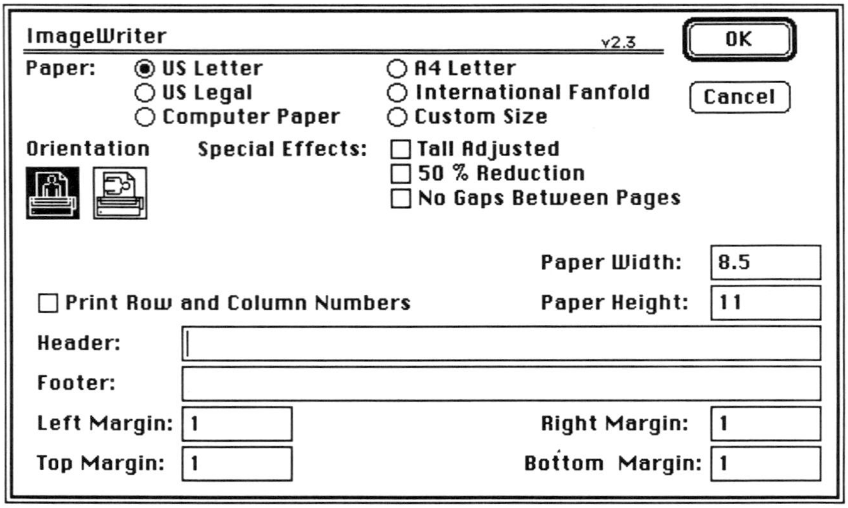

ImageWriter v2.3 OK

Paper: ◉ US Letter ○ A4 Letter
○ US Legal ○ International Fanfold Cancel
○ Computer Paper ○ Custom Size

Orientation Special Effects: ☐ Tall Adjusted
☐ 50 % Reduction
☐ No Gaps Between Pages

Paper Width: 8.5
☐ Print Row and Column Numbers Paper Height: 11
Header:
Footer:
Left Margin: 1 Right Margin: 1
Top Margin: 1 Bottom Margin: 1

Since our spreadsheet area is much wider than it is long, it makes sense to change the printing orientation here.

☐ Click on the wide icon in the Orientation section of the dialog box to print sideways so all columns fit.

☐ Click the OK button.

Scrolling to the right in the spreadsheet now, we see that the page break has moved from column E (April) to column G (June). Changing the printing orientation helped a little, but not enough.

At this point, we have a couple of alternatives. We could either make all the month columns narrower (either by dragging the column dividers individually, or by specifying a new column width with the Column Width... command on the Format menu), or we can reduce the size of the print. Either alternative will let us print more data across a page. For the sake of this example, we'll reduce the print size:

☐ Choose the Page Setup... command from the File menu.

☐ Click the 50% Reduction option in the Special Effects section.

☐ Click the OK button to return to the spreadsheet.

Now, if we scroll to the right, we see that the page break has moved over to column O. That means the whole area will now fit on one page. But even though the 50-percent reduction has solved the problem in our example, you may want to test-print in this mode before you print one of your own spreadsheets: The font used for spreadsheet data is small (9-point) to begin with, and when you reduce it by 50 percent, the results can be very difficult to read, especially if you're printing on an ImageWriter.

For this example, let's assume we can live with the reduced-size print. The problem now is that the page break is actually one column farther to the right than we want it—the page will include the first column of the Business Income area as well. We'll have to insert a new page break so only the summary area is included on the first page.

Remember, when you insert a page break in the spreadsheet, you insert both horizontal and vertical page breaks simultaneously. This means we'll have to select the cell that's just below the bottom row of the summary area (row 18), and just to the right of the totals column in the summary area (column O).

- Select cell O18.
- Choose the Set Page Break command from the Options menu. A new page break appears.

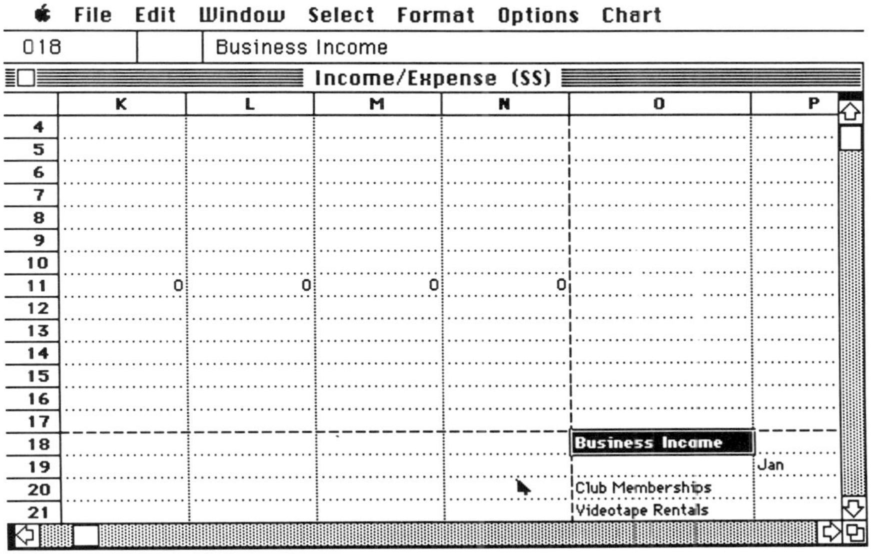

File Edit Window Select Format Options Chart

O18 | Business Income

Income/Expense (SS)

	K	L	M	N	O	P
4						
5						
6						
7						
8						
9						
10						
11	0	0	0	0		
12						
13						
14						
15						
16						
17						
18					Business Income	
19						Jan
20					Club Memberships	
21					Videotape Rentals	

Now, the entire Business Income area will be printed on a new page. From here, we can scroll down the spreadsheet into the other detail areas and insert page breaks in them to make sure each area prints on a new page.

Adding page headers

The final touch before printing is to insert a page header. Since this will be a multiple-page printout, it would be nice to have a page header that identifies the project and numbers the pages.

- ☐ Choose Page Setup... from the File menu. When the Page Setup dialog box appears, you'll notice that the insertion point is blinking in the Header box.
- ☐ Type the header *Al Chroma Expense/Income Report,* but don't press the Return key. (Pressing Return accepts the settings in the Page Setup dialog box and returns you to the spreadsheet.)

We've entered the text of the header now, but we need to tell Works how to format the header. You have to enter special formatting commands in the header window if you want to specify how a header is justified, how pages are numbered, and whether or not a date and time are included in the header. All the formatting commands begin with an ampersand (&) sign. These are the commands:

Command	Results
&L	left justifies the header or footer text
&R	right justifies the header or footer text
&C	centers the header or footer text
&P	prints page numbers in the header or footer
&D	prints the current date (as supplied by the Macintosh clock) in the header or footer
&T	prints the current time (as supplied by the Macintosh clock) in the header or footer
&F	prints the file name in the header or footer
&B	prints the text following this command in boldface
&I	prints the text following this command in italics

Since the ampersand symbol begins formatting commands, you also have to use it if you want to print a single ampersand in a header. If you want Works to print *Expense & Income* in a header, you would have to enter *Expense && Income* in the Header box.

All these commands and procedures apply to both headers and footers. If you want, you can have both a header and a footer in a document. In this case, we'll just finish the header. We've typed the basic header text, but we also want to right-justify the text, make it boldface, and include a date and page number:

- ☐ Click at the beginning of the text in the Header box to move the insertion point there.
- ☐ Type *&R&B* to specify that you want the header text right-justified and boldfaced.
- ☐ Click at the end of the header text, type a space, and then type *- &D - Page &P*. This tells Works to enter the date, followed by the word *Page* and then the page number.

So, the entire header text looks like this:

&R&BAl Chroma Expense/Income Report - &D - Page &P

The header commands that cause text to be added (the date, time, and page number commands) will place those bits of text just where you put the command, so if you want spaces around a date or page number, for example, you must add a space in front of and behind that command. Here, we've set off the date and page number from the header text with dashes. Also, it's a good idea to include the word *Page* in a header before the page number command, so other readers of the document will know that the number that appears there is the page number.

When this header is printed, it will appear in the top, right-hand corner of each page, and will look like this, depending on the date you print:

Al Chroma Expense/Income Report - March 31, 1986 - Page 1

These projects have shown you most of the basic features of the Works spreadsheet in action. (If you want more information about specific functions or operations, consult the Works Reference Manual.) Now let's look at the basic features of the Works database.

C H A P T E R

6

Using the Database

Just as the Works spreadsheet can store, sort, calculate, and otherwise manipulate numbers, the database can store, sort, calculate, and otherwise manipulate facts. Facts can be text, such as names, addresses, or product descriptions, or they can be numbers, such as dates, times, part numbers, or prices. The Works database lets you easily store a wide variety of data, and then retrieve, sort, print, or even calculate it.

DATABASE BASICS

All database programs work fundamentally the same way. You use a database file to store information about people, places, or things. In such a file, you almost always want to store more than one fact about each person, place, or thing. A simple telephone list, for example, would contain two facts about each person: the person's name and the person's telephone number. In a database file, each fact or item of information is stored in a field, and each group of facts about an individual person, place, or thing is stored together as a record.

Before you can store information in any database file, you must structure it in a specific way to accept your data—you must define the fields, or information categories, for your data. Once you define fields for a database file, you can enter your data into them, and then you can retrieve, arrange, or display the data in a variety of ways.

You can display data from a Works database file in two ways. In a form window, you can look at all the data from individual records, one record at a time.

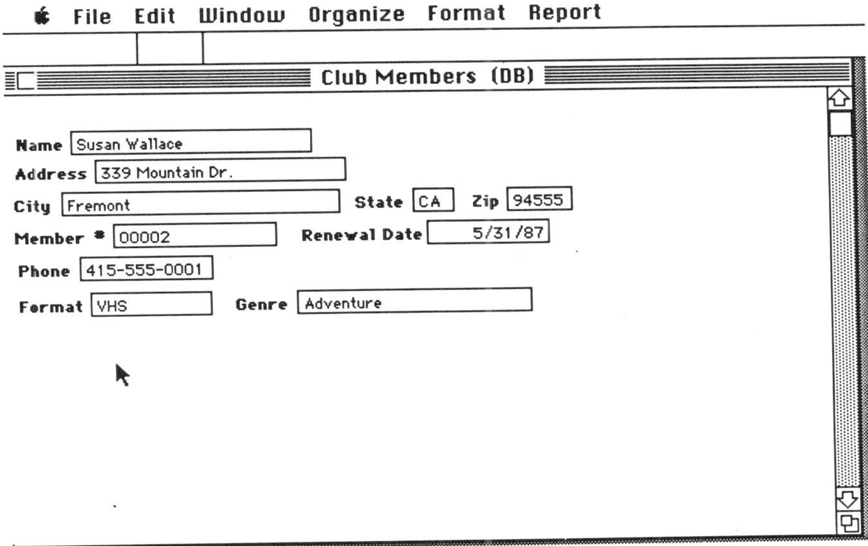

In a list window, you can look at data from several records at a time.

File Edit Window Organize Format Report

Club Members (DB)

Name	Address	City	State	Zip	Phone	Mem
Susan Wallace	339 Mountain Dr.	Fremont	CA	94555	415-555-0001	0000
Renee Lebec	82 Piedmont Ave., #:	Oakland	CA	94666	415-555-0004	0000
Bud Snooter	10327 Park Hills Dr.	San Jose	CA	93333	408-555-0009	0000
Fran Marple	353 Country Estates	Milpitas	CA	94459	408-555-7925	0001
Elias Abou-Ata	15 Claremont St.	San Francisco	CA	94000	415-555-7877	0002
Ed Bernstein	9975 Francis Ct.	San Bruno	CA	94060	415-555-8821	0003
Joe Brubaker	10147 La Rosa Ave.	San Carlos	CA	94606	415-555-1198	0003
Linda Feldman	11223 S. Hindry Blvc	Redwood City	CA	94435	415-555-2891	0003
Steve Marshall	7790 Jacob Way	So. San Francisco	CA	94011	415-555-9900	0002
Nancy Bischel	339 Pardee St.	Hayward	CA	94022	415-555-6666	0003
Sheryl Zack	3359 Geary Blvd., #«	San Francisco	CA	94003	415-555-0007	0000
Mikkel Aaland	35 Clifford Terrace	San Francisco	CA	94444	415-555-1201	0002
Toni Walker	5050 Camino Diablo	San Mateo	CA	94500	415-555-3671	0003
Severina Omega	159 Palm Ave.	Oakland	CA	94600	415-555-5568	0003
Madelyn Korbut	957 Oak Park Dr.	Saratoga	CA	95500	408-555-0121	0001
Steve Chow	42 Jackson St.	San Francisco	CA	94403	415-555-0989	0001
Millard Cuvee	233 Portnoy St.	Burlingame	CA	94400	415-555-9699	0001
Randy Clark	1730 Wawona Ave.	San Francisco	CA	94005	415-555-6730	0003

As you can see, the list window lets you view a lot of information from different records, but it may not show you every field of data in each record it displays. As you'll see later, you can scroll to the right in the list window to view other fields in records, and you can scroll down to view other records or groups of records in the file. In the form window, you see every field in a record, but only one record at a time. You can switch from a form window to a list window by selecting the Show List or Show Form command from the Format menu. These two commands alternate on the Format menu, depending on which type window is active: When a form window is displayed, the Show List command appears on the menu; and when the list window is being displayed, the Show Form command appears on the menu.

To print information from a Works database file, you create a report using the database's Report menu. Reports are designed with a report window, which appears on top of the open database file you're working with and looks like this:

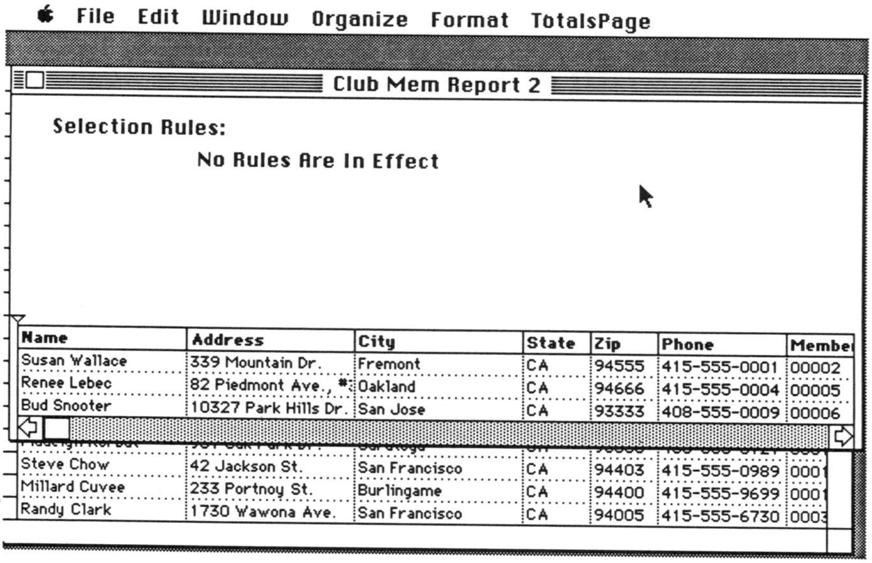

File Edit Window Organize Format TotalsPage

Club Mem Report 2

Selection Rules:

No Rules Are In Effect

Name	Address	City	State	Zip	Phone	Membe
Susan Wallace	339 Mountain Dr.	Fremont	CA	94555	415-555-0001	00002
Renee Lebec	82 Piedmont Ave., #	Oakland	CA	94666	415-555-0004	00005
Bud Snooter	10327 Park Hills Dr.	San Jose	CA	93333	408-555-0009	00006
Steve Chow	42 Jackson St.	San Francisco	CA	94403	415-555-0989	0001
Millard Cuvee	233 Portnoy St.	Burlingame	CA	94400	415-555-9699	0001
Randy Clark	1730 Wawona Ave.	San Francisco	CA	94005	415-555-6730	0003

Using the report window, you can select certain records, or you can select fields of data within records to be included in a printed report. You can also specify calculations in the report, such as the addition of numeric fields. We'll explore these features in detail later in this chapter. First, let's look at the various commands available on the database menus.

A QUICK TOUR OF THE DATABASE MENUS

When you are working with data or creating a new database file, there are seven menus of commands available in the menu bar at the top of the screen. Unlike in the other Works applications, the commands listed on some of the database menus change, depending on whether you're working with a database file in general or whether you're working with a specific report. (We'll look at these differences as we go through the descriptions of each of the menus.)

As mentioned in previous chapters, the Apple menu is the same, no matter which Works application you're working with. So, we'll start our tour with the File menu.

The File menu

The commands on the File menu have the same names in every Works application, but in the database, there are a couple of differences in how they work. When you're defining a file, entering data, or manipulating data with the database, the Page Setup..., Print..., and Print Merge... commands are dimmed, which means they're not available. The Page Setup... and Print... commands are available only when you're working with a database report and have a report window open. The Print Merge... command is active only in the Works word processor.

The Edit menu

The Edit menu is another menu you'll find in every Works application, but it contains some extra commands specific to the database. Several of these commands are not available when you're working on a database report.

As in the other Works applications, you can use the Undo command to cancel a previous action. If you delete a record and then decide you didn't mean to do that, you can choose the Undo command. Undo will cancel your previous command (the command to delete the record), and the record will reappear.

You can use the Cut command to remove data that's in a field, record, or group of records from a file and place it on the Clipboard. When you use the Cut command to remove a record or group of records, those records disappear from the file and any records beneath them move up and are renumbered.

You can use the Copy command when you want to place a copy of a field, record, or group of records on the Clipboard without removing the data from the file. When you're working with a database report, Copy Totals replaces the Copy command. Copy Totals lets you copy the field totals from a report to the Clipboard for transfer into another document so that you can see a report's totals without printing the report. (You can't see the totals in a report window; you must either print the report on paper or copy the totals to another document. We'll see how this works in Chapter 7.)

The Paste command lets you move data from the Clipboard into a database file, beginning at the selected field or record's location. If you have only one field's data from one record on the Clipboard, that data will be inserted into the field you have selected when you use the Paste command. If you cut or copy data from two fields of one record to the Clipboard, the data will be inserted beginning at the field you select and extending to the right into the adjacent field.

Whenever you cut or copy data, a copy of that data remains on the Clipboard until you cut or copy another selection of data. Thus, you can cut one record to the Clipboard, and then paste it into several different locations in a file by using the Paste command repeatedly. If you were putting data into an address file, for example, and several records had the same city and state data, you could enter the data in the first record, copy it to the Clipboard, and then quickly paste it into several other records.

The Clear command removes data from a field, record, or group of records without eliminating the records themselves. When you clear an entire record in a list window, for example, the data in that record is deleted, but the blank record remains.

The Select All command selects all the fields and records in a database file. This command works only in the list window. Select All is useful if you want to cut or copy all of a file's records to the Clipboard.

The Insert Record command inserts a new, blank record above the currently selected record in a list window, or in front of the current record in a form window. You can insert only one blank record at a time with this command.

The last three commands on the Edit menu let you change field names, add fields, or delete fields.

To use the Change Field Name... command, you must select an entire field by clicking on its name. When you select a field and choose the Change Field Name... command, the Field Name box appears, allowing you to enter a new name for that field.

When you choose the Add New Field… command, the Field Name box also appears, allowing you to type the name for a new field. The new field is added to the right of any existing fields in the list window, or below any existing fields in the form window.

To use the Delete Field command, you must select a field by clicking on its name. Once you select a field, you can delete it by choosing the Delete Field command. When you delete a field, you lose all the data stored in that field.

These three commands aren't available when you're working with a database report. Instead, there is a command called Change Report Title…, which lets you change the name you've given to a report.

The Window menu is identical in all three Works applications, so let's skip past it to the Organize menu.

The Organize menu

The Organize menu contains the commands for locating, selecting, or sorting data in the database.

The Find Field… command finds data in any field in any record, according to comparison information you enter. When you choose the Find Field… command, a dialog box appears, allowing you to enter the matching information to locate the data you want. If you want to find all occurrences of the name Bob, for example, you would type *Bob* in the Find Field dialog box as the comparison information. Find Field… finds the first record that contains the comparison information, and presents it on the screen (in a form window) or highlights the matching data (in a list window). To find the next occurrence of the data, you must choose the Find Field… command again and click on the Find Next button. To save time, you can limit the search to text fields only, so that Works doesn't spend time searching fields that contain numbers, times, or dates. The Find Field… command isn't available when you're working with a database report.

The Match Records… command also searches for data that matches comparison information you type into a dialog box, but instead of presenting records one at a time, it presents all the matching records in the list window at the same time. (If there are more matching records than will fit in the list window, you can scroll the window to see them.) This command isn't available when you're working with a database report.

The Record Selection… command is a more sophisticated way of selecting certain records from a database file and listing them on the screen. Unlike the Match Records... command, which locates all of the records that contain your comparison data in any field, the Record Selection... command selects records only if the comparison information is in a specific field and the data meets logical conditions, or selection rules, that you specify, such as a zip code beginning with a certain number or a date falling between two other dates. Once you define some record-selection rules, the command finds all the records meeting those rules and then displays them all at the same time. You can use the Record Selection... command to select certain records to view in a list window, or you can use it to select records to include in a database report. The Record Selection dialog box looks like this:

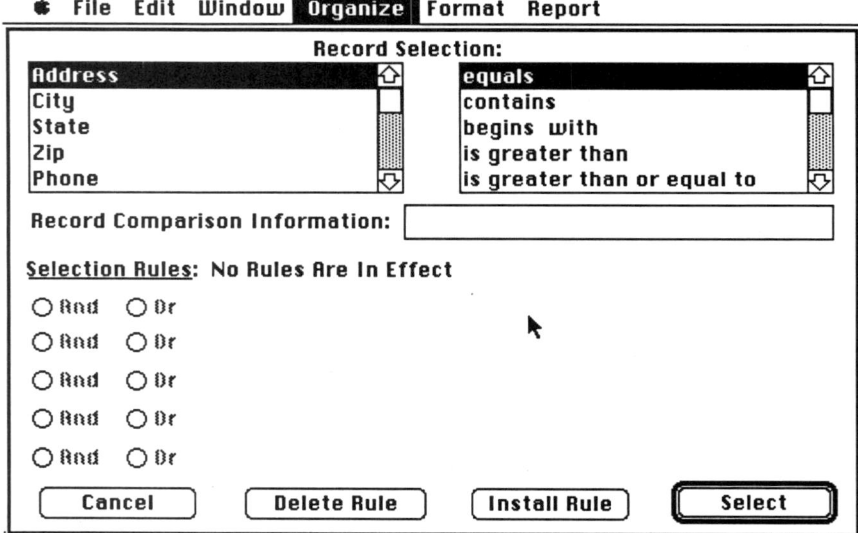

Once you've used the Record Selection... command, if you want to display all the records in the file again, you must choose the Show All Records command. You can also use Show All Records to cancel record-selection rules you've set for a database report.

The Sort... command lets you arrange records in a database file in alphabetical, numeric, or chronological order. If you are sorting data in a text field, you can sort only in alphabetical order. If you're sorting data in a numeric field, you can sort only in numeric order. If you're sorting data in a date or time field, you can sort only in chronological order. The Sort... command isn't available when you're working with a database report.

The Format menu

The Format menu contains a variety of formatting options for the form and list windows when you're working with an entire file, but has far fewer options when you're working with a database report.

The Show Form/Show List command toggles the display between the form window and the list window. (As was mentioned earlier in this chapter, Show Form appears when you're in the list window, Show List when you're in the form window.) You can also toggle the display by double-clicking on the screen or by pressing Command-L.

The Bold Field Name and Bold Field Data commands let you boldface field names, field data, or both in the form window. (Field names are always boldface in the list window, and you can't make data boldface there.) To make a field name or data boldface, you select the field and then choose one of these commands. You can use both commands if you want, so both a field name and its data are boldface. The default setting in the form window is for field names to be boldface, and for field data to be presented in normal text. These two commands aren't available in the list window or in database reports.

The Border Field Name and Border Field Data commands let you specify whether field names or field data should have boxes around them in the form window. Neither command is available in the list window or in database reports. When you use these commands, you choose whether to display a border around every field in the window. You can use both commands so that both the field names and their data have borders around them. The default setting in the form window is for both field names and field data to have borders.

The Show Grid and No Grid commands let you specify whether you want to display a matrix of lines in the list window to separate each field and record. Both commands appear on the menu; a check mark precedes the one that's currently active. The default is Show Grid. These commands are also available when you're working on a report.

The Set Field Attributes... command, available in either the list or form window, lets you select the type of data a field can contain, and it allows you to align the data to the left, right, or in the center of the field, or to underline or boldface the data. To use this command, you must first select a field. Otherwise, the command is dimmed on the menu. As a shortcut, you can double-click on a field name to select this command. The Set Field Attributes... command isn't available in database reports.

The Report menu

The Report menu is the gateway to all reports in the database. It is not available when you're working with a database report.

The Select Report... command produces a list of reports you have defined, and lets you choose one to work with.

If you have a new database file and you haven't defined any reports yet, the New Report... command is the only one available on the Report menu. You can define and store up to eight reports with each database file.

You can use the Duplicate Report... command to produce an exact copy of a previously defined report. This command is helpful when you want to create a complex report that is substantially similar to an existing report—you can duplicate the existing report and then make the changes you want.

The Erase Report... command lets you delete reports you have defined before.

The TotalsPage menu

The TotalsPage menu replaces the Report menu in the menu bar when you're working with a database report. It does not appear when you're working in any other type of database window.

The Total on Field Change command works in conjunction with the Sum This Field command to produce subtotals of numeric fields whenever the name or number in another field changes. If you had an inventory that was divided into several classes of parts, for example, and you wanted a subtotal of the number of parts in each class, you would use the Sum This Field command on the field containing the part quantities, and then use the Total on Field Change command on the field containing the names of parts classes. This way, the database would produce a subtotal in the quantity field whenever the data in the class field changed. We'll see how this works in Chapter 7.

Total-1st Char Field is similar to the Total on Field Change command. Total-1st Char Field produces a subtotal only when the first character in a field changes. This command is useful when the first digit of a part number is a code that divides an inventory into classes. A company's widgets, for example, might be numbered X-1, X-2, X-3, and so on, while its doodads might be numbered Y-1, Y-2, and Y-3. If you wanted to produce subtotals of all widgets or doodads, you would use the Total-1st Char Field command, and the database would wait until it had printed all the product codes beginning with the same letter or number before it produced a total.

The Sum This Field command produces a total for all of the data in any numeric field. To use this command, you select the numeric field you want to sum, and then choose the Sum This Field command from the TotalsPage menu. Field totals appear only when you print a report, or when you use Copy Totals to move them to the Clipboard. You can then see the totals by using the Show Clipboard command or pasting the totals into another document.

KEYBOARD SHORTCUTS

As in the word processor and spreadsheet, Works offers Command-key equivalents for many database menu commands, allowing you to use the keyboard instead of the mouse to choose a command from a menu. The database keyboard equivalents are shown in Figure 6-1.

Action	*Command*	*Menu*	*Keyboard Equivalent*
Open a file	Open...	File	Command-O
Save a file	Save	File	Command-S
Print a file	Print...	File	Command-P
Quit Works	Quit	File	Command-Q
Undo a command	Undo	Edit	Command-Z
Cut data	Cut	Edit	Command-X
Copy data	Copy	Edit	Command-C
Paste data	Paste	Edit	Command-V
Insert a record	Insert Record	Edit	Command-I
Change the size of a window	Full Window/ Small Window	Window	Command-W
Find data in any field	Find Field ...	Organize	Command-F
Find data in a specific field	Match Records...	Organize	Command-M
Sort data	Sort ...	Organize	Command-A
Toggle between the form and list windows	Show Form/ Show List	Format	Command-L

Figure 6-1. *Fourteen Works database commands have keyboard equivalents.*

SAMPLE DATABASE

To see how to set up and use a Works database file, let's look at a quick example.

Creating the database

Suppose we want to store a bunch of names, addresses, and telephone numbers in the Works database. We would:

- ☐ Load Microsoft Works.
- ☐ Select the New... command from the File menu.
- ☐ Double-click on the database icon. A Field Name window will appear.

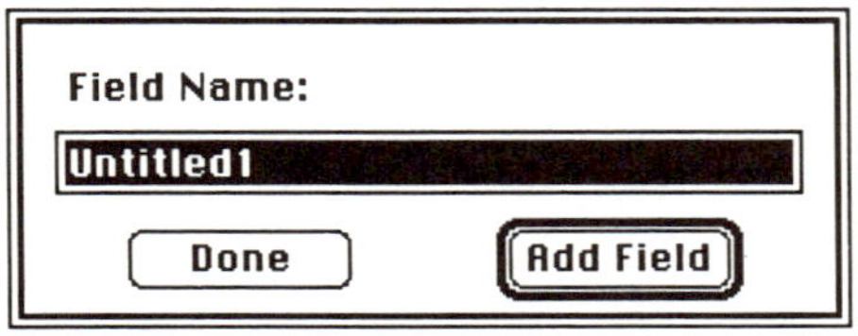

Field Name:
Untitled1
Done
Add Field

We want a field and label for each category of information for our file. The file will contain names, telephone numbers, and addresses, so let's use these categories as our field names.

- ☐ Type the field name *Name* and press the Return key. A new field with this name appears in the database-file window. (Pressing Return is the same as clicking the Add Field button in the Field Name window.)
- ☐ Type the field name *Phone* and press the Return key. This new field is added to the database-file window.
- ☐ Enter the field names *Address, City, State,* and *Zip.* Press Return after you type each name.
- ☐ Click the Done button in the Field Name window to tell Works you are finished naming fields for this file. The Field Name

window disappears, and the database-file window appears, ready to store information.

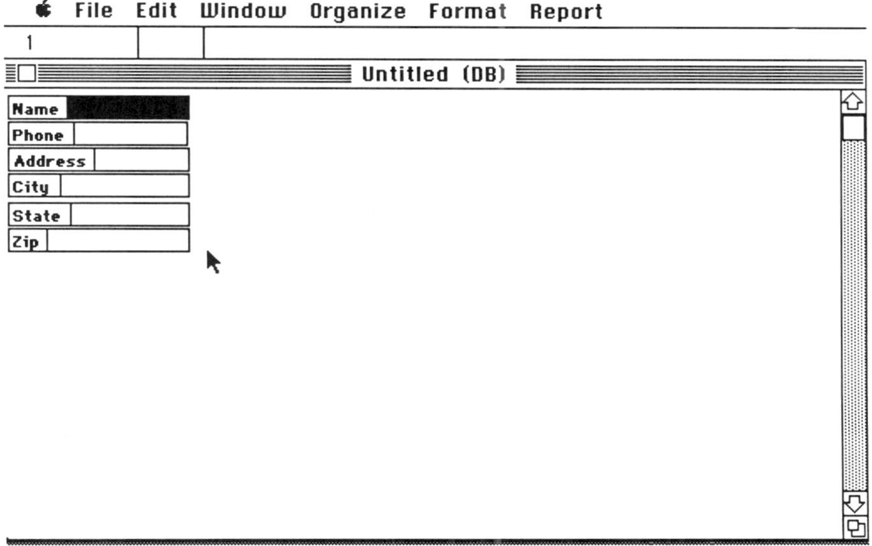

Now, we can enter a few names and addresses.

- Click on the Name field to select it, if it isn't already selected.
- Type the name *Joe Jones*, and press the Return key. The name is entered in the Name field and the Phone field below is automatically selected next.

You can move the selection from one field to the next in either the form window or the list window by pressing Return (to move the selection from top to bottom, down the screen) or the Tab key (to move the selection from left to right, across the screen). You can also move the selection up one field at a time by pressing Shift-Return. The list window can usually display only a few fields at a time—the rest of the fields in a given file are off the screen to the right. To view off-screen fields, you can either continue pressing the Tab key to move the selection across the screen one field at a time, or you can use the scroll bar at the bottom of the window. By pressing Shift and Tab at the same time, you move from right to left one field at a time. To move from one record to the next in the form window (or to display records farther down in the file in the list window), you can use the scroll bar at the right side of the window.

☐ Type the phone number *555-1111*, and press the Return key. The number is entered, and the Address field is selected.

☐ Enter *12 Main St.*, *Belmont*, and *CA* in the Address, City, and State fields, respectively, following the same procedure.

These five items of information are now stored in the file.

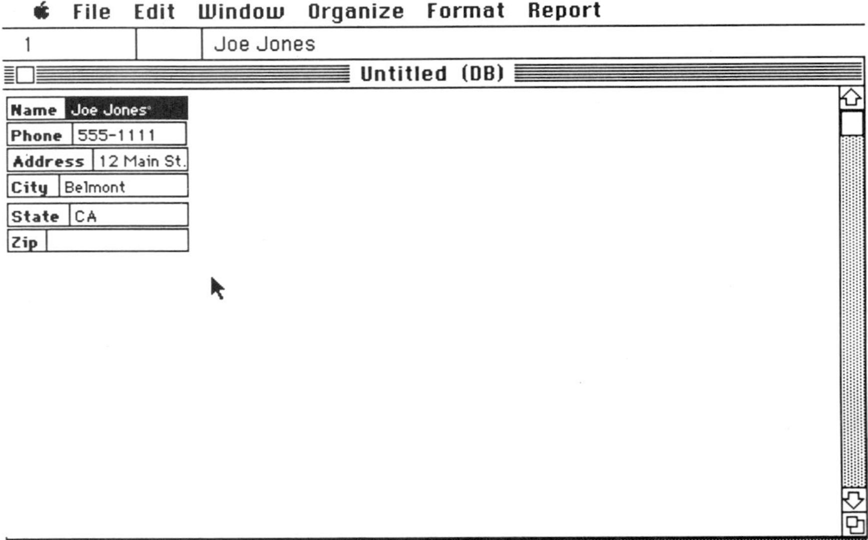

Now, we can enter the last item of information for this record:

☐ Select the Zip field if it isn't already selected.

☐ Type the zip code, *94444*, and press the Return key. The information is entered, and a new, blank record is displayed.

Whenever you fill in the last field in a Works database record and press Return, that record is stored away and a new, blank record is displayed. This lets you enter a lot of records into the file easily, since you're always presented with a new record when you finish filling in the current record. Most database programs keep track of information by numbering the records in each file. In the Works database, the number of the current record is always displayed in the upper-left corner of the database window, as long as one of the fields in the record is selected. (The maximum number of records in a file depends on the size of each record and the amount of memory you have available.)

Using the database

Once you've stored information in a database file, you can then arrange it, retrieve it, or display it in a number of ways. As we've already seen, you can use the Find Field... command from the Organize menu to find individual facts by typing information and asking the program to locate any records that contain that information. If you wanted to find Joe Jones's phone number in our sample file, for example, and all you could remember was that his last name was Jones, you could ask Works to find every record that contains Jones.

Of course, telling Works to find the name Jones might not be very efficient, because you might have dozens of Joneses in the file, and Works would find every one of them. So, you might want to use a more efficient way to locate this information, by supplying more specific comparison information. For example, you might remember that the Jones you want lives on Main Street. If you did, you could use Works' Record Selection... command in the Organize menu to find all the records that contain both the name Jones and a Main Street address.

You can also sort and calculate information in a database file. If you had entered the names and addresses in a file in no particular order, you could sort the records so they were in alphabetical order by name, in ascending numerical order by zip code, or in other ways, based on the contents of one field. Our sample file doesn't contain any information we might want to calculate, but as you'll see in Chapter 7, you can also use arithmetic operators and Works spreadsheet functions to calculate one or more fields in a database file. In an inventory file, for example, you might multiply the contents of the Quantity field by the contents of the Price field to produce a new field called Total Amount.

Finally, you can report data, or print it out, very flexibly. Database programs let you print all the records in a file, or only selected groups of records or certain fields from records. Usually, you can arrange fields so they are printed in specific places on a page, and you can apply calculations to reports so quantities or costs are subtotaled throughout the report or summed at the end of the report.

These features of the Works database are common to most database programs. For example, all database programs let you store, retrieve, arrange, and print data. The differences between Works' database and other databases lie in the ease and flexibility with which you can work with and format your data with Works.

ADVANTAGES OF THE WORKS DATABASE

The Works database offers several data-handling advantages over other programs in its price and performance class.

The database is fast

Database files in Works are stored entirely in random-access memory, or RAM, as you work on them. So you don't have to wait for portions of a file to be read into RAM from a disk when you search for or select information. This means that the Works database will find, sort, and select records faster than most other database programs. Files can be much larger with programs that maintain parts of open database files on disk. The size of a given file is limited to the amount of available disk space, rather than the amount of available RAM space. But you can build fairly large files with Works. The actual maximum size of any database file will depend on the number of fields in each file and the amount of data in each field. But if each record in your file contained about 100 characters of data, you could build a file containing about 2,000 records on a 512K Mac, and you could store about 6,000 records on a 1Mb Mac Plus. This capacity is more than adequate for most personal, small business, and analytical tasks. If you occasionally need more space than this, there are ways to get it, as we'll see later in this chapter.

The database is flexible

Most personal computer users aren't experts at database management, and even the experts are bound to make mistakes once in a while. A key advantage to the Works database is that you can change the structure of a file after you've begun entering information into it. Suppose you begin a file and enter a few records, only to discover that you really need three more fields. In many other database programs, you can't add, delete, or rename fields once you've defined a file. But with Works, you can.

Suppose we wanted to add a field called Age to the sample name and address file described earlier in this chapter. To add a field in the form window:

- Point to an area below the current group of fields. (You can point to any blank area in the form window to add a field.)
- Hold down the mouse button and drag the pointer to the right. As you do, a new field is outlined on the screen.
- When the field outline is the size you want, release the mouse button. The Field Name window will appear.

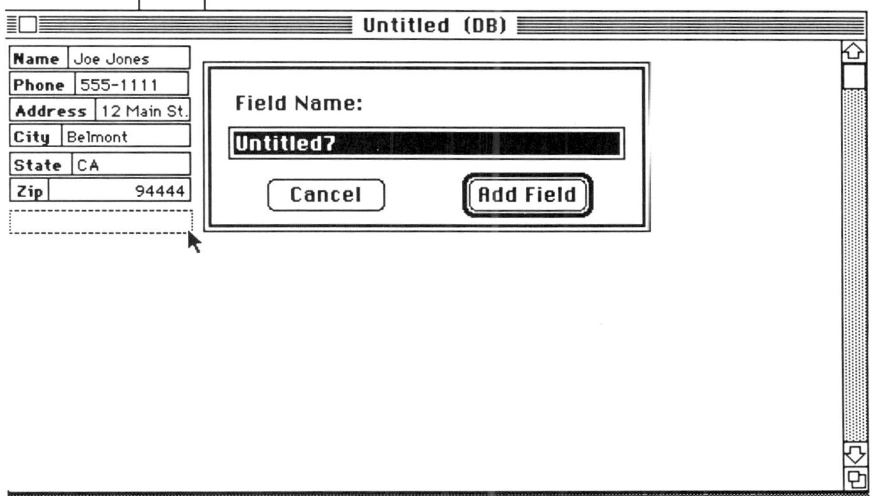

- Type the name for the new field (in this case, *Age*).
- Press the Return key or click the Add Field button in the Field Name box. The Field Name box disappears, and the field name is added to the field you outlined.

To add a field in the list window:

- Choose Show List from the Format menu to display the list window.

- ☐ Choose the Add New Field... command from the Edit menu. The Field Name window will appear.
- ☐ Type the name for the new field, and then press the Return key or click the Add Field button. The Field Name box disappears, and the field is added to the right of any existing fields in the list window. (If the field you added is off-screen to the right and you want to make sure it's there, you can use the scroll bar at the bottom of the screen to bring it into view.)

You can also rearrange fields. Suppose we wanted the Phone field in our address file at the bottom of the form window screen, instead of under the Name field:

- ☐ Choose the Show Form command from the Format menu.
- ☐ Place the pointer on top of the Phone field name. The pointer becomes a hand.

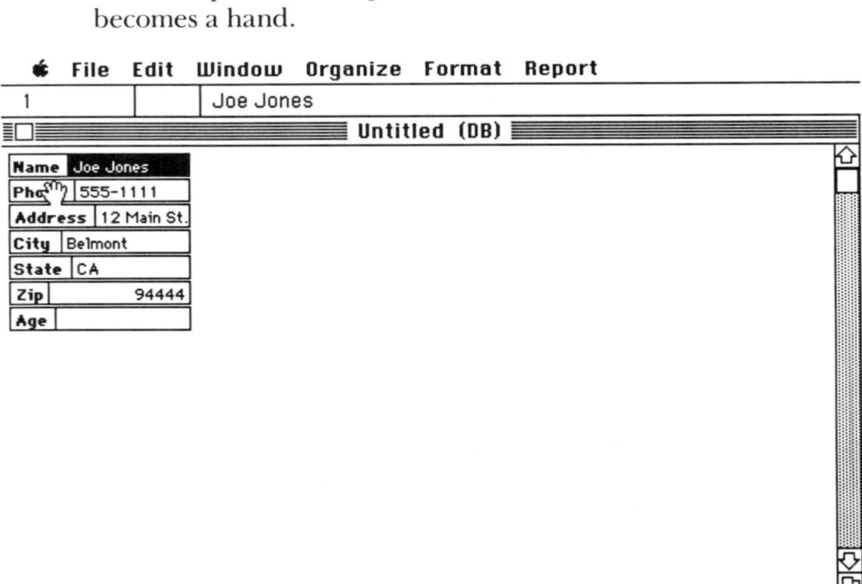

- ☐ Hold down the mouse button, and drag the pointer to the field's new location (in this case, underneath the new Age field).

- Release the mouse button. The field is now in its new location.

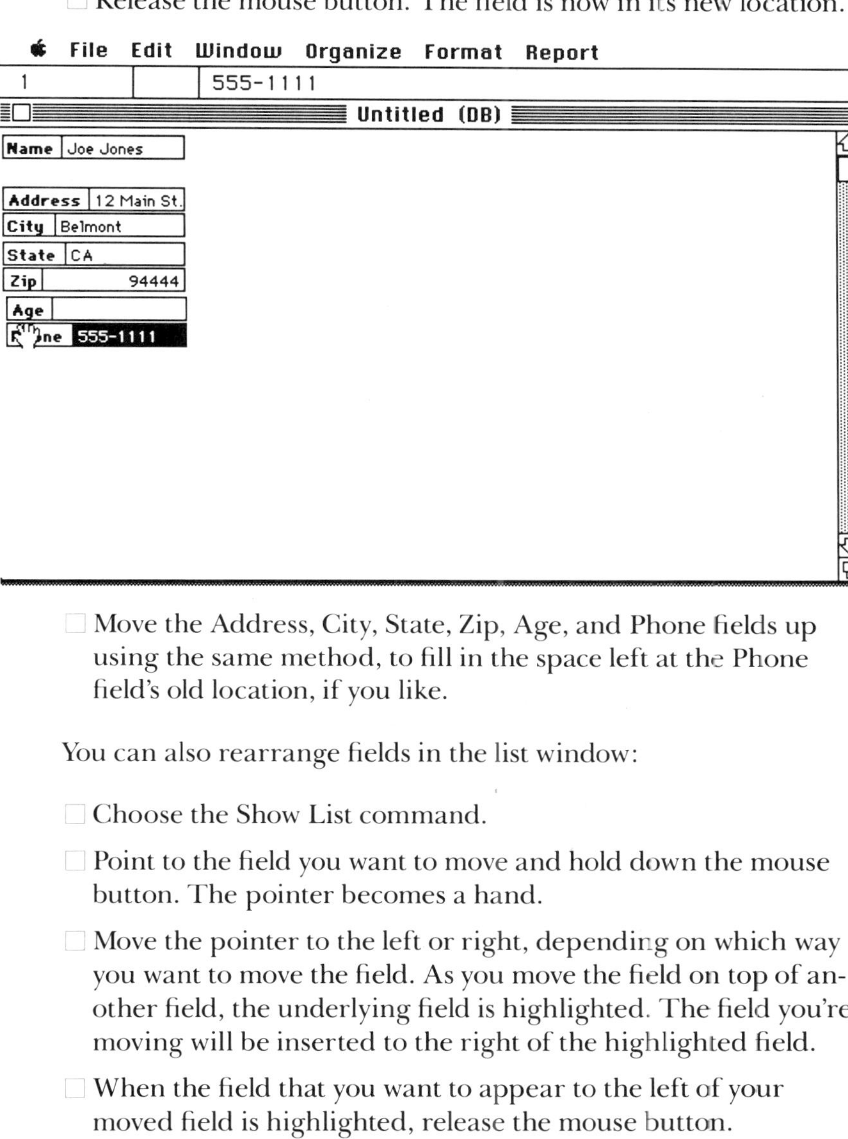

- Move the Address, City, State, Zip, Age, and Phone fields up using the same method, to fill in the space left at the Phone field's old location, if you like.

You can also rearrange fields in the list window:

- Choose the Show List command.
- Point to the field you want to move and hold down the mouse button. The pointer becomes a hand.
- Move the pointer to the left or right, depending on which way you want to move the field. As you move the field on top of another field, the underlying field is highlighted. The field you're moving will be inserted to the right of the highlighted field.
- When the field that you want to appear to the left of your moved field is highlighted, release the mouse button.

Finally, you can also make fields larger so they can hold more data. To see this, let's go back to the form window by choosing the Show Form command. When we created the fields in our sample database file, Works automatically made the fields the default width. As we enter names, however, some of those fields might not be wide enough to display our data. (Works will store field data up to 248 characters long, but it can't display the data if the field isn't wide enough.) Suppose we enter the name John Krumholtzenthaler in a new record in the file. (To enter a new record in the form window, drag the right-hand scroll box to the bottom of the scroll bar—a blank record will appear.) The Name field isn't wide enough to display the whole name, but Works has stored the whole name (as indicated in the entry bar).

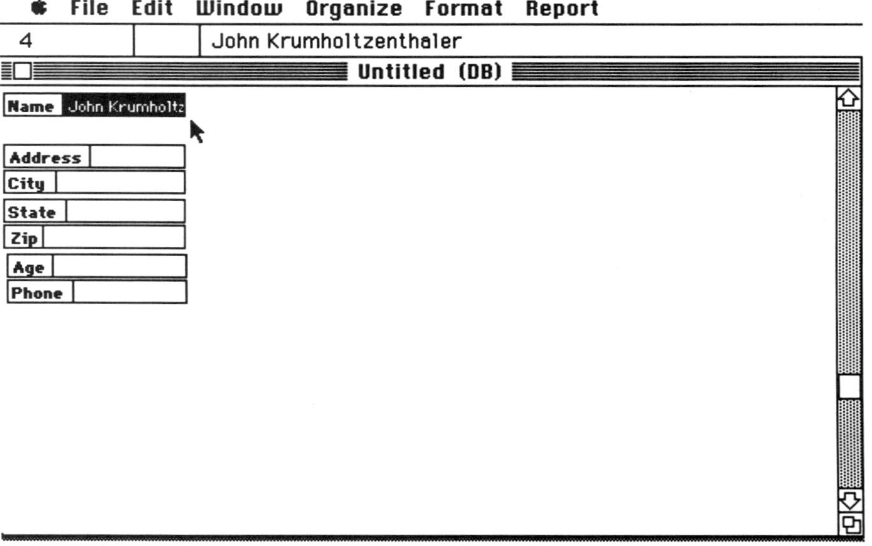

To make this field wider:

- Place the pointer on the right edge of the field. The pointer turns into a right-pointing arrow.
- Hold down the mouse button, and drag the edge of the field to the right to make the field wider. The field is outlined as you drag the mouse.
- When the field outline looks big enough, release the mouse button, and the field will be displayed with its new width.

You can also make fields wider in the list window by dragging the dividing line between one field and another.

Being able to change the database's structure means you won't have painted yourself into a corner when you make a mistake in setting up your database file. If you want to add a field to a file, for instance, you don't have to define a new file all over again—you can simply add the field. Instead of requiring you to make all your data organization decisions before you begin storing information, Works lets you begin a file, store some data, and then modify the file or the data as your needs grow.

The database is simple

Database management can become a very complex affair, but never with Microsoft Works. As we saw in the sample name and address file, creating a file and storing information is extremely easy. You can select a record or field to work on simply by clicking on it. To select a record in the list window:

- With the list window active, click on the small, blank box directly to the left of the record you want to select.

If you want to select a group of fields or records in the list window, you can drag the mouse across them. To select the two records of our sample address file, for example:

- Point to the box to the left of the first record at the top of the window, and hold down the mouse button.
- Drag the mouse pointer down to the second record, and release it. Both records are selected.

You can also move records within a file or between files by cutting and pasting with the Clipboard:

- Select the record or records you want to move.
- Choose the Cut command or the Copy command from the Edit menu (or press Command-X or Command-C, respectively) to cut or copy the selected record or records to the Clipboard.
- Select the new location for the records in the current file, or open a different database file and select a destination there.
- Choose the Paste command from the Edit menu (or press Command-V). The records you cut or copied will be inserted at the new location.

You can arrange or select data in many ways

You can sort, search for, or select data by choosing a menu command and then typing in the comparison information or clicking an option. Suppose we wanted to arrange the records in our address file alphabetically by name, for example:

- ☐ Click on the field name Name to select this field.
- ☐ Choose the Sort... command from the Organize menu (or press Command-A). The Sort box appears.

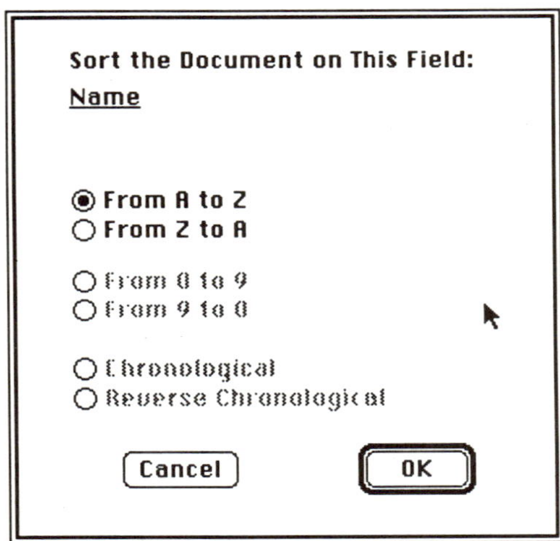

- ☐ The option to sort from A to Z is already selected (this is the default when you sort a text field), so either press Return or click the OK button to sort the field. All the database records will be rearranged in alphabetical order by the names in the Name field.

You can calculate data in a variety of ways

Works lets you add calculated fields to records, so you can calculate two numeric fields and produce a new field containing the result. Unlike the displays in many other database programs, the Works screen instantly shows the results of calculations. And when it comes time to print a report of your data, you can create subtotals of numeric data in different fields as well as grand totals at the end of the report. We'll explore these features more in Chapter 7.

It's easy to print and format your data

Works gives you several options for looking at or printing out your data without a lot of hassle. To print selected data from a database file, you must create a report:

☐ Choose the New Report... command from the Report menu. A new database report window appears.

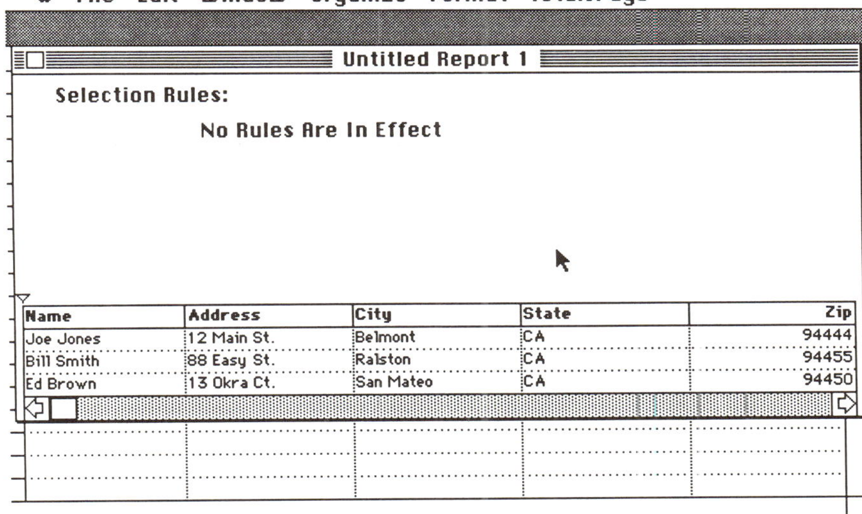

If you want to rearrange the categories in a report, you simply click on them and drag them. (The procedure is exactly like rearranging the fields in a list window.) You can also sort or select records in a report, just as you can when you're looking at a database file.

You can easily format the same field in every record

You can adjust the formatting of individual fields or the type of data a field will contain with the Set Field Attributes... command from the

Format menu. Suppose you wanted to center all the street addresses in our sample address file:

- ☐ If the form window is showing, double-click on the screen to change to a list window.
- ☐ Double-click on an entry in the Address field. The Set Field Attributes window opens.

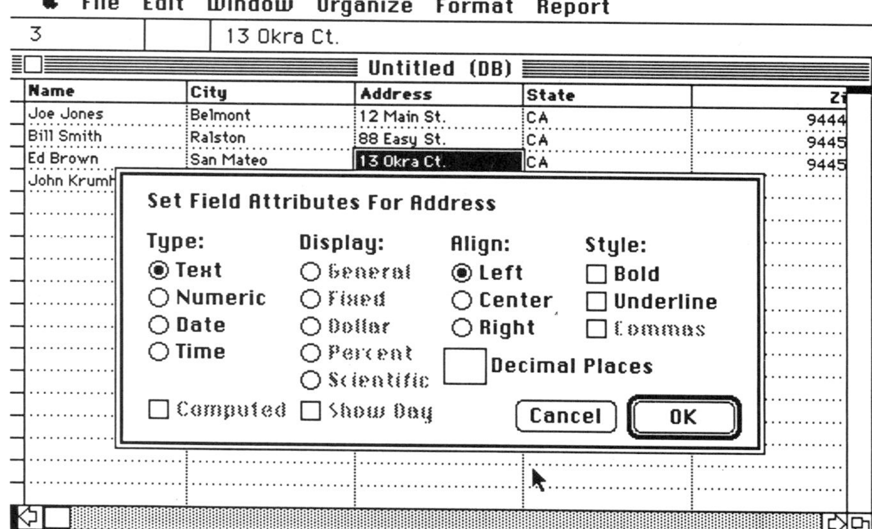

- ☐ Click the Center option under the Align heading.
- ☐ Press Return or click the OK button. The entries in the Address field will be centered.

You can use this procedure to align or otherwise format field data in the form window.

With the Set Field Attributes... command, you can tell Works that fields will contain numbers, times, or dates, instead of text. If you don't set the attributes of a field, Works assumes you are entering text information, but if you set the attributes to numbers, dates, or times, you can then sort that data numerically or chronologically.

You can get a lot of data on a printed page

Thanks to the 50% Reduction and wide Orientation options in the Page Setup dialog box, you can print database reports that are much wider than those from other programs. The 50% Reduction option lets you print your data with smaller characters, so more of them will fit on a page, and the wide Orientation option lets you print the data sideways down the length of your paper, instead of across its width. To choose one of these options:

- Choose the New Report... command from the Report menu.
- Choose the Page Setup... command from the File menu. The Page Setup dialog box appears.
- Click the wide option icon in the Orientation area of the Page Setup dialog box to print a database report sideways, or click the 50% Reduction option in the Special Effects area of the window to select the reduced print size. You can select both options at the same time, if you wish, to squeeze the most data on a page.

WHAT THE DATABASE WON'T DO—AND WHAT TO DO ABOUT IT

The Works database is a simple, flexible data-handling tool that will meet most of the needs of most users, but it is by no means the most sophisticated database program around.

The database doesn't evaluate your entries

More powerful database programs can evaluate the data entered into them. Some database programs can be set up to accept only 5-digit zip codes in a field, for example, or to check each record in the file each time you enter a new one, and then warn you when there is a duplicate. Works' data-evaluation capabilities are far more limited. If you set a field's attributes to inform Works that a field contains a certain type of data (text, dates, times, or numbers), Works will warn you if you enter an inappropriate type of data. If, for example, we set the Zip field in our address file so that Works expects it to contain numbers, and we try to enter text, Works will warn us, like this:

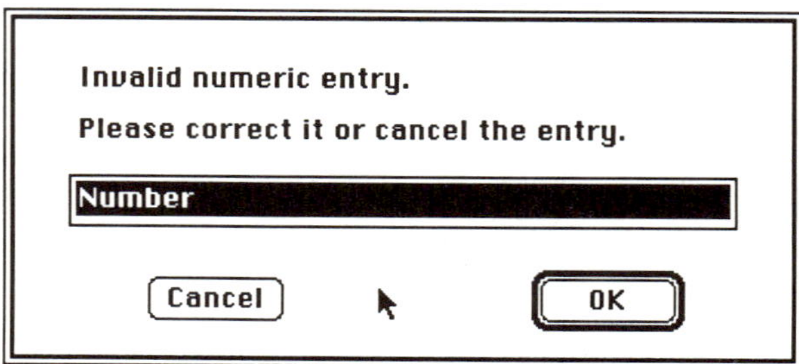

Data evaluation is a nice feature, but it doesn't completely prevent mistakes. With Works, you can set fields to accept only dates, times, or numbers, but just as with any other database file, you should check the entire file periodically for mistakes. When you do want to look at a whole file quickly, you can use the list window display.

The ability to check for duplicate records is perhaps the handiest data-evaluation feature. Works doesn't check duplication automatically, but it's easy to check this yourself. Suppose we want to check for duplicate entries in our address file:

- Display the file's list window.
- Select the Name field by clicking on the field name.
- Choose the Sort... command from the Organize menu.
- Press Return to accept the default sorting option (A-Z). Works sorts the records in the file alphabetically by name. Now, you can scan the file in a list window and check for duplicate entries. Since the file is sorted by name, you'll find any duplicate names next to each other in the Name field.

Works can't compare data

Works is a non-relational, as opposed to a relational, program. Relational database programs allow you to create a number of different files and then have the program compare, or relate information, among them. If you had one file containing employee salaries and another file containing employee education records, you could ask the program to correlate salaries with education histories and produce a ranked list that showed each employee, his salary, and his educational level. With Works, you can't relate information between files automatically. To produce an employee/salary/education list from two different files, you must combine the information manually.

You can, however add new information to an existing database file whenever you want by adding new fields, and you can cut and paste data between files. Suppose, for example, that we had a separate file containing names and employee numbers (in a field called Employee Number), and we wanted to merge the employee numbers with our existing address file:

- ☐ Open the file containing the employee numbers.
- ☐ Click on the Name field to select it.
- ☐ Choose the Sort... command from the Organize menu, and select the A-Z option, then press the Return key so that the entire file is sorted by name.
- ☐ Select all the data in the Employee Number field by clicking on the field name. (Note that this doesn't select the field name itself, only the data contained in that field.)
- ☐ Choose the Copy command from the Edit menu to copy the data to the Clipboard.
- ☐ Open the address file.
- ☐ Double-click on the screen to switch to the list window.
- ☐ Sort the file on the Name field with the A-Z option.
- ☐ Choose the Add New Field... command from the Edit menu. The Field Name box will appear.
- ☐ Type *Employee Number* (or another name, if you like) as the new field name, and press the Return key. The new field is added at the right of the existing fields in the list window.
- ☐ Click in the bottom scroll bar to move the Employee Number field into view, if it isn't in view already.
- ☐ Click on the Employee Number field in the first record.
- ☐ Choose the Paste command from the Edit menu. The employee numbers will be pasted from the Clipboard, and since both of the files are sorted in the same order, the numbers will match the correct employees.

A record can't be more than one screen long in a form window

In some other database programs, you can design screen forms that occupy several successive "pages," or screens, putting some fields on the first page, some on the second, and so on. This allows you to group fields on different screens. With Works, you have to lay all your cards on the table at the same time, and you can use only one table—all fields in a file must be on the same screen in the form window.

You could run out of file space

Since the database maintains files entirely in RAM, you could run out of file space if you collect too many records. If you run out of file space, a dialog box appears on the screen warning you that you're out of memory, and suggesting that you close one or more files on the desktop to make more room. When your files become particularly large (say, over 2,000 records in the database), you should periodically check the About MS-Works... desk accessory on the Apple menu to see how much memory is left. This helps you keep from running out of memory when you're in the middle of working with a file.

If you do run out of memory, you will have to close some files on the desktop to free up Works so you can continue. But if you only have one huge file open at the time, your only option will be to close that file. This is a problem, since it prevents you from making that large file smaller to allow you to work with it again. You can't reduce the size of a large file by copying some of its data through the Clipboard and another file. The Clipboard shares RAM with your open files, and if there isn't any RAM left for files, there won't be any RAM left for the Clipboard.

To avoid this predicament, check the About MS-Works... desk accessory from time to time. Then, when you see that your database file is beginning to use up most of your Mac's memory, you can split it into two parts. Suppose, for example, that you have a customer file with 2,500 names in it, and you see by checking the About MS-Works... desk accessory that you're almost out of memory. To deal with the problem, you can split the file into two files, each of which will contain half of the records.

☐ Open the original customer file.

☐ Create a new file with exactly the same fields in it.

- ☐ Sort the original file on the Name field, in alphabetical order.
- ☐ Select all the records with names beginning with N-Z, and cut them to the Clipboard.
- ☐ Activate the new file's window (it should be in a list window—if it isn't, choose Show List).
- ☐ Select the first field in the first record.
- ☐ Paste the records from the Clipboard into the new file.

By doing this, you create two files with the same fields, each of which contains half of your records. If the first file is called Customers, you can name the second file Customers2 to help you remember which file is which. Now, you have twice the room to store new names (although, since the file space was a function of the amount of desktop space available, you'll only be able to have one of these files open at a time if they get much bigger).

BASIC DATABASE TIPS

As you build your experience with Works, you'll discover a variety of shortcuts and operating tips that make your database work more efficient. The following tips apply to database work in general, and they'll get you started on your way to using the Works database as effectively as possible.

Use efficient field names

When you name fields in a database file, make the names as descriptive and efficient as possible. You want a name to identify a field, but you don't want it to take up any more space on the screen than necessary. A good example is the name State. In most cases, the data you would store in a State field would be two-letter state name abbreviations, such as CA, NY, or TX. If you use the name State, the field name will be twice as long as the field data, and when you display records in the list window, the State field will be wider than it needs to be. You could just as easily use the abbreviation ST, in which case the field name would be no longer than the field data, and you wouldn't waste any extra screen space. As a rule, try to keep field names as short as, or shorter than, the data you'll be storing.

Use field names to divide your data in useful ways

Although Works lets you add and delete fields from a database file whenever you want, you can help minimize such changes by planning ahead. When you decide how many fields your file will have and what the field names will be, think about how you might want to sort or select data in the future. Suppose you want to be able to sort or select records based on a person's last name. If you only create one field called Name, you'll have to enter the last names first (Smith, John, instead of John Smith) in order to sort on last names. This is because Works sorts text fields by the first letter in the field. To make life easy for a sort like this, it would be better to specify two fields, First Name and Last Name. That way, you could always sort on the Last Name field easily. You might also want to separate area code and telephone number data into two fields, so you could sort on area codes as well as on telephone number prefixes.

Customize the form window for easy data entry

Although fields are simply placed one on top of the other in the order in which you define them in the form window, you can drag fields around the screen to relocate them. By relocating fields, you can place them in the most logical order for your data-entry needs.

If you usually only fill out half of the fields in a new record, you should place those fields in the same part of the form window so that you can move easily from one field to the next. You can rearrange fields any time, so you can adjust the layout of a form window as your data-entry needs change. You might also want to rearrange fields in a form window to match a paper form you are using. If the form window is laid out like the paper form, you can fill in data in the same way you're used to filling it in on paper.

Use the Tab and Return keys to move from field to field

Depending on where you want the selection to move when you are entering data, you can use either the Tab or Return key to accept each entry. If you're in the list window and you want to fill out all the fields in one record, use the Tab key to enter data. (As mentioned earlier in this chapter, the Tab key moves the selection one field to the right after it enters your data in the current field.) When the current field is the rightmost field in the list window, the Tab key moves the selection to the first field on the left in the record below. If, on the other hand, you want to enter data into one field in several records in the list window, you should use the Return key. (Again, Return moves the selection into the field below after it enters your data in the current field.) If the last record in a file is selected and you press the Return key, the selection moves down to the same field in the new record below. So, you can insert data into several new records this way.

DATABASE SPECIFICATIONS

Here are some specifications you may want to refer to as you use the database.

Maximum file size: Approximately 2,000 records (512K Mac); 6,000 records (Mac Plus)—actual limit depends on specific file contents.

Maximum field length: 256 characters

Maximum number of fields in a record: 60

Maximum number of stored reports per database file: 8

Maximum number of record selection rules: 6

Maximum paper height: 300 inches (with Custom Size paper option)

Minimum paper height: 1 inch

Maximum paper width: 15 inches

Minimum paper width: 1 inch

Default paper size: US Letter (8½ by 11 inches)

Default top, bottom, left, and right margins: 1 inch

Default font: 9-point Geneva

Number of fonts available: 1

Maximum length of search strings: 80 characters

Maximum length of headers or footers: 99 characters

Range of numbered pages in a document: 1 through 9,999

CHAPTER 7

Database Projects

The Works database is extremely flexible when it comes to arranging, selecting, and even calculating data. In this chapter, we'll see just how flexible the database can be, as we help Al Chroma with a variety of business and personal projects.

A CALENDAR

With all the activity involved in getting the Videorama off the ground (personal appointments, employee interviews, due dates for various license fees and bills, and vendor appointments), Al has found that he has far more things to do than he can remember, and he's having trouble organizing his day-to-day activities. A calendar is the obvious answer, and with the Works database, Al can make a calendar that will quickly produce daily "do" lists as well as lay out his schedule for the weeks and months ahead. Because he can have up to ten Works files on the desktop at a time, Al can load his calendar file every day and leave it on the desktop so it's instantly available whenever he needs it.

Creating the calendar file

The calendar file we'll create is really very simple in terms of the number of data fields it contains. The secret lies in formatting the fields and creating useful reports. Let's begin by creating the file itself:

- ☐ Load Microsoft Works.
- ☐ Click on the database icon, and then click the New button. The Field Name window appears, ready for you to enter field names for the new file.

Before we enter field names, we need to think about the types of data we'll want to store in the calendar file. Calendars store dates and times of events, along with descriptions of the events themselves. So let's begin this file with three field names: Date, Time, and Event.

- Type the field name *Date* in the Field Name window, and press Return or click the Add Field button to add this field to the database file. The field appears in the form window, and the Field Name window reappears, ready for the second field name.
- Type the field name *Time* in the Field Name window, and press the Return key to add it to the file.
- Type the field name *Event* and press the Return key to add it to the file. This is the final field you want to add to the file at this point, so click the Done button in the Field Name window. The Field Name window disappears, and the form window is displayed with these three fields in it.

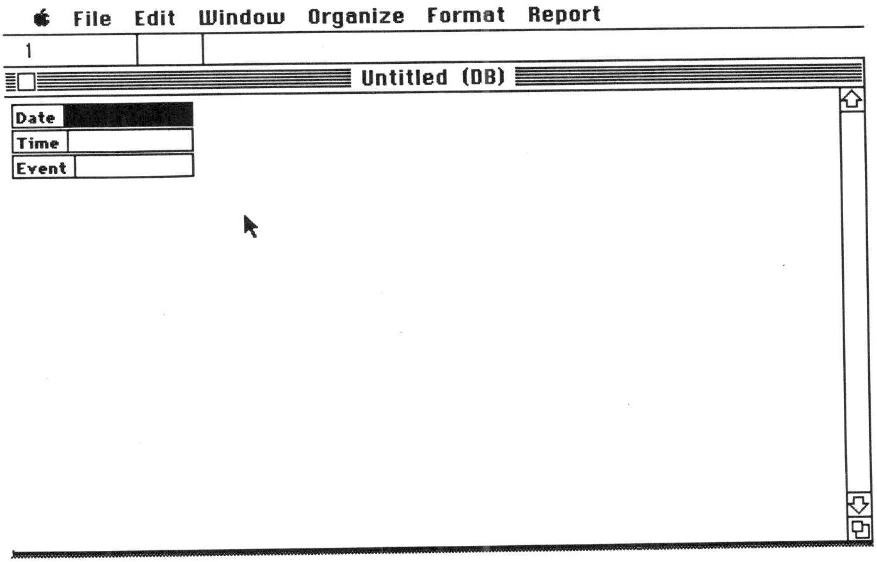

File Edit Window Organize Format Report

Untitled (DB)

Date

Time

Event

Before we begin entering appointment information into this file, we need to adjust each field so that the file is as useful as possible. The file contains date and time information. By using the Set Field Attributes... command, we can tell Works that the Date and Time fields contain date and time information. This will allow us to sort these fields in chronological order, and it will let us specify certain formats for the dates and times we enter.

□ Click on the Date field to select it.

□ Choose the Set Field Attributes... command from the Format menu. The Set Field Attributes dialog box appears.

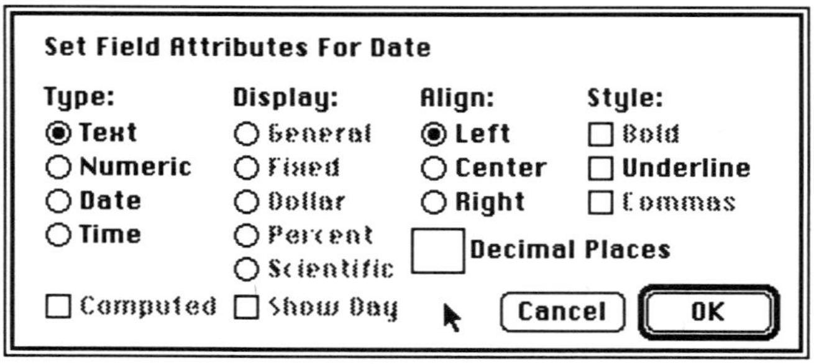

Set Field Attributes For Date

Type:	Display:	Align:	Style:
◉ Text	○ General	◉ Left	□ Bold
○ Numeric	○ Fixed	○ Center	□ Underline
○ Date	○ Dollar	○ Right	□ Commas
○ Time	○ Percent	□ Decimal Places	
	○ Scientific		
□ Computed	□ Show Day	Cancel	OK

□ To tell Works that the Date field will contain date information, click the Date option in the Type area. When you do, the options in the Display area change to Short, Medium, and Long.

The Short, Medium, and Long options are three different formats in which Works can present dates. The formats look like this:

Format	*Example*
Short	3/24/86
Medium	Mar 24, 1986
Long	March 24, 1986

Since this is a calendar file, we'll want fairly descriptive dates, so we'll select the Medium option.

□ Click the Medium button.

You can also tell Works to calculate the day of the week for a date you enter and to display it along with the date in a field. You specify this format by clicking the Show Day box at the bottom of the Set Field Attributes dialog box. Works will display the day with a date only when you have selected either Medium or Long as the date format. When you click the box next to Show Day, the day will be displayed in the date format you have selected, as follows:

Format	*Example*
Medium	Mon, Mar 24, 1986
Long	Monday, March 24, 1986

□ Click the Show Day box.

The other options in the Set Field Attributes dialog box control how data is aligned in a field and whether or not the data is enhanced with underlining and other style options. The default alignment option is Left, meaning data is aligned with the left edge of data fields. Left alignment is fine for a calendar, so we don't need to change it. The only Style options available in this dialog box when you set the data type to Date are bold and underlining. Let's leave the Style options alone for now. (If you want to make data appear in boldface within a field, you can select Bold Field Data from the Format menu.) To confirm these field-attribute settings, either click the OK button in the lower-right corner of the dialog box or press the Return key.

The next field in the file will contain time data, so you'll want to set the field attributes for it as well:

□ Click on the Time field to select it, and then choose the Set Field Attributes... command from the Format menu.

□ Click the Time option in the Type area.

□ Press the Return key to confirm this change and return to the form window.

The third field will contain only text, and the default field data type is text; so we don't have to change this field's attributes. Now we're ready to enter some data into the file. Let's suppose Al has made an appointment with his dentist for 9:00 in the morning on March 24.

□ Click on the Date field to select it, and type *3/24/86*. Press the Return key. Works will automatically convert this entry to the Medium date format and display it in the window.

When you specify a certain data type for a field, Works expects you to enter that data in a particular format. Since we specified Date data for this field, Works will accept dates in any of these formats:

- 03/24/86
- 3-24-86
- 03/24/1986
- Mon, Mar 24, 1986
- Mar 24, 1986
- Mar 24, 86
- March 24, 1986
- March 24, 86
- Monday, March 24, 1986
- Monday, March 24, 86

Works will convert any of these formats to the display format you selected in the Set Field Attributes dialog box.

When we enter this date in our first record, however, there's a problem: Works converts the date to the Medium format, but the field isn't wide enough to display the whole date.

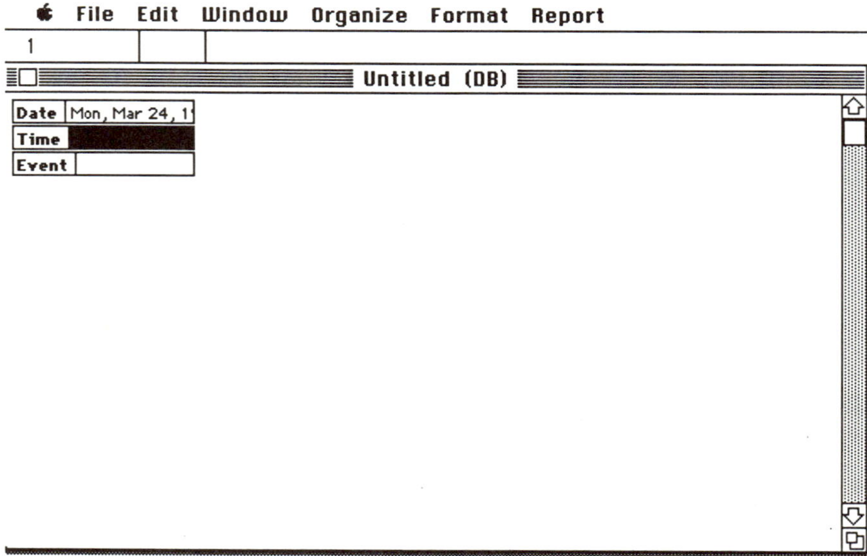

To see the entire date, we'll widen this field:

- Place the pointer on the right edge of the Date field. The pointer changes to a double arrow.
- Hold down the mouse button and drag the edge of the field to the right about three inches.
- Release the mouse button. The entire date is displayed.

You can make any field wider or narrower at any time in the form window by dragging the field's right edge. While we're at it, we might as well widen the other two fields in this file:

- Drag the right edge of the Time field about an inch right.
- Drag the right edge of the Event field to the right edge of the screen. (This field will sometimes contain a lot of data, so you'll want all the room you can get.)

Now we can enter the other two items of information.

- Click on the Time field, enter *9:00*, and press Return. Works converts this entry to 9:00 AM and selects the Event field.

Works uses a 24-hour clock to convert times, so if you enter any time up to 12:00 without specifying either AM or PM, Works assumes you mean AM. To enter times after noon, you can either use military (24-hour clock) time or type *PM* after them. For example:

If you type:	***Works shows:***
9:00	9:00 AM
21:00	9:00 PM
9:00 PM	9:00 PM
09:00	9:00 AM
09:0	9:00 AM

The best course is to specify AM or PM when you enter times.

Finally, you can enter the text describing the calendar event itself. The Event field should already be selected, so:

- Type *Dentist Appointment-Dr. Hesselschwerdt, 12th & Broadway, 6th Floor.*

Notice that this entry is longer than the space in the database's entry bar will allow. When you type more data than will fit in the entry bar, the entry bar expands to reveal an extra line below.

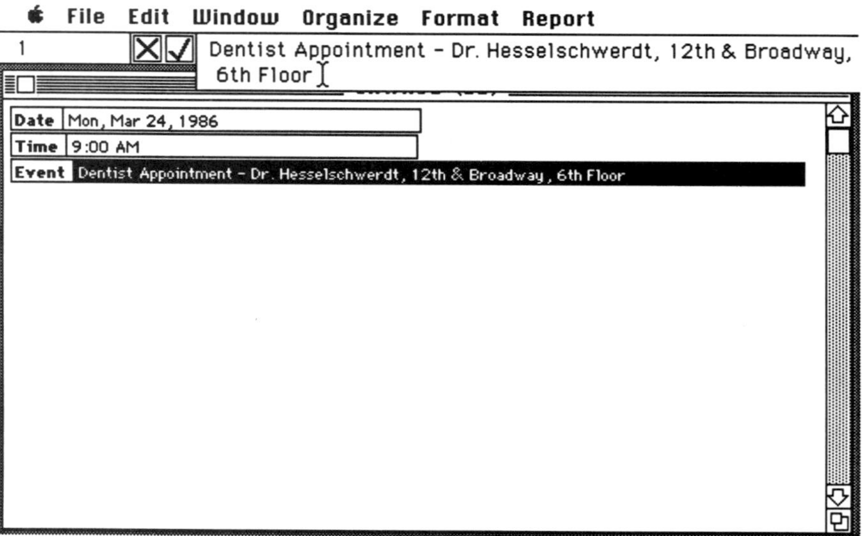

You can enter up to 256 characters of data into any database field. The entry bar can expand to be up to three lines deep. When a data field is not wide enough to display an entry, Works still stores the entry (as long as 256 characters), but displays only what fits in the field. You can view the full entry by selecting the field and looking at the entry bar, where all the field's data is displayed.

☐ Press the Return key to enter this data.

From here on, entering data into this file is simply a matter of typing in each appointment as we make it. For now, let's save the file with the name Calendar.

☐ Choose the Save command from the File menu. A dialog box appears, prompting you to type a name for the new file.

☐ Type the name *Calendar*, and then either click the Save button or press the Return key. The file will be saved to the current disk drive.

Using the calendar file

Now, let's assume that Al has made a couple of weeks' worth of appointments and entered them into the Calendar file. He entered the appointments as they were made, which means they weren't always entered in the order in which they will occur. Now he wants to see how his calendar shapes up for the next few months. To do that, he will want to look at a lot of appointments at once and then sort them chronologically.

The form window is showing because we were working with the form window when we saved the file. We want to see the list window, though, so:

- ☐ Double-click in a blank part of the form window. The display changes to the list window.

Double-clicking in a blank part of the screen is a fast way to change from the form window to the list window, and vice versa. Of course, you can also use Show Form or Show List from the Format menu to change displays, or you can press Command-L.

In a list window, the file looks like this:

File Edit Window Organize Format Report

Calendar (DB)

Date	Time	Event	
Mon, Mar 24, 1986	9:00 AM	Dentist Appointment - Dr. Hesselschwe	
Fri, Apr 4, 1986	9:00 AM	3-day sale begins	
Thu, May 15, 1986		Anna's Birthday	
Fri, Aug 15, 1986		Vacation Begins	
Sun, Aug 31, 1986		Back from Vacation	
Mon, Sep 15, 1986	10:00 AM	Check with landlord on building status	
Thu, Mar 27, 1986	6:30 PM	Dinner with the Jacksons, their house	
Sun, Jun 1, 1986	1:00 PM	Felicia's Wedding - St. Mary's	
Mon, Mar 31, 1986	2:00 PM	Income Tax Preparation - Don Rose	
Tue, Mar 25, 1986	10:15 AM	Interview VCR Technician	
Wed, Mar 26, 1986	12:00 PM	Lunch with Cousin Lou, Antoine's	
Tue, Mar 25, 1986	4:00 PM	MCA Video salesman	
Mon, Mar 31, 1986		Payroll tax installment due	
Tue, Sep 30, 1986		Payroll tax installment due	
Sat, Mar 29, 1986	12:00 PM	Projectionists' Union Picnic	
Wed, Sep 3, 1986	12:00 PM	Tony's Retirement Lunch - Bingo's	
Wed, Apr 2, 1986	3:00 PM	UA Video Salesman	

- ☐ Enter the rest of the appointments as shown.

With the list window showing, we can see that the appointments are out of order. We also notice that not very much of the first Event entry is visible, because the Event field is too narrow. So, before we sort the Event field, let's widen it.

☐ Point to the vertical line that marks the right edge of the Event field. The pointer changes to a double arrow.

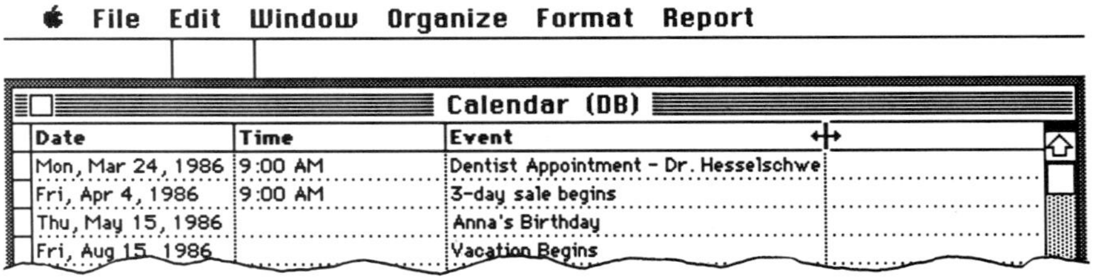

File Edit Window Organize Format Report

Calendar (DB)

Date	Time	Event	
Mon, Mar 24, 1986	9:00 AM	Dentist Appointment - Dr. Hesselschwe	
Fri, Apr 4, 1986	9:00 AM	3-day sale begins	
Thu, May 15, 1986		Anna's Birthday	
Fri, Aug 15, 1986		Vacation Begins	

☐ Hold down the mouse button and drag the line over to the right edge of the screen.

☐ Release the mouse button to change the field width.

You can also make fields narrower by dragging dividing lines to the left.

Now that we can see more of the Event data, let's sort the file so the records are in chronological order by date.

☐ Click on the Date field name to select that field.

☐ Choose the Sort... command from the Organize menu. The Sort dialog box appears.

When you sort a Date- or Time-type field the only options available are Chronological and Reverse Chronological. The Chronological option is the default, so it is selected.

☐ Click the OK button or press the Return key. The records are sorted chronologically on the Date field.

 File Edit Window Organize Format Report

Calendar (DB)

Date	Time	Event
Mon, Mar 24, 1986	9:00 AM	Dentist Appointment - Dr. Hesselschwerdt, 12th & Broadway
Tue, Mar 25, 1986	10:15 AM	Interview VCR Technician
Tue, Mar 25, 1986	4:00 PM	MCA Video Salesman
Tue, Mar 25, 1986	3:30 PM	Video Listing to printer
Wed, Mar 26, 1986	12:00 PM	Lunch with Cousin Lou, Antoine's
Thu, Mar 27, 1986	6:30 PM	Dinner with the Jacksons, their house
Sat, Mar 29, 1986	12:00 PM	Projectionists' Union Picnic
Mon, Mar 31, 1986	2:00 PM	Income Tax Preparation - Don Rose
Mon, Mar 31, 1986		Payroll tax installment due
Wed, Apr 2, 1986	3:00 PM	UA Video Salesman
Fri, Apr 4, 1986	9:00 AM	3-day sale begins
Thu, May 15, 1986		Anna's Birthday
Sun, Jun 1, 1986	1:00 PM	Felicia's Wedding - St. Mary's
Fri, Aug 15, 1986		Vacation Begins
Sun, Aug 31, 1986		Back from Vacation
Wed, Sep 3, 1986	12:00 PM	Tony's Retirement Lunch - Bingo's
Mon, Sep 15, 1986	10:00 AM	Check with landlord on building status

At this point, Al can scan the list window to see all his appointments on a certain date. There's still one problem, however. Works will only sort one database field at a time, and although we've sorted dates, some of the times within those dates aren't in chronological order. For instance, you can see that on March 25, some of the times are out of order. To arrange the records so both fields are in chronological order by date and time, you have to sort the file twice—once by time and once by date.

☐ Click the Time field name to select this field.

☐ Choose the Sort... command from the Organize menu.

☐ Press Return to select the default option to sort in chronological order. The records will be sorted by time of day.

☐ Click the Date field name to select this field.

☐ Sort the Date field in chronological order. The records are now sorted by date, and within each date, they remain sorted by time.

Now these records are useful to look at in the list window. But it might also be handy to print out a report for a certain day so Al can carry a list of his daily appointments with him. Ordinarily, you would create a report format to print out selected records from a database file. But since there are only a few appointments in any given day on this calendar, you can do something a little simpler, especially since the file is already sorted in chronological order.

Before selecting the records, let's make the most of the screen space by making the Time field a little narrower and then widening the Event field again, using the same techniques we used to make the Event field its present size. That way, you can see all the Event data on the screen.

☐ Drag the right border of the Time field to the left and the border of the Event field to the right.

Now, suppose we want to print out a list of Al's appointments for March 25:

☐ Choose the Match Records... command from the Organize menu. A dialog box appears.

☐ Type the information you want to match (in this case, *Mar 25*).

☐ The matching information you want Works to find is in a date field, and normally the Match Records... command searches all types of fields. (If you want to make certain that Works searches only text fields in the file, click the Search Text Fields Only box.)

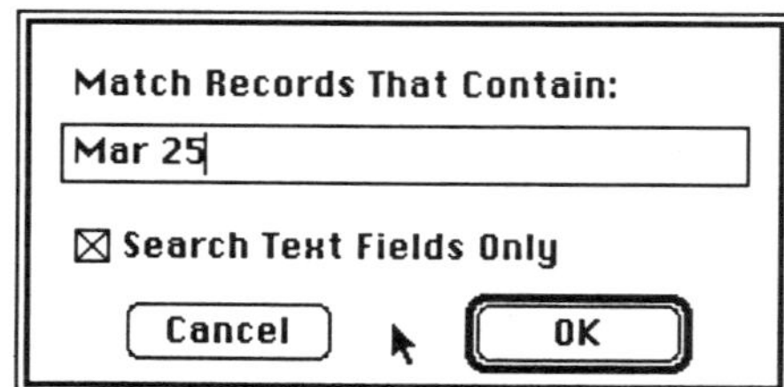

☐ Press the Return key or click the OK button. The records that contain the date Mar 25 will be selected from the file and displayed on the screen.

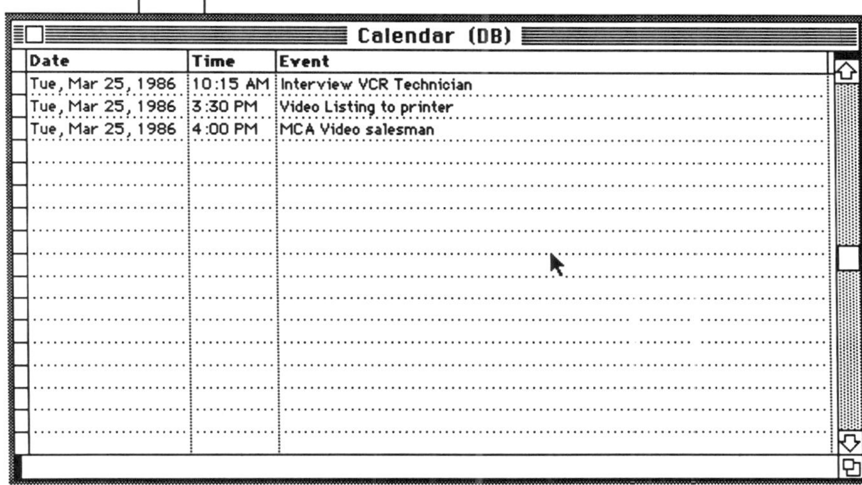

Now you can print them out quickly:

☐ Select the Print Window command from the File menu. The records you selected, along with the field names, will be printed.

This is a quick way to print a few records from a database file. The Print Window command prints only records that are showing on the screen, so this option is suitable only when you are printing fewer than 18 records (the maximum number of records that can be displayed in a list window at one time). To redisplay all the records in a file, you have to choose the Show All Records command again. When you do, the check mark next to Match Records... on the Organize menu disappears, and all the file's records are displayed again.

A VIDEO CLUB MEMBER FILE

Al wants to keep track of everyone who joins the Videorama's video club, so he's set up a simple file that does this. In the list window, Al's file looks like the screen display in Figure 7-1.

File Edit Window Organize Format Report

Club Members (DB)

Name	Address	City	ST	Zip	Phone	Memb #	Renew Date
Joe Brubaker	1047 La Rosa Ave.	San Carlos	CA	94606	415-555-1198	00033	6/6/87
Randy Clark	1730 Wawona Ave.	Belmont	CA	94005	415-555-6730	00034	6/6/87
Gary Carlston	23 Palou Ct.	San Rafael	CA	94599	415-555-7810	00029	6/5/87
Alice Villalobos	43518 Trimble Ct.	Santa Clara	CA	94505	408-555-8932	00015	6/2/87
Fred Bolton	3359 Warnocke St	San Jose	CA	95555	408-555-0000	00001	5/31/87
Kelly Stiern	4402 Bandley St.	Los Altos	CA	95505	408-555-4445	00026	6/5/87
Brad Baldwin	5770 Pinckney St.	San Bruno	CA	94060	415-555-0098	00028	6/5/87

Figure 7-1. *A video club membership file can be displayed in the list window.*

Creating the membership file

To follow along with this exercise, you need to create a sample file such as the one shown in Figure 7-1, using the procedures outlined for the Calendar file. Here's a summary of the steps:

- ☐ Open a new database file.
- ☐ Create fields titled Name, Address, City, ST, Zip, Phone, Memb #, and Renew Date.
- ☐ Type in the data shown in Figure 7-1.

- Drag the field dividing markers to the left so the list window of the file looks like the one in Figure 7-1.
- Choose the Save As... command from the File menu, type the file name *Club Members*, and press Return to save the file to disk.

Now, you're ready to continue.

The fields in one record in this file (displayed in the form window) look like this:

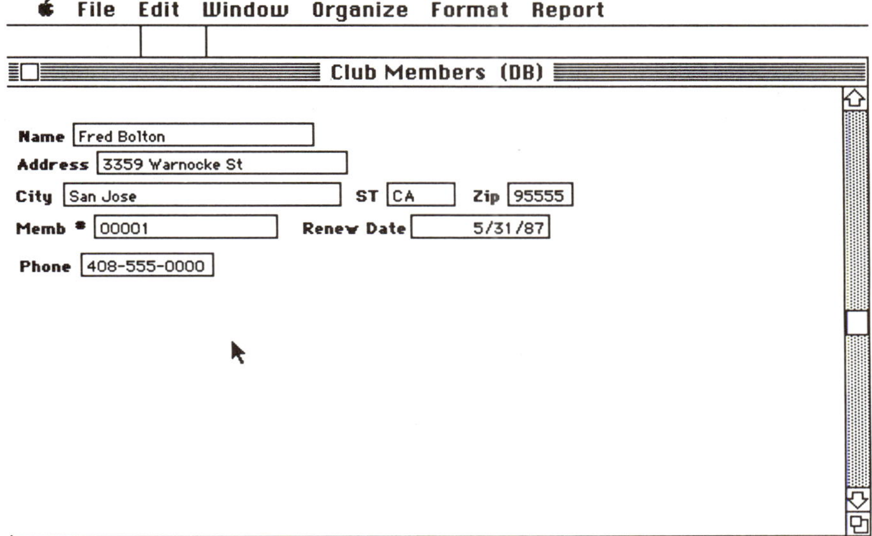

To see it yourself, select the record for Fred Bolton and choose the Show Form command from the Format menu.

Rearranging the fields

After entering a few records, Al discovers there are a few problems with this file. For one thing, a couple of employees have suggested that the Phone field should be next to the Name field so that they can find phone numbers more easily when they call a member about a reserved videotape. Fortunately, this is an easy modification to make in the form window.

- ☐ Place the pointer on top of the Phone field name. The pointer turns into a hand.
- ☐ Hold down the mouse button and drag the Phone field until it is to the right of the Name field.

As you hold down the mouse button, you'll notice that an outline appears around the field name and data, like this:

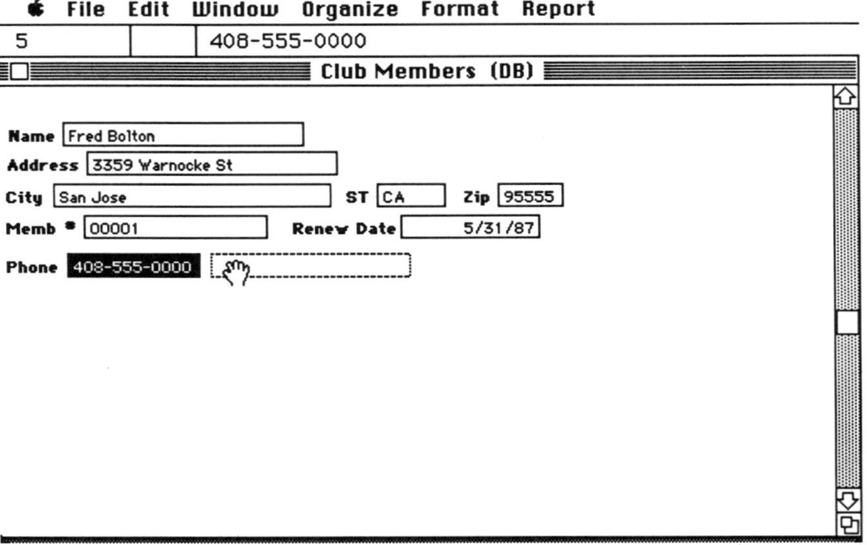

The outline shows you the overall size of the field you're moving. This is important, because you can't place one field on top of another field on the screen. If you try to, you'll get a warning that says you can't. By seeing the field outline, you can determine just where the edge of a field is, and you won't place part of it over another field when you move it.

☐ When the Phone field is to the right of the Name field, release the mouse button. The field moves to its new position, like this:

File Edit Window Organize Format Report
5 408-555-0000
Club Members (DB)
Name Fred Bolton Phone 408-555-0000
Address 3359 Warnocke St
City San Jose ST CA Zip 95555
Memb # 00001 Renew Date 5/31/87

Adding fields

Now that the form is a little more useful, Al has something else he wants to do. Since a lot of storage space is still left in this file, he wants to add more fields to store other useful information. One field will specify a customer's videotape format. This will help Al decide how many Beta-format tapes and how many VHS-format tapes to stock. Another field that will help Al in his purchasing decisions is one that records the favorite film genre of each customer. Let's add these fields to the file in the form window.

☐ Point to the blank area directly below the Memb # field and hold down the mouse button. The pointer changes to a right-pointing arrow.

☐ Drag the pointer to the right. As you drag, a dotted outline of a new field appears.

□ Drag the pointer until the field outline is about two inches long, then release the mouse button. The Field Name box appears, ready for you to type in the new field name.

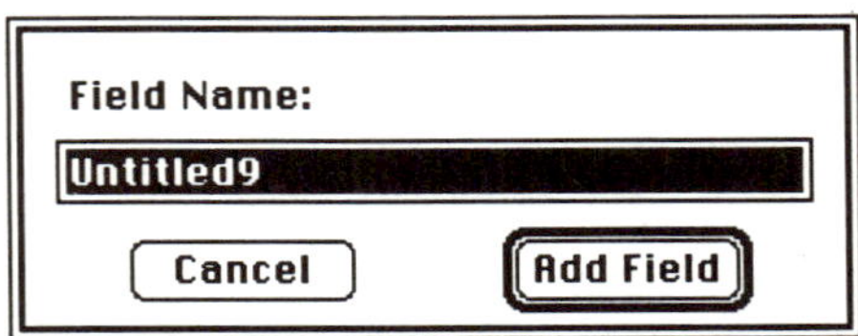

□ Type the field name *Format*, and press the Return key or click the Add Field button to add the new field. The new field appears in place of the outline on the screen.

□ Place the pointer to the right of the Format field, and repeat the steps for adding a new field.

□ Type the field name *Genre*, and press the Return key. The second new field is added to the file.

Now Al can record these added bits of information with each new video club member, and he can also add the information to existing records. To add information as easily as possible, Al will use the list window.

□ Double-click in a blank area of the form window, and the display changes to the list window.

Viewing wide files

The problem with the list window as it is currently set up is that you can't see the new Format and Genre fields, because they're off the screen to the right. And if you scroll to the right so you can see these fields, you can no longer see the Name field in each record. This will make it hard to match each video club member's name with the proper Format and Genre information.

We could rearrange the list window so that these two fields appear after the Name field. As explained in Chapter 6, you rearrange fields by pointing to their names, holding down the mouse button, and dragging to the left or right. But there's another way to see both the left and right parts of a file on the screen at the same time: Split the window into two panes.

- ☐ Point to the split bar in the lower-left corner of the list window (the black bar to the left of the left-hand arrow in the bottom scroll box), and hold down the mouse button.
- ☐ Drag the split bar to the middle of the list window. As you drag, a vertical dotted line appears.
- ☐ When the dotted line is at the middle of the list window, release the mouse button. The dotted line is replaced by two solid lines, and the screen divides into two side-by-side panes.

File Edit Window Organize Format Report

Club Members (DB)

Name	Address	City	ST	Zip	Phone	Memb #	Renew Date
Joe Brubaker	1047 La Rosa Ave.	San Carlos	CA	94606	415-555-1198	00033	6/6/87
Randy Clark	1730 Wawona Ave.	Belmont	CA	94005	415-555-6730	00034	6/6/87
Gary Carlston	23 Palou Ct.	San Rafael	CA	94599	415-555-7810	00029	6/5/87
Alice Villalobos	43518 Trimble Ct.	Santa Clara	CA	94505	408-555-8932	00015	6/2/87
Fred Bolton	3359 Warnocke St	San Jose	CA	95555	408-555-0000	00001	5/31/87
Kelly Stiern	4402 Bandley St.	Los Altos	CA	95505	408-555-4445	00026	6/5/87
Brad Baldwin	5770 Pinckney St.	San Bruno	CA	94060	415-555-0098	00028	6/5/87

You can also divide the list window horizontally by pulling down the split bar located at the top of the right-hand scroll bar. Splitting the window horizontally allows you to view two separate groups of records on the screen at once. You can also use both split bars at once, to view four different parts of a file on the screen at a time.

Now, we can scroll the two windows independently to display two different parts of the file. The names in the records are already showing in the left window, so all we have to do is scroll the right window until the Format and Genre fields appear. With all the pertinent fields showing for each record, it will be easy to enter the new Format and Genre information into the existing records.

Creating a report

Let's assume that Al has updated all the records in this file and that he's ready to take advantage of Works' sorting and reporting features.

- ☐ To follow along with this part of the exercise, enter the Format and Genre information shown here:

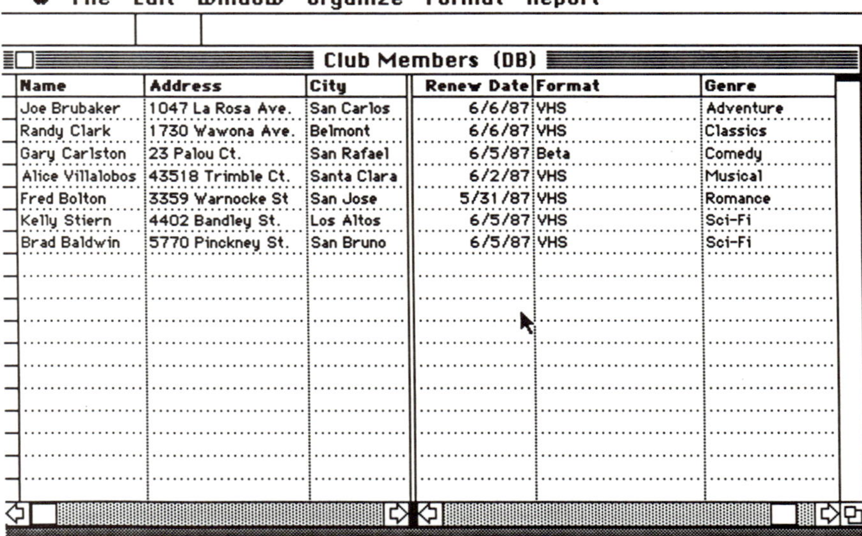

Name	Address	City	Renew Date	Format	Genre
Joe Brubaker	1047 La Rosa Ave.	San Carlos	6/6/87	VHS	Adventure
Randy Clark	1730 Wawona Ave.	Belmont	6/6/87	VHS	Classics
Gary Carlston	23 Palou Ct.	San Rafael	6/5/87	Beta	Comedy
Alice Villalobos	43518 Trimble Ct.	Santa Clara	6/2/87	VHS	Musical
Fred Bolton	3359 Warnocke St	San Jose	5/31/87	VHS	Romance
Kelly Stiern	4402 Bandley St.	Los Altos	6/5/87	VHS	Sci-Fi
Brad Baldwin	5770 Pinckney St.	San Bruno	6/5/87	VHS	Sci-Fi

Al has an opportunity to acquire a special collection of classic comedies in VHS format, and he wants to find out if there are enough club members who like classics or comedies (and whose tape format is VHS) to support the purchase.

☐ Choose the New Report... command from the Report menu. A report window appears.

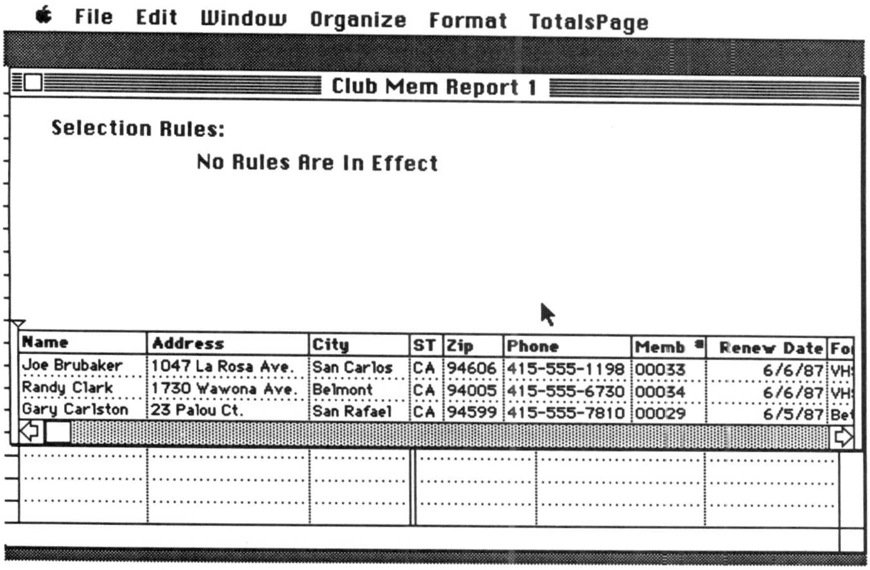

File Edit Window Organize Format TotalsPage

Club Mem Report 1

Selection Rules:

No Rules Are In Effect

Name	Address	City	ST	Zip	Phone	Memb #	Renew Date	Fo
Joe Brubaker	1047 La Rosa Ave.	San Carlos	CA	94606	415-555-1198	00033	6/6/87	VH
Randy Clark	1730 Wawona Ave.	Belmont	CA	94005	415-555-6730	00034	6/6/87	VH
Gary Carlston	23 Palou Ct.	San Rafael	CA	94599	415-555-7810	00029	6/5/87	Be

First, we need to decide which fields of data should appear in the report. Since Al wants to know how many people like comedies or classics in VHS format, the address, telephone number, and member number information is irrelevant for this report—the report should include only the Name, Format, and Genre fields.

You can tell which fields will be included in a database report by looking above the field names in the report window. There, you'll see a pair of downward-pointing triangles (called edge markers). The left and right edge markers indicate the left and right limits of the report—all fields between these markers will be included in the report. (You may have to scroll to the right to see the right edge marker.)

We can see that this report already includes the Name field. But if we scroll to the right, we can see that the right edge marker is located over the middle of the Format field so that the complete Format and Genre fields aren't currently included. To change this, we need to move the Format and Genre fields to the left.

☐ Click on the Format field to select it.

☐ Drag the field to the left until it is on top of the Address field.

- ☐ Release the mouse button. The Format field is inserted between the Name and Address fields.
- ☐ Repeat these same three steps with the Genre field to insert it to the right of the Format field.

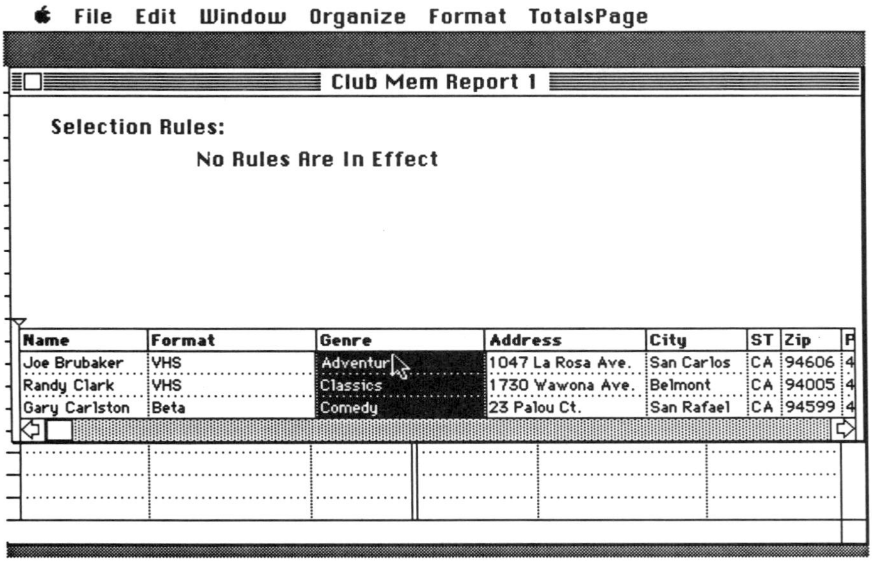

Now, the three fields we want are next to each other, and all of them will be included in the report. As you can see, though, the report still contains fields we don't want included. To eliminate the unwanted fields, we can do either of two things: Drag the field dividers of the three fields until they are so wide that they occupy the entire report (that is, so the right edge of the Genre field lines up with the right edge marker); or use the Page Setup... command from the File menu to change the margins of the report so there is only enough room in it for the three fields we want to include.

Let's use the Page Setup... command to narrow the report's width first.

- ☐ Choose the Page Setup... command from the File menu. The Page Setup dialog box appears.

☐ Double-click in the Right Margin box to select it.

☐ Type the number *3*. This sets the right margin at 3 inches.

☐ Press the Return key to confirm this change and to close the Page Setup dialog box.

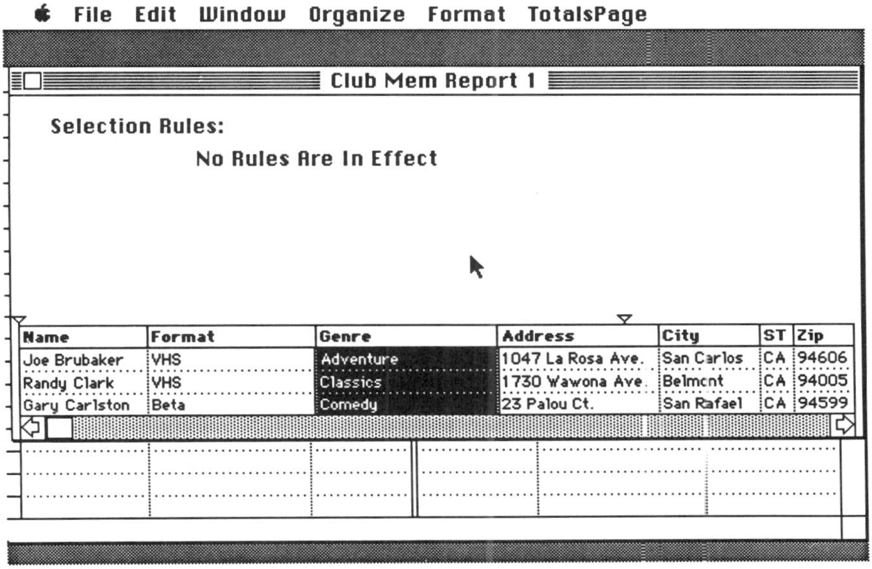

When the Page Setup dialog box disappears and the report is displayed again, you'll notice that the edge marker at the report's right limit has moved left to the Address field. That's because we changed the right margin with the Page Setup... command, and changing the margins affects the amount of data that you can fit into each line of a report.

At this point, the report still includes part of the Address field, however. To eliminate all of the Address field from the report, we can just widen the Genre field:

☐ Place the pointer on the dividing line between the Genre and Address field names.

☐ Hold down the mouse button, and drag the dividing line until it is underneath the right edge marker.

☐ Release the mouse button. The Genre field now extends all the way to the edge of the report.

Now that the report contains only the fields that interest us, we need to select specific records. We'll use Works' record-selection rules to do this.

☐ Choose Record Selection... from the Organize menu. The Record Selection box appears.

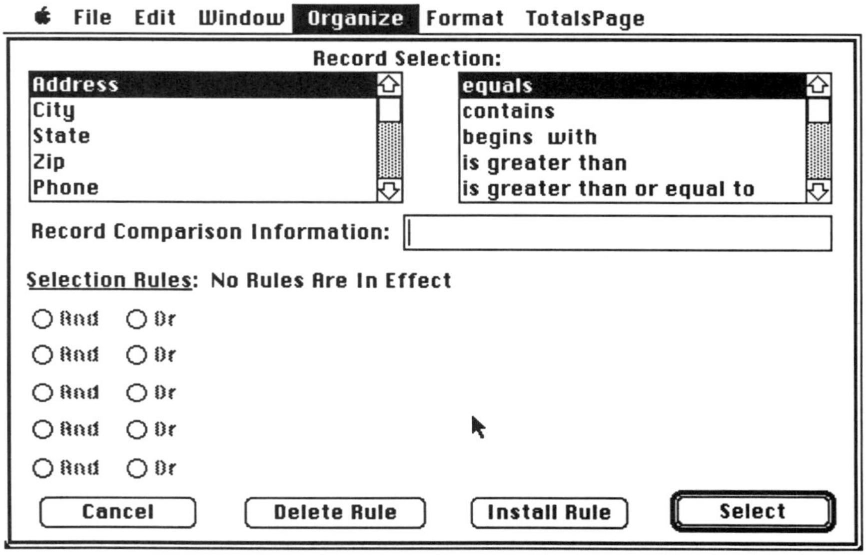

The Record Selection box contains a list of the field names in the file from which you're reporting and a list of logical operators. You choose the field upon which you want record-selection criteria to be based, then you choose the logical operator, and finally you enter the comparison information that will determine whether a record is selected. (A record is selected if the field you choose matches the criteria you've specified.) You can have up to six record-selection rules in a report, so you can be very specific in selecting data from a file. The first rule we want to use in Al's tape report will select only the records in which the Format field contains the entry *VHS*.

☐ Scroll down the list of fields in the Record Selection box until the Format name is showing.

☐ Click on the Format name to select it.

We want the Format field's data to equal *VHS* (to use Works' own terminology). The equal sign is already selected in the list of logical operators, so we can skip the second part of the rule-making process this time and go on to the third part:

- ☐ Enter the comparison information, *VHS*, in the window below the logical operator box. Do NOT press the Return key. Doing so selects the records according to the current rules, and you aren't finished entering rules yet.
- ☐ Click the Install Rule button at the bottom of the box. The rule is now installed, and you can see it spelled out in the Record Selection box.

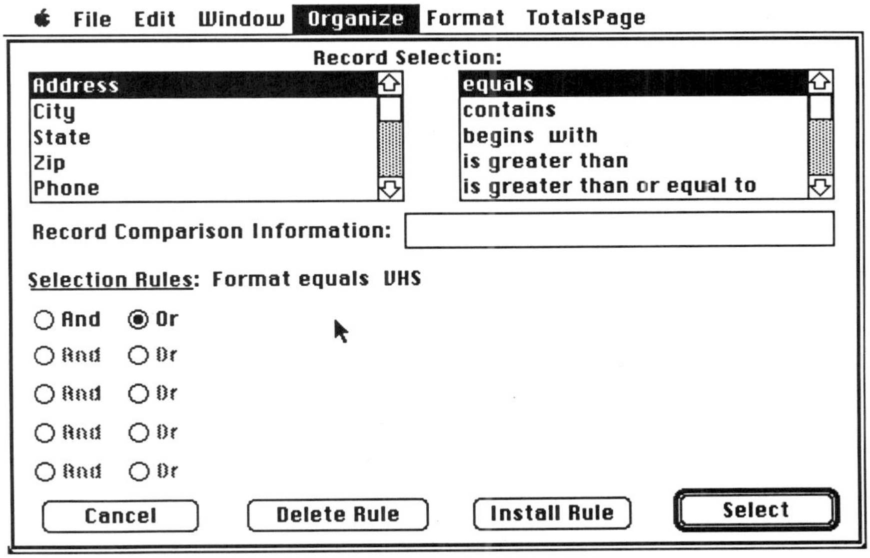

File Edit Window Organize Format TotalsPage

Record Selection:

Address
City
State
Zip
Phone

equals
contains
begins with
is greater than
is greater than or equal to

Record Comparison Information:

Selection Rules: Format equals VHS

And Or
And Or
And Or
And Or
And Or

Cancel Delete Rule Install Rule Select

We've now installed one rule, but we're not ready to select records yet. We also want the selection based on the Genre field—that is, we want only records in which the Genre field contains either *Comedy* or *Classics*. You'll notice that below the first rule are some And and Or buttons. These are connectors that link rules. The first group shows the Or button selected, which means that the selection would be based on either the first rule (Format equals VHS) or a second rule you specify. But we want Works to use both the first rule and a second rule.

- ☐ Click the And button to select it.

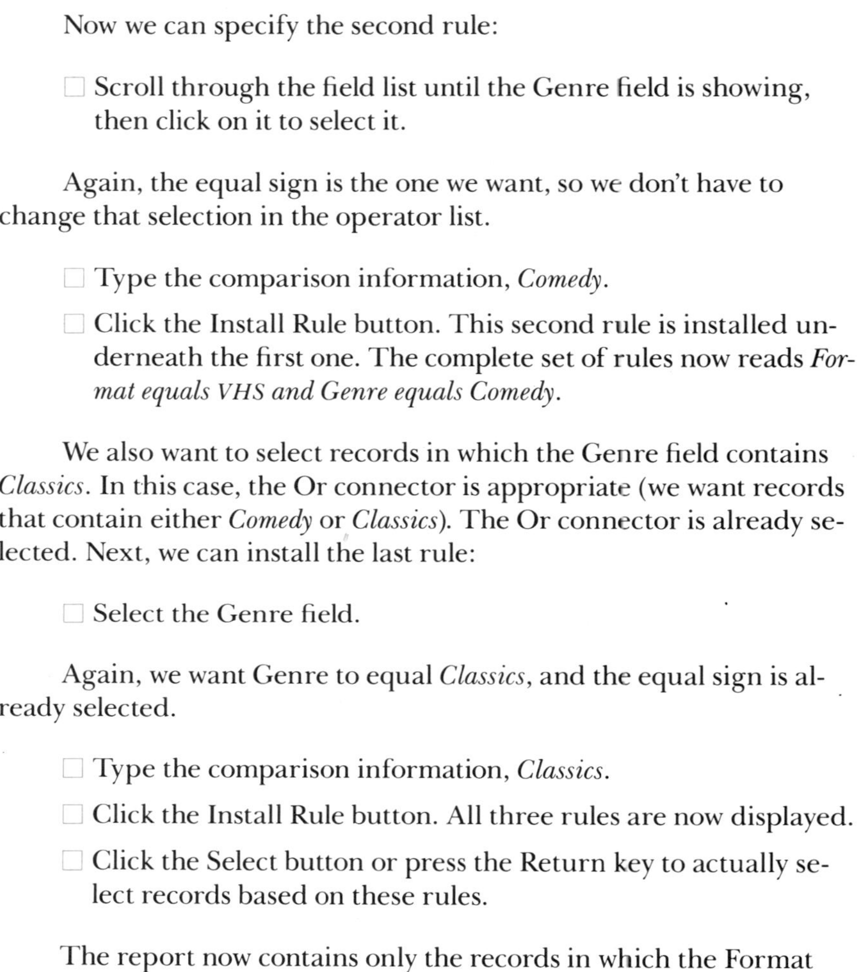

Now we can specify the second rule:

- Scroll through the field list until the Genre field is showing, then click on it to select it.

Again, the equal sign is the one we want, so we don't have to change that selection in the operator list.

- Type the comparison information, *Comedy*.
- Click the Install Rule button. This second rule is installed underneath the first one. The complete set of rules now reads *Format equals VHS and Genre equals Comedy*.

We also want to select records in which the Genre field contains *Classics*. In this case, the Or connector is appropriate (we want records that contain either *Comedy* or *Classics*). The Or connector is already selected. Next, we can install the last rule:

- Select the Genre field.

Again, we want Genre to equal *Classics*, and the equal sign is already selected.

- Type the comparison information, *Classics*.
- Click the Install Rule button. All three rules are now displayed.
- Click the Select button or press the Return key to actually select records based on these rules.

The report now contains only the records in which the Format field contains *VHS* and the Genre field contains either *Comedy* or *Classics*. All other records are left out. We've also formatted the report so that only the Name, Format, and Genre fields are included. The only other thing to do is sort the data so that all records with the same Genre data are together. This way, it will be easy to count the number of records for each genre. (The report we've created contains only one record. Read the next section to see how you'd sort multiple records.)

Works doesn't allow data-sorting in a report window, so we'll have to select the database file window from the Window menu and sort the data there.

- ☐ Choose the Club Members file from the Window menu.
- ☐ Click on the Genre field name to select that field.
- ☐ Choose the Sort... command from the Organize menu. The default sorting method is from A through Z, which is what we want. Press the Return key to sort the file this way. The records will be sorted on the Genre field from A through Z, placing all records with the same genre data together.
- ☐ Choose Club Mem Report 1 from the Window menu to return to the report window.

Naming the report

The report is almost ready to print out, but let's change the name so it's more descriptive. That way, it will be easy to remember what the report is for when we want to use it again.

- ☐ Choose the Change Report Title... command from the Edit menu.
- ☐ Type the name *Comedy & Classics in VHS*, and press the Return key. The report is renamed.

The report will be stored with this name when you close and save the Club Members file. You can recall the report any time the file is open by choosing Select Report... from the Report menu and then selecting this report from the list of stored reports.

Printing the report

To print the report, choose the Print... command from the File menu. The report will be printed with the margins you set with the Page Setup... command.

A TAX LEDGER

Now that Al is in business for himself, he has a lot of expenses that could be tax-deductible. One way to track deductible expenses along with income is to store a record of each transaction in a database file. The database's sorting and reporting features will then make it easy to zero in on tax-deductible expenses and taxable income when tax time rolls around.

To be useful, this file must contain enough fields so that Al can include information about each type of expense or income, its purpose, its amount, and the date. The list window of this file is shown in Figure 7-2.

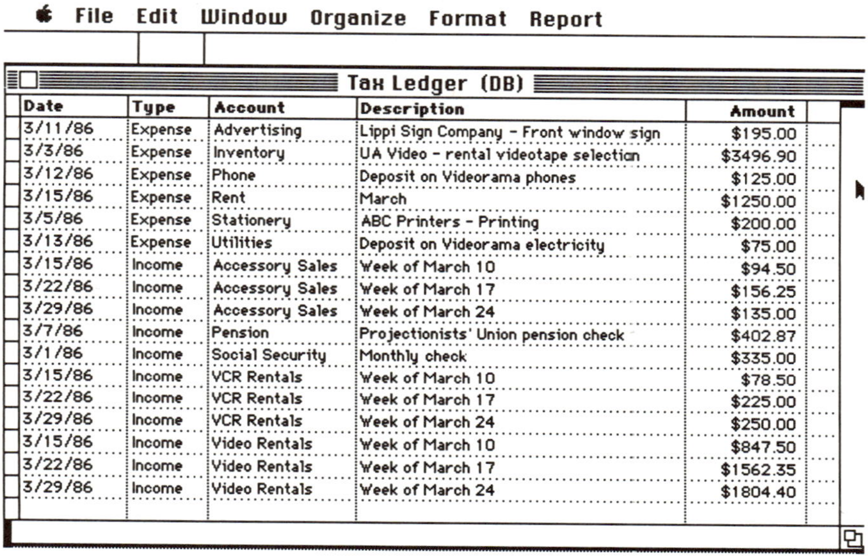

 File Edit Window Organize Format Report

Tax Ledger (DB)

Date	Type	Account	Description	Amount
3/11/86	Expense	Advertising	Lippi Sign Company - Front window sign	$195.00
3/3/86	Expense	Inventory	UA Video - rental videotape selection	$3496.90
3/12/86	Expense	Phone	Deposit on Videorama phones	$125.00
3/15/86	Expense	Rent	March	$1250.00
3/5/86	Expense	Stationery	ABC Printers - Printing	$200.00
3/13/86	Expense	Utilities	Deposit on Videorama electricity	$75.00
3/15/86	Income	Accessory Sales	Week of March 10	$94.50
3/22/86	Income	Accessory Sales	Week of March 17	$156.25
3/29/86	Income	Accessory Sales	Week of March 24	$135.00
3/7/86	Income	Pension	Projectionists' Union pension check	$402.87
3/1/86	Income	Social Security	Monthly check	$335.00
3/15/86	Income	VCR Rentals	Week of March 10	$78.50
3/22/86	Income	VCR Rentals	Week of March 17	$225.00
3/29/86	Income	VCR Rentals	Week of March 24	$250.00
3/15/86	Income	Video Rentals	Week of March 10	$847.50
3/22/86	Income	Video Rentals	Week of March 17	$1562.35
3/29/86	Income	Video Rentals	Week of March 24	$1804.40

Figure 7-2. *You can use the database to create a simple ledger of taxable income and expenses.*

Creating the database file

To follow along with this exercise, you must create a database file like the one Al has. Here are the steps:

- ☐ Open a new database file.
- ☐ Define fields named Date, Type, Account, Description, and Amount.
- ☐ Select the Date field and use the Set Field Attributes… command from the Format menu to make this a date-type field.

- ☐ Select the Amount field and use the Set Field Attributes... command from the Format menu to make this a numeric field formatted for dollars.
- ☐ Type in the 17 records of information shown in Figure 7-2.
- ☐ Choose the Save As... command, and save the file to disk with the name Tax Ledger.

Now you're ready to continue.

With these fields, Al can sort or select tax-related data in many ways. The Type field separates income from expenses, so he can generate reports that total only expenses or only income. The Account field breaks up expenses or income by purpose or source, so he can produce reports that list just utilities expenses or only Social Security income. The Description field lets him zero in on specific transactions. By using the Set Field Attributes... command, Al has identified the Date field as a date-type field (so records can be sorted or selected chronologically), and he's identified the Amount field as a numeric field with the Dollar format (so he can total expense amounts).

Most of the transactions to be recorded in this file will be transferred from a checkbook. Al can go through his checkbook every week or so and update the file with all the expenses that are deductible. When he has cash expenses, he can get the information from receipts. As for income, he can use bank- and savings-account statements as a source of deposit information, or he can use cash-register tapes from the Videorama. As he gathers information, Al can manipulate the data in this file in a number of useful ways. Let's look at a couple of examples.

Viewing selected records

Suppose Al wants to determine quickly how much money he has spent on the videotapes he rents. Because he's been careful to specify the videotape rental in the description of expenses related to it, all he has to do is select all the records that contain those words.

- ☐ Choose the Match Records... command from the Organize menu. A dialog box appears, asking you to type in comparison information Works will use to match records.

☐ Type the word *videotape*, and then press the Return key. The dialog box disappears, and only the record that contains the word *videotape* appears on the screen.

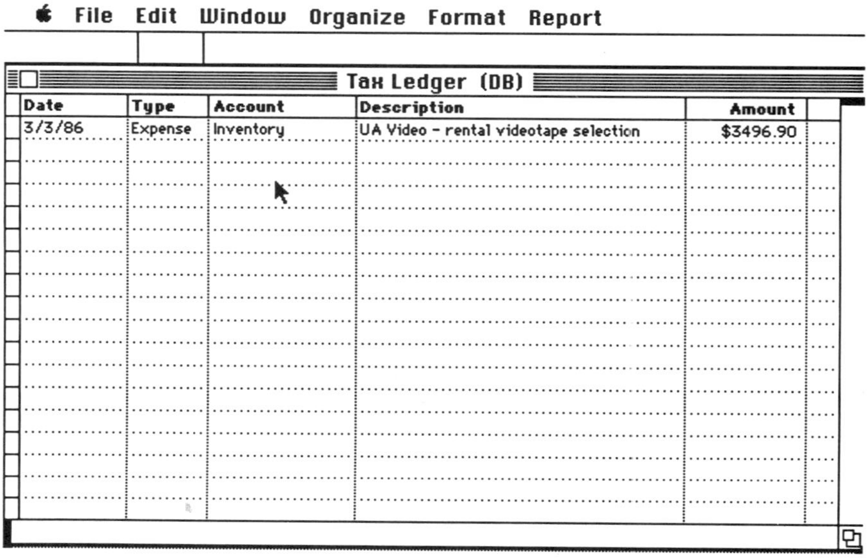

 File Edit Window Organize Format Report

Tax Ledger (DB)

Date	Type	Account	Description	Amount
3/3/86	Expense	Inventory	UA Video - rental videotape selection	$3496.90

Notice that the Match Records... command displays only records from the file that match the criteria you type in. When you're ready to view the entire file again, choose the Match Records... command a second time to display the entire file's records as before.

If you want to locate comparison information as it appears in the file (rather than displaying only records that match that information), use the Find Field... command from the Organize menu. This command finds any field that contains the comparison information you type and highlights that field, one record at a time. The records are not selected out of the file and displayed separately. If we had used the

Find Field… command with the videotape comparison information, the list window would have looked like this:

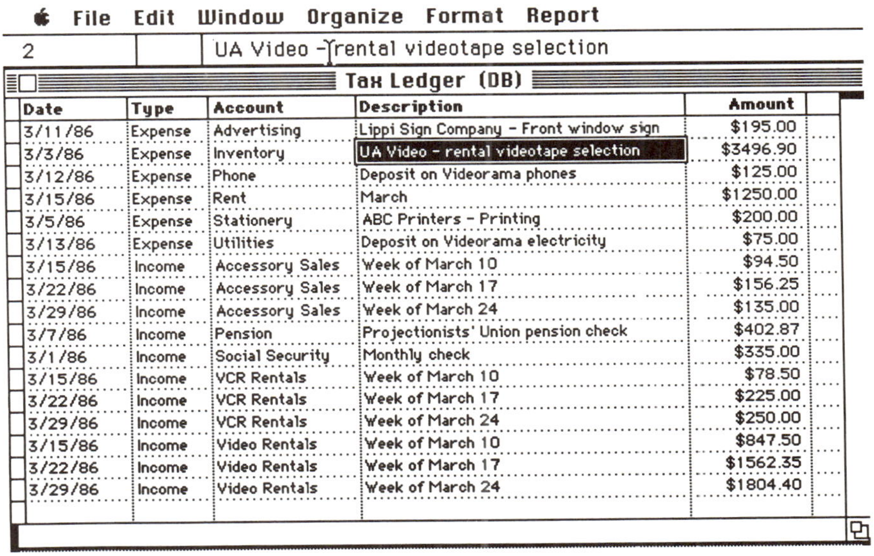

File Edit Window Organize Format Report

2 | | UA Video - rental videotape selection

Tax Ledger (DB)

Date	Type	Account	Description	Amount
3/11/86	Expense	Advertising	Lippi Sign Company - Front window sign	$195.00
3/3/86	Expense	Inventory	UA Video - rental videotape selection	$3496.90
3/12/86	Expense	Phone	Deposit on Videorama phones	$125.00
3/15/86	Expense	Rent	March	$1250.00
3/5/86	Expense	Stationery	ABC Printers - Printing	$200.00
3/13/86	Expense	Utilities	Deposit on Videorama electricity	$75.00
3/15/86	Income	Accessory Sales	Week of March 10	$94.50
3/22/86	Income	Accessory Sales	Week of March 17	$156.25
3/29/86	Income	Accessory Sales	Week of March 24	$135.00
3/7/86	Income	Pension	Projectionists' Union pension check	$402.87
3/1/86	Income	Social Security	Monthly check	$335.00
3/15/86	Income	VCR Rentals	Week of March 10	$78.50
3/22/86	Income	VCR Rentals	Week of March 17	$225.00
3/29/86	Income	VCR Rentals	Week of March 24	$250.00
3/15/86	Income	Video Rentals	Week of March 10	$847.50
3/22/86	Income	Video Rentals	Week of March 17	$1562.35
3/29/86	Income	Video Rentals	Week of March 24	$1804.40

You can use Find Field… in either the list or form window.

Creating a monthly income report

Now, let's help Al create a monthly income report. Al's income comes from a few different sources, but let's assume he simply wants a quick way to total each month's income and view it without printing out the report. In this report, let's say he wants to create a total of all the income transactions for the month of March. That means we'll have to use Works' record-selection rules to select only records for which (in Works' terminology again) the Type field equals Income, and where the Date field is greater than or equal to March 1 and less than or equal to March 31. After you select the records, you'll want to sum the Amount field to produce an income total from all the selected transaction records. Also, it would be nice if all the transaction records were in chronological order.

You can't sort records in a report window—you have to do your sorting with the database file itself. So, we'll start by arranging the records in the Tax Ledger file.

- ☐ Click on the Date field name to select that field in the list window.
- ☐ Press Command-A (a shortcut for selecting the Sort... command from the Organize menu). The Sort dialog box appears.

Because we selected a date field (and the field's attributes identify it as containing date-type data), the Sort dialog box option is set to sort the file in chronological order. This is the order you want, so:

- ☐ Press the Return key to sort the file.

Now, we can create the report:

- ☐ Choose the New Report... command from the Report menu. The report window opens.

There is no scroll bar at the bottom of the report window because all the fields in this report fit inside the edge markers. We don't have to rearrange any fields—we can simply include every field in the report.

- ☐ Choose Record Selection... from the Organize menu. The Record Selection box appears.

We want to create a rule that says: "Type equals Income and Date is greater than or equal to 3/1/86 and less than or equal to 3/31/86."

- Following the steps detailed for the video-club-member file earlier in this chapter, complete the Record Selection box like this:

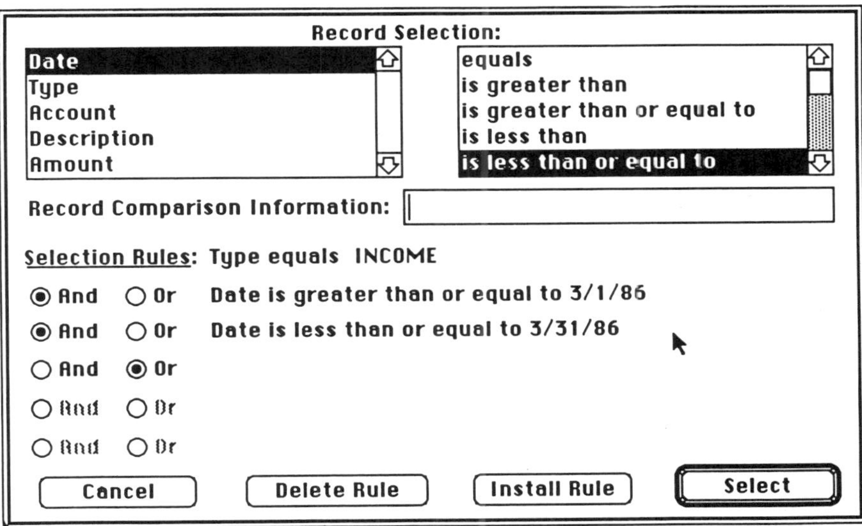

- After installing these rules, press the Return key to select the records.

With the records selected, you can now sum the income amounts to produce a total for the month.

- Click on the Amount field name to select this field.
- Choose Sum This Field from the TotalsPage menu. This tells Works to add all the Amount values and produce a total at the end of the report.
- Choose the Change Report Title... command from the Edit menu, and type the new title, *Monthly Income*. Then press the Return key.

Monthly Income is a more descriptive name for this report and will make it easy to remember what the report is for.

This report is now ready to print out on paper, but let's assume we just want to get a quick look at the total income without actually printing the report. We can do this by using the Copy Totals command and then viewing the report totals in the Clipboard.

- Choose the Copy Totals command from the Edit menu (or press Command-C as a shortcut). This copies all field totals you've specified in the report to the Clipboard.
- Choose the Show Clipboard command from the Window menu. The Clipboard window opens, and the report total is shown in a one-line record. To view the total, either scroll the Clipboard window to the right or make the window larger.

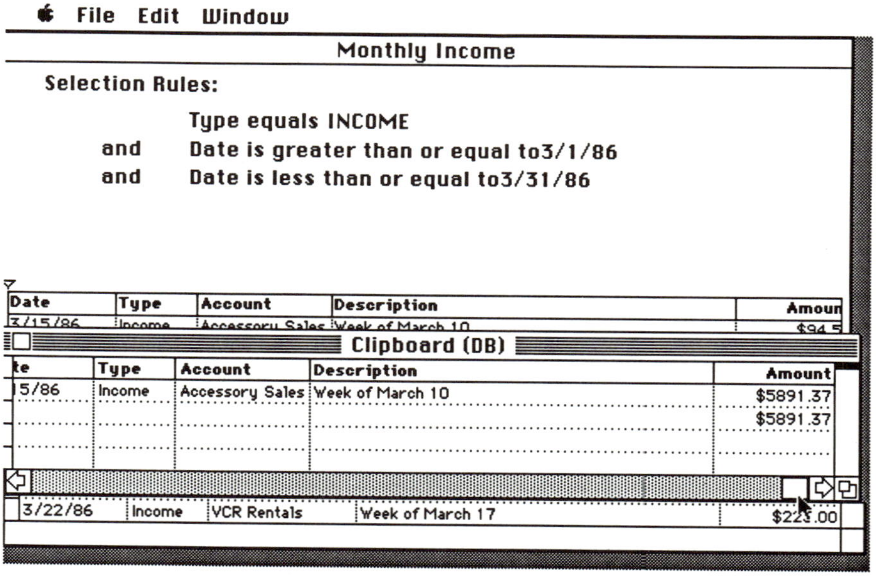

File Edit Window

Monthly Income

Selection Rules:

Type equals INCOME
and Date is greater than or equal to3/1/86
and Date is less than or equal to3/31/86

Clipboard (DB)

te	Type	Account	Description	Amount
5/86	Income	Accessory Sales	Week of March 10	$5891.37
				$5891.37

3/22/86	Income	VCR Rentals	Week of March 17	$223.00

Preparing an income-and-expense report

Now, let's suppose Al wants to get ready for tax time. This will involve printing a report that shows each of his expense and income categories, with subtotals for each account type. We don't need to use record-selection rules here because we want to include all the records in the file. But we'll have to arrange the totals a little differently in this report. Before specifying the totals, though, we have to re-sort the records in this file.

When you print a report from a Works database file, the records are printed in the order that they occupy in the file at that time. In this income-and-expense report, we want the records printed in two groups: all the expense records in one group and all the income records in another group. This way, we can produce separate totals for each group. Also, we want all the records grouped by account so that we can produce subtotals of expenses or incomes by account name. And finally, it will be most useful if we arrange the records in chronological order within each account.

What this amounts to is a three-level sort of the file: We want records sorted by transaction type (expense or income), within types by account, and within accounts by date. Works sorts only one field at a time, so we'll have to sort the Tax Ledger file three times on three different fields. Remember, in a multi-level sort, you sort the least important field first, and the most important field last. In this case, the least important field is Date, and the most important field is Type.

- ☐ Click on the Date field name.
- ☐ Press Command-A (a shortcut for choosing the Sort... command from the Organize menu). Since this is a date-type field, the sort selection is chronological, which is what you want.
- ☐ Press the Return key to sort the file chronologically.
- ☐ Click on the Account field name.
- ☐ Press Command-A, and then press the Return key to sort the Account field from A to Z. This will group all the records by account.
- ☐ Click on the Type field name.
- ☐ Press Command-A, and press the Return key to sort the Type field from A to Z. This will separate all the records into two groups: Expense and Income.

Now that the records are arranged properly, you can create the report itself.

- ☐ Choose the New Report... command from the Report menu.
- ☐ As before, all the fields fit between the edge markers in this report. We want to include them all, but we need to drag the

field dividing lines to change the widths of the fields in the report so that as much information is shown in the report as possible.

- ☐ Narrow the Date, Type, Account, and Amount fields a bit so that there's room between the edge markers to make the Description field wide enough to show most of its data.
- ☐ Click on the Amount field name to select this field.
- ☐ Choose the Sum This Field command from the TotalsPage menu. (This command may already have a check mark next to it from earlier in the exercise. If so, the field is already being summed, and you don't need to select the command again.)

At this point, the report will produce a grand total of all the expenses and income amounts for the entire year because Works will add together all the values in the Amount field. Naturally, we don't want income and expenses added together, so we'll have to specify subtotals that will show sums of each account.

You can control when Works generates a subtotal using the Total On Field Change command, which tells Works to insert a subtotal in a field whenever the contents of a second field change. In this file, we want subtotals to appear at the end of each account group (so the report shows subtotals for rent, utilities, advertising, and other expense categories). To create these subtotals we'll use the Total On Field Change command for the Account field.

- ☐ Click on the Account field name to select this field.
- ☐ Choose the Total On Field Change command from the TotalsPage menu.

Now, the report will produce a subtotal whenever the contents of the Account field change. Because the records are sorted into account groups, a subtotal will appear at the end of each group.

The report is almost ready to print out, but we need to take care of some final formatting chores. First, the report could use a more descriptive name.

- Choose the Change Report Title... command from the Edit menu.
- Type *Income/Expense Report* and press the Return key to change the report name.

Since this report contains an entire year's transactions, it will cover several pages. Accounts containing only a few transactions will occupy only a few lines, but other accounts (such as the weekly income records) will occupy more than one page. You could set up the report so that a new printed page begins after each subtotal. This would make it easier to keep each account's printed records separate. To do this, you would choose the New Page After Total command from the TotalsPage menu. But for our purposes in this example, we'll let several totals appear on the same printed page.

The only other thing left to do is specify a header for the report. Since the report will cover several pages, a header will help identify the separate pages as belonging to the same report, and it will also let you number the pages and date the report.

- Choose the Page Setup... command from the File menu. The Page Setup dialog box appears.

The Paper and Margin settings are the way we want them, but we need to supply header information.

- The insertion point is already blinking in the header entry line, so type *&LIncome/Expense Report - &D - Page &P* as the header.

The ampersand commands in the header information tell Works to automatically do certain things. The *&L* tells Works to left justify the header text, the *&D* tells Works to print the current date, and the *&P* tells Works to print the current page number. Thus, this header will contain the title Income/Expense Report, followed by the date, followed by the word *Page,* and the page number. The Page Setup box now looks like this:

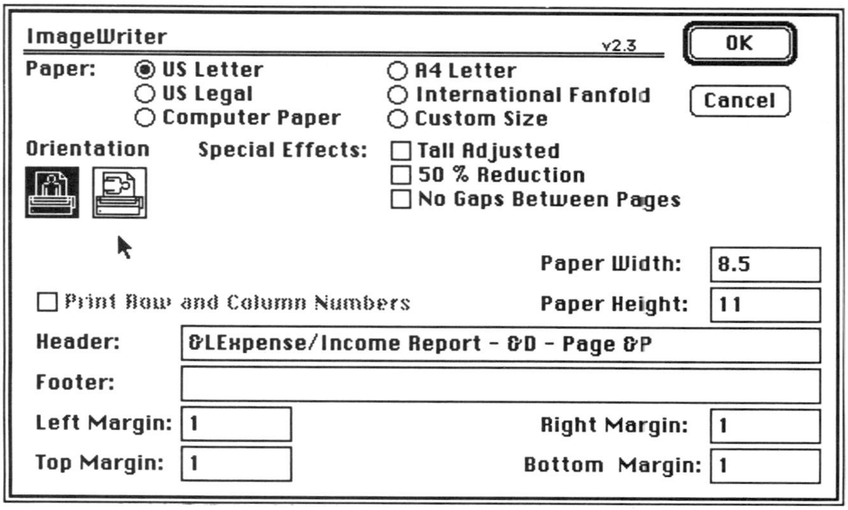

ImageWriter v2.3 OK Cancel
Paper: (•) US Letter ( ) US Legal ( ) Computer Paper ( ) A4 Letter ( ) International Fanfold ( ) Custom Size
Orientation
Special Effects: [ ] Tall Adjusted [ ] 50 % Reduction [ ] No Gaps Between Pages
Paper Width: 8.5
[ ] Print Row and Column Numbers
Paper Height: 11
Header: &LExpense/Income Report - &D - Page &P
Footer:
Left Margin: 1 Right Margin: 1
Top Margin: 1 Bottom Margin: 1

□ Press the Return key or click the OK button to store these changes to the page setup.

Now, to print the report:

□ Choose the Print... command from the File menu. The Print dialog box appears:

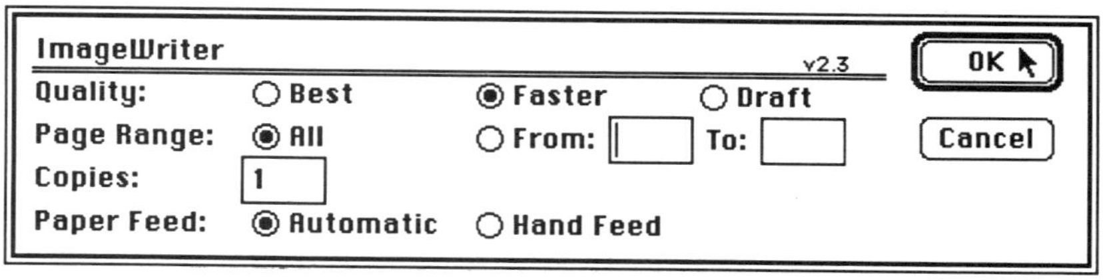

ImageWriter v2.3 OK Cancel
Quality: ( ) Best (•) Faster ( ) Draft
Page Range: (•) All ( ) From: To:
Copies: 1
Paper Feed: (•) Automatic ( ) Hand Feed

□ Select the quality of print you want.

□ Click the All button to print all the pages in the report.

□ Choose the paper-feed type that corresponds to the kind of paper and printer you're using.

□ Press Return or click the OK button to print the report.

When the report is printed, all the accounts will be subtotaled, and the Income and Expense groups will have totals. A sample page from the printed report is shown in Figure 7-3.

Income/Expense Report - July 9, 1986 - Page 1

Date	Type	Account	Description	Amount
3/11/86	Expense	Advertising	Lippi Sign Company - Front window sign	$195.00
				$195.00
3/3/86	Expense	Inventory	UA Video - rental videotape selection	$3496.90
				$3496.90
3/12/86	Expense	Phone	Deposit on Videorama phones	$125.00
				$125.00
3/15/86	Expense	Rent	March	$1250.00
				$1250.00
3/5/86	Expense	Stationery	ABC Printers - Printing	$200.00
				$200.00
3/13/86	Expense	Utilities	Deposit on Videorama electricity	$75.00
				$75.00
3/15/86	Income	Accessory Sales	Week of March 10	$94.50
3/22/86	Income	Accessory Sales	Week of March 17	$156.25
3/29/86	Income	Accessory Sales	Week of March 24	$135.00
				$385.75
3/7/86	Income	Pension	Projectionists' Union pension check	$402.87
				$402.87
3/1/86	Income	Social Security	Monthly check	$335.00
				$335.00
3/15/86	Income	VCR Rentals	Week of March 10	$78.50
3/22/86	Income	VCR Rentals	Week of March 17	$225.00
3/29/86	Income	VCR Rentals	Week of March 24	$250.00
				$553.50
3/15/86	Income	Video Rentals	Week of March 10	$847.50
3/22/86	Income	Video Rentals	Week of March 17	$1562.35
3/29/86	Income	Video Rentals	Week of March 24	$1804.40
				$4214.25
				$11233.27

Figure 7-3. *The Income/Expense report breaks down all the transaction records in the Tax Ledger file by account name and transaction type.*

Although we've set up this report for a year-end summary, you could also use the record-selection rules in Works to prepare reports like this for each month, quarter, or six-month period. All you would have to do is to specify record-selection rules that match information in the Date field with the dates you want to report on.

A VIDEOTAPE INVENTORY

One last example will expand on the simple inventory-valuation worksheet we looked at in Chapter 5. By maintaining inventory data in the database instead of on the spreadsheet, you can store text information more easily, and you can search for or sort the data in more ways.

Let's assume Al has the inventory file shown in Figure 7-4.

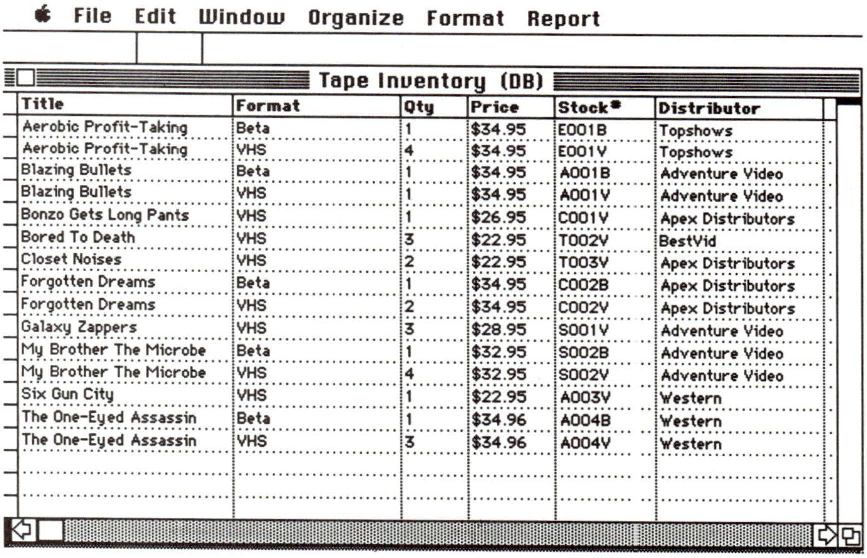

File Edit Window Organize Format Report

Tape Inventory (DB)

Title	Format	Qty	Price	Stock#	Distributor
Aerobic Profit-Taking	Beta	1	$34.95	E001B	Topshows
Aerobic Profit-Taking	VHS	4	$34.95	E001V	Topshows
Blazing Bullets	Beta	1	$34.95	A001B	Adventure Video
Blazing Bullets	VHS	1	$34.95	A001V	Adventure Video
Bonzo Gets Long Pants	VHS	1	$26.95	C001V	Apex Distributors
Bored To Death	VHS	3	$22.95	T002V	BestVid
Closet Noises	VHS	2	$22.95	T003V	Apex Distributors
Forgotten Dreams	Beta	1	$34.95	C002B	Apex Distributors
Forgotten Dreams	VHS	2	$34.95	C002V	Apex Distributors
Galaxy Zappers	VHS	3	$28.95	S001V	Adventure Video
My Brother The Microbe	Beta	1	$32.95	S002B	Adventure Video
My Brother The Microbe	VHS	4	$32.95	S002V	Adventure Video
Six Gun City	VHS	1	$22.95	A003V	Western
The One-Eyed Assassin	Beta	1	$34.96	A004B	Western
The One-Eyed Assassin	VHS	3	$34.96	A004V	Western

Figure 7-4. *An inventory file can be displayed in the list window.*

To follow along with this exercise, you must create a database file like the one shown in Figure 7-4. Here are the steps:

- ☐ Open a new database file, and create fields named Title, Format, Qty, Price, Stock #, and Distributor.
- ☐ Select the Qty field and then use the Set Field Attributes... command on the Format menu to make this a numeric field.

- Select the Price field and then use the Set Field Attributes… command on the Format menu to make this a numeric field formatted as dollars.
- Type the data into the records, as shown in Figure 7-4.
- Choose the Save As… command and save the file to disk with the name Tape Inventory.

Now you're ready to proceed.

The file shows each tape title, format, quantity, price, stock number, and distributor, but something is missing. As it is, this file can't possibly produce a report that shows how much Al's videotape inventory is worth—it shows the quantity of tapes and their prices, but it doesn't calculate their values.

When you want to calculate new values from existing values in a database file, you have to create a special kind of field – called a calculated field. Calculated fields contain information that comes from calculating data in two or more other fields. To calculate the value of tapes in the inventory, we have to create a new field. Let's call it Value.

- Choose the Add New Field… command from the Edit menu. The Field Name box appears.
- Type the name *Value*, and press the Return key. The new field is added to the file, to the right of the Distributor field.

This new field doesn't contain any data yet, and we won't have to type any data into it. We want the Value field to contain the total value of the tapes in each record. Therefore, in each record, we want to multiply the contents of the Qty (quantity) field by the contents of the Price field to produce the total value of tapes. To do this, we have to specify that the new Value field is a calculated field, and then we'll enter a formula that tells the database how to arrive at the values to be stored there.

- Click on the Value field to select it.
- Choose Set Field Attributes… from the Format menu. The Set Field Attributes dialog box appears.
- The Value field will contain a dollar value computed from the Qty and Price fields, so click on the Numeric type and Dollar

display options. The default number of decimal places is 2, which is what you want.

- To tell Works this will be a computed field, click the Computed box at the bottom of the Set Field Attributes dialog box. The settings now look like this:

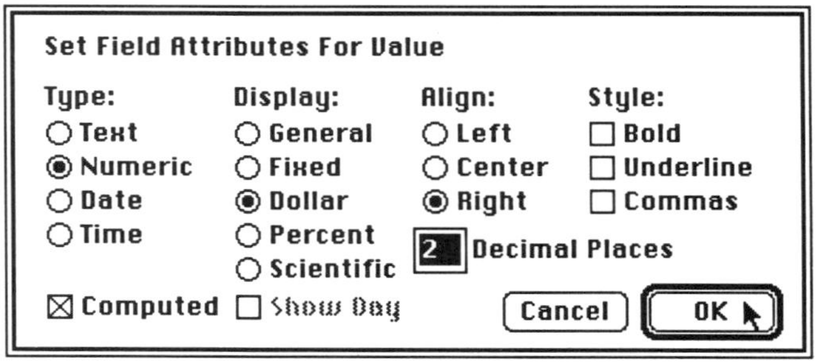

Set Field Attributes For Value

Type:	Display:	Align:	Style:
○ Text	○ General	○ Left	☐ Bold
◉ Numeric	○ Fixed	○ Center	☐ Underline
○ Date	◉ Dollar	◉ Right	☐ Commas
○ Time	○ Percent	2 Decimal Places	
	○ Scientific		

☒ Computed ☐ Show Day Cancel OK

- Press the Return key to confirm these Set Field Attributes settings. The dialog box disappears.

Since we specified a computed field, we still have to enter the formula for the calculation. Works is expecting this, and the insertion point is blinking next to an equal sign in the entry bar at the top of the file window.

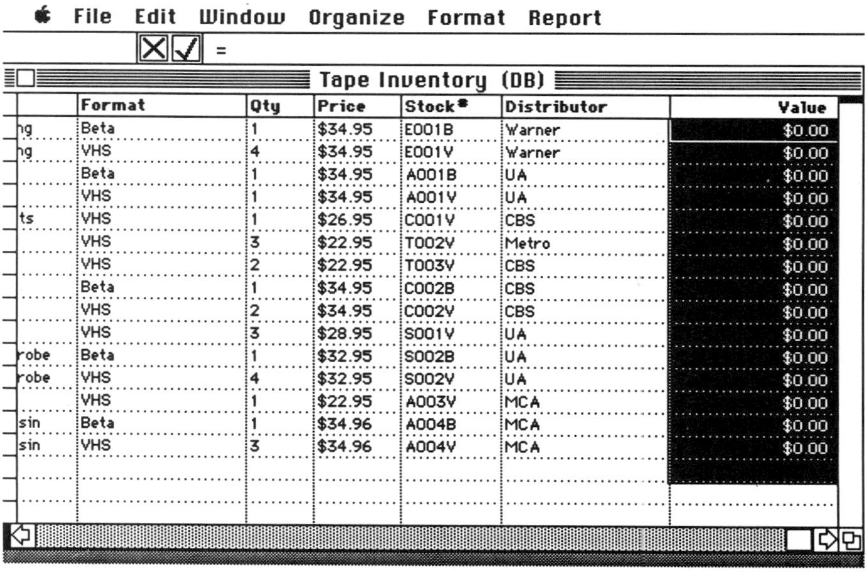

File Edit Window Organize Format Report

=

Tape Inventory (DB)

	Format	Qty	Price	Stock#	Distributor	Value
ng	Beta	1	$34.95	E001B	Warner	$0.00
ng	VHS	4	$34.95	E001V	Warner	$0.00
	Beta	1	$34.95	A001B	UA	$0.00
	VHS	1	$34.95	A001V	UA	$0.00
ts	VHS	1	$26.95	C001V	CBS	$0.00
	VHS	3	$22.95	T002V	Metro	$0.00
	VHS	2	$22.95	T003V	CBS	$0.00
	Beta	1	$34.95	C002B	CBS	$0.00
	VHS	2	$34.95	C002V	CBS	$0.00
	VHS	3	$28.95	S001V	UA	$0.00
robe	Beta	1	$32.95	S002B	UA	$0.00
robe	VHS	4	$32.95	S002V	UA	$0.00
	VHS	1	$22.95	A003V	MCA	$0.00
sin	Beta	1	$34.96	A004B	MCA	$0.00
sin	VHS	3	$34.96	A004V	MCA	$0.00

We want Works to multiply the Qty field by the Price field, so enter the formula that way, using the field names in place of values in the formula.

☐ Type *Qty∗Price* in the entry bar. This tells Works to multiply the Qty field by the Price field and to place the result in the new computed field, Value.

☐ Press the Return key or click the enter box to enter the formula. Works does the calculations, and the new values appear.

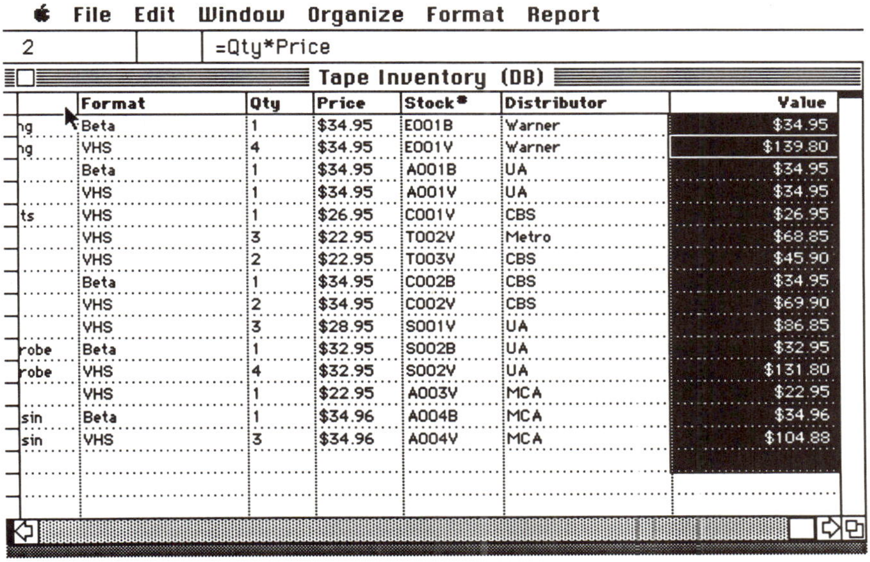

File Edit Window Organize Format Report

2 | =Qty*Price

Tape Inventory (DB)

	Format	Qty	Price	Stock#	Distributor	Value
ng	Beta	1	$34.95	E001B	Warner	$34.95
ng	VHS	4	$34.95	E001V	Warner	$139.80
	Beta	1	$34.95	A001B	UA	$34.95
	VHS	1	$34.95	A001V	UA	$34.95
ts	VHS	1	$26.95	C001V	CBS	$26.95
	VHS	3	$22.95	T002V	Metro	$68.85
	VHS	2	$22.95	T003V	CBS	$45.90
	Beta	1	$34.95	C002B	CBS	$34.95
	VHS	2	$34.95	C002V	CBS	$69.90
	VHS	3	$28.95	S001V	UA	$86.85
robe	Beta	1	$32.95	S002B	UA	$32.95
robe	VHS	4	$32.95	S002V	UA	$131.80
	VHS	1	$22.95	A003V	MCA	$22.95
sin	Beta	1	$34.96	A004B	MCA	$34.96
sin	VHS	3	$34.96	A004V	MCA	$104.88

Now, the calculating formula is stored with this file, and its results will always be placed in the Value field. If we change an entry in the Qty or Price field in a record, the calculated value in the Value field in the affected record will change as well. The general rules for calculating fields in a database file are:

- The fields being calculated must be numeric-type fields, as indicated with the Set Field Attributes... command.
- You specify fields to be calculated by using their exact field names.
- You can use arithmetic operators or spreadsheet functions to calculate fields. (The operators are +, −, ∗, and / for adding,

subtracting, multiplying, and dividing.) When you use spreadsheet functions, you must use the same formula format as in the spreadsheet, except that you specify field names instead of cell coordinates. You have to type the function names into calculated-field formulas by hand. (See Chapters 4 and 5 for details about using spreadsheet formulas and functions.)

With the calculated field added, this file becomes much more useful. We can now determine how much the entire inventory is worth by specifying a field total on the Value field. We can also count the total number of tapes by specifying a field total on the Qty field.

The Stock # field will allow us to produce subtotals of tape amounts and values by tape genre (Adventure, History, Classics, and so on). The stock number entries are coded to indicate each tape's genre (the letter at the beginning of each stock number indicates which genre group the tape belongs to).

Let's create a report that shows total quantities and values of tapes by genre and that includes grand totals for the entire report. First, we'll sort the file on the Stock # field so that the records are arranged in groups by genre.

- ☐ Click on the Stock # field name to select this field.
- ☐ Choose the Sort... command from the Organize menu, or press Command-A. The Sort dialog box appears.
- ☐ The Stock # field is a text field, and the default sort order is from A to Z, which is what you want, so press the Return key to sort the file.

Now, let's create the report.

- ☐ Choose the New Report... command from the Report menu. A report window opens.

As we can see by scrolling the report to the right, all fields in the file fit within this report's edge markers. We don't have to worry about rearranging fields or changing the report's margins to accommodate data. (If all the fields in your report window don't fit inside the edge markers, make one or more fields narrower by dragging field dividing lines to the left.)

☐ Click on the Value field name to select this field.

☐ Choose the Sum This Field command from the TotalsPage menu. Works will now total the values in this field at the end of the report. Remember, Works doesn't show report totals on the screen—you have to either print the report or use the Copy Totals command to put the totals on the Clipboard and then view them there.

☐ Click on the Qty field name to select this field.

☐ Choose the Sum This Field command from the TotalsPage menu. Works will now total the tape quantities in this field at the end of the report.

We've set up this report to calculate grand totals of tape quantities and values, but we also want it to produce subtotals by genre group. (Genre groups are determined by the first character in the stock numbers.) We've already sorted the file on the Stock # field, so the tapes are arranged in genre groups. All we have to do now is give Works some subtotaling instructions.

☐ Click on the Stock # field name to select this field.

☐ Choose the Total-1st Char Field command from the TotalsPage menu.

We used the Total-1st Char Field command rather than the Total On Field Change command we used in the Tax Ledger report earlier in this chapter because we want Works to produce a subtotal each time the first character in the Stock # field changes. If we used the Total On Field Change command to produce subtotals, Works would print a total after each record.

To finish preparing this report, let's specify a header with the Page Setup… command.

☐ Choose the Page Setup… command from the File menu.

☐ Type *&CInventory Report—&D—Page &P* as the header information. This tells Works to center the header on the page (the &C command), print the date between two dashes (the &D command), and print the page number after the word *Page* (the &P command).

- Click the OK button or press the Return key to store the page setup changes.

The report is now ready to print. We can either print it on paper or we can copy the totals to the Clipboard for a quick check of the inventory value. Let's do a quick check.

- Choose the Copy Totals command from the Edit menu. The report totals are copied to the Clipboard.
- Choose the Show Clipboard command from the Window menu.
- Enlarge the Clipboard window and scroll it to the right so that both the Qty and Value fields are showing. You'll see that all the subtotals and grand totals are there.

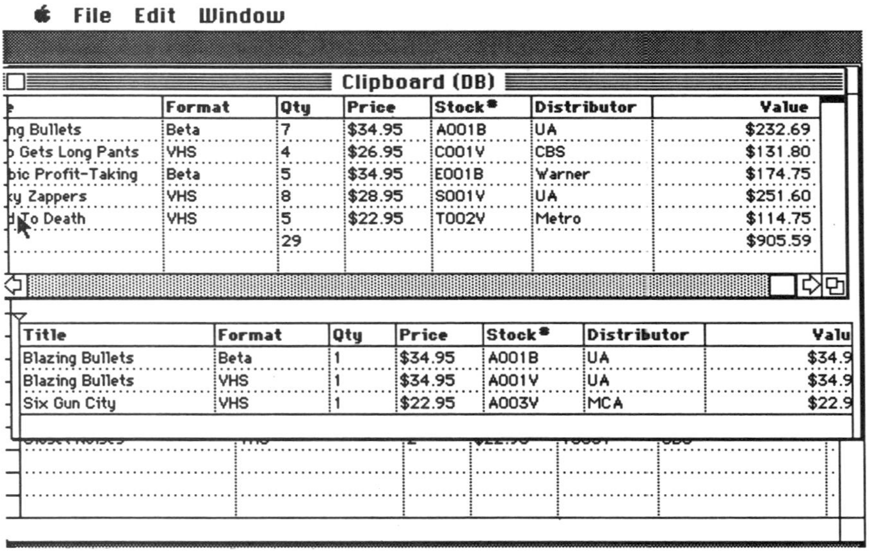

File Edit Window

Clipboard (DB)

	Format	Qty	Price	Stock#	Distributor	Value
ng Bullets	Beta	7	$34.95	A001B	UA	$232.69
Gets Long Pants	VHS	4	$26.95	C001V	CBS	$131.80
bic Profit-Taking	Beta	5	$34.95	E001B	Warner	$174.75
y Zappers	VHS	8	$28.95	S001V	UA	$251.60
d To Death	VHS	5	$22.95	T002V	Metro	$114.75
		29				$905.59

Title	Format	Qty	Price	Stock#	Distributor	Valu
Blazing Bullets	Beta	1	$34.95	A001B	UA	$34.9
Blazing Bullets	VHS	1	$34.95	A001V	UA	$34.9
Six Gun City	VHS	1	$22.95	A003V	MCA	$22.9

If all the fields in the database report aren't shown on the Clipboard, even after you scroll to the right, they are not included in the report. To check this, click the close box on the Clipboard window and look at the report window. Scroll to the right, and look at the position of the right edge marker. Any fields that are either partially or completely to the right of the marker won't be copied to the Clipboard.

In this way, the Copy Totals command is just like printing—you only copy the portion of the database report that falls within the edge markers. To include more fields in the report, either drag the field-divider markers to the left to narrow the fields in the report window (and thus include more fields inside the edge markers), or rearrange the fields in the report, moving fields that aren't important to the right of the edge marker.

Although the Copy Totals command only shows subtotals and the grand total in the report, rather than each record, the printed report itself will show all the records, with subtotals and grand totals included, as shown in Figure 7-5.

Inventory Report--August 21, 1986--Page 1

Title	Format	Qty	Price	Stock #	Distributor	Value
Blazing Bullets	Beta	1	$34.95	A001B	Adventure Vide	$34.95
Blazing Bullets	VHS	1	$34.95	A001V	Adventure Vide	$34.95
Six Gun City	VHS	1	$22.95	A003V	Western	$22.95
The One-Eyed Assassin	Beta	1	$34.96	A004B	Western	$34.96
The One-Eyed Assassin	VHS	3	$34.96	A004V	Western	$104.88
		7				$232.69
Bonzo Gets Long Pants	VHS	1	$26.95	C001V	Apex Distributo	$26.95
Forgotten Dreams	Beta	1	$34.95	C002B	Apex Distributo	$34.95
Forgotten Dreams	VHS	2	$34.95	C002V	Apex Distributo	$69.90
		4				$131.80
Aerobic Profit-Taking	Beta	1	$34.95	E001B	Topshows	$34.95
Aerobic Profit-Taking	VHS	4	$34.95	E001V	Topshows	$139.80
		5				$174.75
Galaxy Zappers	VHS	3	$28.95	S001V	Adventure Vide	$86.85
My Brother The Microbe	Beta	1	$32.95	S002B	Adventure Vide	$32.95
My Brother The Microbe	VHS	4	$32.95	S002V	Adventure Vide	$131.80
		8				$251.60
Bored To Death	VHS	3	$22.95	T002V	BestVid	$68.85
Closet Noises	VHS	2	$22.95	T003V	Apex Distributo	$45.90
		5				$174.75
		29				$905.59

Figure 7-5. *A report on an inventory file can show subtotals and grand totals.*

CHAPTER 8

Using the Communications Application

It's fine to be able to create and store Works spreadsheet, database, and word-processor files for your own use, but sometimes you'll want to share your files with other computer users, or you'll want access to files or information that are stored in another computer. The communications module in Microsoft Works lets you use your Macintosh to communicate with other computers over standard telephone lines. Just as you use a telephone to exchange spoken information with other people, your Mac can use the telephone to exchange digitized data with other computers. With the communications part of Works, you can send your spreadsheet, word-processor, or database files to other computers. You can also transmit files you've created with other Macintosh programs, such as MacPaint. And you can use Works to access other computers, so you can read files stored in those computers and sent to you electronically. Before we get into the specifics of communications with Microsoft Works, let's look at personal-computer communications in general.

HOW COMPUTERS USE THE TELEPHONE

Telephones are designed to transmit spoken sounds, which is fine for allowing people to talk to each other. But computers store and represent information as silent electrical impulses. In order to communicate over a telephone line, a computer must be given a "voice" with a device called a modem. A modem (short for MOdulator/DEModulator) translates the electrical data stored in a computer into sounds that can be transmitted via telephone lines. In order to use the communications module in Works to transmit data, you must have a modem connected to your Macintosh. You can buy a modem from your Apple dealer or from any computer specialty store. A few specific modems are discussed in the Appendix of this book.

At first glance, communications looks like a simple application for a computer, because there aren't as many commands and options in a communications program as there are in a spreadsheet, database, or word processor. But, despite outward appearances, communications is very complex because it involves more potential trouble spots than other applications. If something doesn't work right in a database, spreadsheet, or word-processor file, you know that you have a problem with one of only two types of interaction: Either you have given a wrong command (the interaction between you and your software) or there is a problem in the interaction between your hardware and software. With communications, these two types of interaction are only the beginning.

Using a communications program and modem to exchange data with another computer involves five types of interaction:

- You interact with the communications software.
- The communications software and your computer interact.
- The computer and software interact with the modem.
- The modem interacts with the telephone line.
- Your computer and modem interact via the telephone line with another computer and modem.

Once the modem is properly connected and turned on, it receives instructions from you (through the software) about how to format and send data to other computers. These instructions (or protocols) can include:

- the speed at which data is sent from the computer to the modem;
- the speed at which data is sent from the modem to the telephone line;
- the data format—that is, the number of electrical impulses it takes to transmit each piece of data (a number in a spreadsheet or a character in a word-processor file, for example), and the method by which each individual piece of data is separated from the others;
- the data type—that is, whether a file being sent is a text file, which can contain only characters, or a binary file, which can also contain graphics or program instructions; and
- the presence or absence of special error-correcting routines that help verify the accuracy of data sent.

The quality of the telephone connection also plays a part in communications. Since the modem is translating computer data into sounds, a noisy telephone line can be a problem—one of the communicating modems may not be able to "hear" the other modem's tones properly because of interference on the line. When this happens, some of the data is garbled, or the transmission may be broken off.

Even if you have set up your software and modem to send data properly, the modem and computer at the other end of the line must be set to match your transmission rate and other protocols. Otherwise, the two modems can exchange tones, but they can't understand each other. It's like having your modem transmitting in English while the modem at the other end of the line is set to receive in Spanish.

To communicate effectively, things must go smoothly with all of these types of interaction. Fortunately, today's modems, computers, and communications software automate much of the process. Most modems, for example, can automatically adjust their transmission speeds to match the transmission speed of the modem at the other end of the line. Most communications programs have error-checking facilities, which help compensate for noisy telephone lines and ensure accurate data transmission by verifying each piece of data as it is sent and by re-transmitting data that was garbled. And the transmission protocols (data size and so forth) are fairly standard, so the number of possible settings is limited.

To see how you can control some of these facets of communications with Works, let's look at the menu commands.

A QUICK TOUR OF THE COMMUNICATIONS MENUS

The communications module has fewer menus than any other Works application. The first four menus from the left edge of the menu bar are either identical or very similar to the same menus in other Works applications. However, on the File menu, the Page Setup..., Print..., and Print Merge... commands are dimmed, because you can't print an entire file directly from a communications document.

And on the Edit menu, the Undo command is dimmed when you're using a communications document, because it's not active. Once you issue an editing command, such as Cut, Copy, or Clear, you can't undo it. The Select All command selects all the text that is visible on the screen in a communications document. But once text has scrolled off the screen, you can't select it or re-display it.

The Communications menu

The Communications menu is the real control center of the communications application in Works.

The Echo On and Echo Off commands determine whether information you are sending is displayed (echoed) on your screen. The type of echo depends on how the other (or remote) computer's echo (or duplex) function is set. If you type data to transmit and don't see it on your screen, change the setting to Echo On. On the other hand, if each character you type is displayed twice on the screen, change the setting to Echo Off.

The Dial... command displays the telephone list you've stored for the current communications document. When the telephone list is displayed, you can click the Dial button next to any of the numbers, and Works will dial the number for you.

The Hang Up command disconnects the modem from the telephone line, just as hanging up a telephone receiver disconnects a regular telephone call. Use this command when you have finished communicating.

The Answer Phone command sets your modem to automatically answer the telephone when it rings. Use this command when you are expecting some other computer to call your computer and you want your Mac to answer the phone.

The Capture Text... command lets you receive and save a text file as a Works word-processor file. The Send Text... command lets you transmit text files. You can also use these commands to send or receive standard Works word-processor, spreadsheet, or database files, as well as standard text files created by other programs. When you begin receiving a text file, the Capture Text... command changes to End Text Capture. You must choose the End Text Capture command to save the file to disk.

The Receive File... and Send File... commands let you receive and send binary files. Use these commands when you want to send or receive MacPaint files, BASIC programs, Scrapbook files, and other non-text files. When you use the Send File... or Receive File... command, you have the choice of using either the MacBinary or the Xmodem error-correcting protocol. Xmodem is a very common error-checking protocol, and it can be used to communicate with a variety of other computers. Works has two Xmodem protocols: Xmodem Text and Xmodem Data. You use the Xmodem Text protocol when you're sending or receiving text characters only, and you use Xmodem Data when you're sending or receiving text characters and formatting information. The MacBinary protocol can be used only when you're communicating with another Mac that is also using this protocol. When you use the Receive File... command and open a receiving file on disk, the Receive File... command changes to Cancel Receive, and you must choose Cancel Receive before the file will be saved to disk.

The Settings... command displays a dialog box in which you indicate communications settings, such as the transmission speed (or baud rate), data size, stop bits, parity, and other protocols.

Keyboard shortcuts

Just as in the other Works applications, the Communications module's menus have many keyboard equivalents that allow you to issue menu commands directly from the keyboard. The keyboard equivalents are shown in Figure 8-1.

Action	*Command*	*Menu*	*Keyboard Equivalent*
Open a file	Open ...	File	Command-O
Save a file	Save	File	Command-S
Quit Microsoft Works	Quit	File	Command-Q
Cut text to the Clipboard	Cut	Edit	Command-X
Copy text to the Clipboard	Copy	Edit	Command-C
Paste text from the Clipboard	Paste	Edit	Command-V
Change the size of the display window	Full Window/ Small Window	Window	Command-W

Figure 8-1. *Seven of Works' communications commands have keyboard equivalents.*

Now let's look at how to set up your modem and use some of these commands.

HOOKING UP A MODEM

The first thing to do if you want to use Works to communicate is to get a modem and hook it up to your Mac. There are several brands of modems from which to choose. Some of them are discussed in the Appendix of this book. Basically, though, all modems let your Mac communicate with other computers—the differences lie in the variety of transmission speeds you can use, the types of software commands each modem understands, and the presence or absence of extra convenience features.

Modem transmission speeds are measured in bits per second (bps, also called baud). Today's personal computer modems transmit at speeds from 110 to 9600 baud. Most personal-computer communications take place at either 300 or 1200 baud, with a small but growing number of transmissions at 2400 baud or higher. If you buy a modem that transmits at 300 and 1200 baud, you will be able to communicate with virtually every other personal-computer modem.

Modems are programmed internally to accept certain control commands from the communications software you use. These commands instruct the modem about its transmission speed, data format, and so forth. The most common set of commands in use for personal computers is called the Hayes command set. (Hayes Microcomputer Products of Norcross, Georgia, was the first major supplier of microcomputer modems, and most subsequent manufacturers have used its command set.) Microsoft Works uses the Hayes command set, so be sure that the modem you buy uses Hayes commands.

Beyond these two essential considerations, you can choose from a variety of modems, depending on the price and extra features you want. Some modems, for example, contain built-in memories that let you capture incoming data in the modem itself or store outgoing transmissions so that they can be sent later. Other modems have built-in error-correcting circuitry.

Once you've bought a modem, you need to hook it up, following these steps:

- ☐ Connect one end of the data cable to the modem and the other end to the Mac's telephone port (the one on the rear of the Mac with the telephone handset icon above it).
- ☐ Connect one end of the telephone cable to the modem and the other end to a standard modular telephone jack. If your phone

location doesn't have a standard modular jack, you can buy an adapter from a telephone supply store.

- Connect the modem's power-supply cord to a standard AC electrical outlet.
- Check your modem's manual to see if there are any switches that must be set on the modem.

That's all there is to setting up the modem. Now, you must set up the Works communications software.

Specifying communications settings

As with every other Works application, you begin communications by opening a new document.

- Load Microsoft Works.
- Click on the Communications icon.
- Click on the New button.

When you open a new communications document, the Communications Settings dialog box appears.

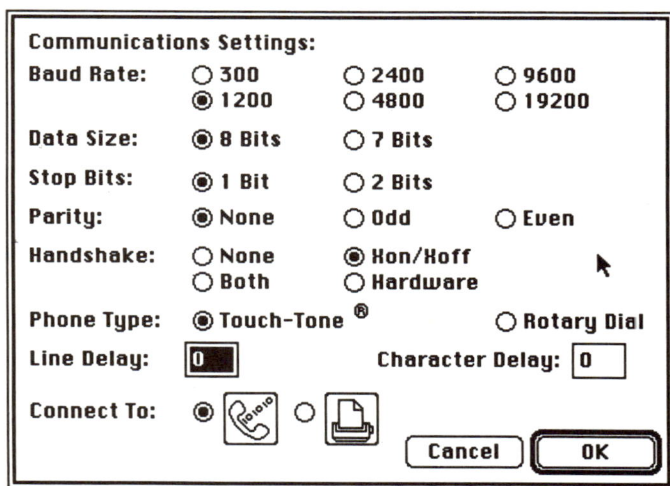

This box is where you indicate all the basic settings that let Works interact properly with your modem. You can re-display this dialog box at any time by choosing Settings... from the Communications menu.

Beginning at the top of the dialog box, you click the option in each area to set the program so that it instructs your modem to transmit properly. When the settings are the way you want them, click OK.

The Baud Rate setting is the speed at which you'll transmit your data. There are two things to remember about the Baud Rate setting: You and the person you're communicating with must transmit data at the same rate, and your modem must be capable of handling the rate you select. If you choose the 9600 baud rate, for example, and your modem transmits only up to 1200 baud, then you will transmit data at 1200 baud. The most common transmission rate is 1200 baud, so Works automatically selects this setting when the dialog box appears. Clicking any other option tells Works to instruct your modem to send data at that rate instead.

The Data Size, Stop Bits, and Parity settings indicate the form each item, or character, of data will take as it is transmitted. These settings must be the same on both the sender's and receiver's software for the communication to take place. The Data Size is the size (in bits, or electrical impulses) of each character of information. Data can be represented in either 7-bit or 8-bit groups. The Stop Bits setting specifies the presence and number of bits that indicate where one character ends and the next one begins. The Parity setting lets you specify the presence and number of bits used to check for transmission errors. The most common settings for these three items are 8 Bits for Data Size, 1 Bit for Stop Bits, and None for Parity, so the dialog box contains these default selections when it first appears. You can set these options any way, as long as the computer with which you're communicating is set the same way. When you communicate with an information service, such as MCI Mail or Dow Jones News/Retrieval, you will have to set your Works settings to match the settings of that service.

The Handshake setting determines how Works and the computer with which you communicate will indicate when each computer, in turn, has stopped transmitting and is waiting for an answer. Most personal computer applications use Xon/Xoff, or software, handshaking (each computer sends a special character to indicate when it's finished sending), and Works defaults to this option when the dialog box first appears with each new document. Use Hardware Handshake when you transmit via a cable hooked directly to another computer.

The Phone Type setting lets you specify whether your telephone line uses rotary or Touch-Tone dialing. Most telephone systems support Touch-Tone dialing now, so that is the default setting. If your system uses rotary dialing, you'll have to change this option.

The Line Delay and Character Delay options let you place pauses in the transmission so that your computer will wait a specified number of seconds after transmitting each line or character. Normally, no line or character delay is needed, so the default entries here are 0. To enter a delay value, double-click in the Line Delay or Character Delay box to select it and then type the number of seconds you want. DO NOT press the Return key until you've finished changing settings; pressing Return confirms all the settings and makes the dialog box disappear.

The Connect To area lets you specify which port your modem is using. Works assumes you connected your modem's data cable to the telephone port, and defaults to this option. If you connected your modem's data cable to the printer port (the one with the printer icon over it), click that option in the Connect To area.

To review, then, if you accept all the default settings in the Communications Settings dialog box, Works will instruct the modem to transmit at 1200 baud, using a data format of eight data bits, one stop bit, and no parity bits, with Xon/Xoff handshaking, using a Touch-Tone phone system, with no line or character delays, and connecting to the modem port on the Mac.

To save these settings, click OK or press Return. The dialog box disappears, leaving the blank communications document.

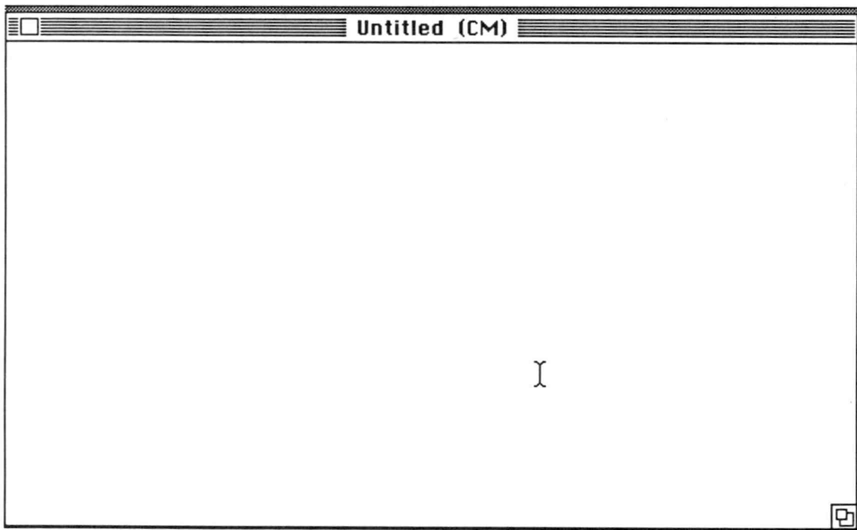

Calling another personal computer

Now, you're ready to communicate. Let's assume you want to call a friend's computer.

☐ Choose the Dial... command from the Communications menu. A list of telephone number blanks appears.

	Name:	Phone Number:
Dial		
Dial		
Dial		
Dial		
Dial		
Dial		
Dial		
Dial		

Cancel OK

The telephone list can store up to eight names and phone numbers. When the phone list first appears, the insertion point is blinking in the first Name blank on the list, waiting for you to enter the name of the person or information service whose number you want to store. (If you want to follow along on your own computer with the example in this chapter, you'll need to enter a phone number—either an actual number of a friend with a modem or the fictitious number used in the example.) Once you type in a name and telephone number and press the Return key, the name and number are stored automatically.

☐ Type the name *Joe Jones*, and press the Tab key. The insertion point moves to the Phone Number blank to the right.

☐ Type the phone number, *5554545*, and press the Tab key. The insertion point moves to the Name blank in the second row, and the Dial button for the first name/number entry is no longer dimmed, indicating that you can now click this button to dial that number.

Notice that you didn't include a dash to separate the prefix in the phone number. When you enter phone numbers in Works, you don't need to use dashes between prefixes and area codes—just type all the numbers one after another.

At this point, you could continue entering more names and telephone numbers, or you could put the phone list away by clicking the OK button in the lower-right corner of the dialog box or by pressing the Return key. Instead, you want Works to dial Joe Jones's number, so:

- ☐ Click the Dial button next to Joe Jones's name. The phone list disappears, and the blank communications document screen is displayed again. Works reports that it is dialing the telephone number by displaying the message on the screen.

If Joe Jones's computer answers the phone (and his computer software is using the same settings as yours), his modem and your modem will exchange acknowledgment signals, and the message *CONNECT* will appear on your screen. You can then type messages on your Mac, and Joe's computer will receive them. If Joe types a message, you'll see it on your screen. Of course, typing messages while you're connected is a tedious process, so you may well want to send text files you have stored on disk. Once you are connected, you can use some of the Communications menu's other options to send or receive data.

Calling an information service

For most individuals, commercial information services, such as CompuServe or The Source, are the main reason for communicating via a personal computer. These services are large mainframe computers that store thousands of computer files and programs, as varied as magazine excerpts, stock quotations, games, special-interest bulletin boards, and shop-at-home services. You can also use many commercial information services to communicate with other personal computer users, either in an online, interactive mode (in which you type a message, and the other user reads the message as you type and then responds to it), or through electronic mail (in which you send a message to another user's electronic mailbox to be read later).

To call a commercial information service, you need Works and a modem, of course, but you also need a password or other information that identifies you as a subscriber. Commercial services require you to have a subscription before you can use them, and the password or other user identification number you get when you subscribe allows you to access, or log-on to, that system. The four most popular commercial services are CompuServe, Dow Jones News/Retrieval, The Source, and MCI Mail.

Once you receive your password or other access information, look it over to familiarize yourself with how the information service works. In particular, learn how to issue commands to see various types of information, what to type to access the service, and how to exit the service when you've finished. When you're ready to communicate:

- ☐ Check your modem cables to make sure everything is plugged in.
- ☐ Load Microsoft Works.
- ☐ Click on the Communications icon, and then click the New button. A blank communications document appears, with the Communications Settings dialog box displayed.

The information kit you get from the service to which you've subscribed will tell you how to set up your modem and communications program for proper communications. Most services let you transmit at either 300 or 1200 baud, and most services use 8-bit data with one stop bit and no parity bits. When you open a new communications document with Works, the Communications Settings box contains the default settings of 1200 baud, eight data bits, one stop bit, and no parity bits, so you don't have to change these settings on the screen.

- ☐ The Handshake setting in the dialog box is automatically set to Xon/Xoff. This is also the type of handshaking commercial services use, so leave this setting as it is.
- ☐ Set the Phone Type option to match the type of telephone service you have, as in the previous example.
- ☐ With most information services, you don't need to specify a line delay or character delay when you transmit—the service can receive your data as fast as you can send it. These two delay options are set to zero automatically, so you don't need to change them.
- ☐ Set the Connect To option to match the port to which your modem is connected, as in the previous example.

- ☐ Click the OK button or press the Return key to store these communications settings. The dialog box disappears, and you're ready to begin communicating.
- ☐ Choose the Dial... command from the Communications menu. The telephone list appears.
- ☐ Type the name of the information service in the first name blank, and press the Tab key.
- ☐ Type the telephone number of the information service in the Phone Number blank. Your information service may have different access telephone numbers for different parts of the country, so choose the one that is in your local dialing area.
- ☐ Once you've typed the phone number, the Dial button next to the top name/phone number line will be shown in normal text (instead of gray text), indicating that you can now dial this number. Click the Dial button. The telephone list disappears, and Works dials the number you entered in the first blank.

If everything is working properly and your modem is equipped with a speaker, you will hear a dial tone, followed by the sound of the telephone number being dialed. When the commercial information service answers, there will be a high-pitched acknowledgment signal. Your modem will respond with a similar sound, and you will be connected.

At this point, the information service will prompt you to enter a user name, user number, or password. The prompt will look something like this:

```
User Name?
```

- ☐ Type the user name you received in the service's information packet when you subscribed. You should be able to see the user name on your screen when you type it. If you can't see it, choose Echo On from the Communications menu. If, on the other hand, you see double letters (*JJOONNEESS* instead of *JONES,* for example), choose the Echo Off command from the Communications menu.

- After you type the name, press the Return key. The information service will evaluate your entry to make sure it is valid, and then it will probably ask you for a password with a prompt something like this:

Password?

- Type the password you were given when you subscribed to the information service. Usually, you can't see the password on your screen when you type it. This is to prevent someone from looking over your shoulder and learning your password. (If you can see your password on the screen as you type, choose the Echo Off command from the Communications menu.)
- Once you type the password, press the Return key.

After a few seconds, the information service will respond. If your user name and password are valid, you will see a message something like this:

Welcome to MCI Mail

You are now connected to the system, and you can proceed to select options from the system's menus or issue commands to access information on the system.

If the system is particularly busy when you call, it may take some time for you to get a response to your typed commands or log-on information. Information services and other mainframe computers can handle dozens of users at the same time, but the more people using the computer, the longer it takes for the computer to respond. Be patient. It doesn't do any good to re-type information if you aren't getting a response as fast as you'd like—you'll only be transmitting those same characters again, and the system will have to respond to the second set of characters after it responds to the first set.

Sending files

There are two ways to transmit files with Works: You can send text, which is a stream of characters, symbols, or numbers without any formatting, or you can send a file, which is everything in a file, including formatting and program instructions. If you want to send only the data in a Works word-processor, spreadsheet, or database file, use the Send Text... command. You can also send files created in other programs and then converted to text files, which allows you to send regular-text files to a different kind of computer or to another Macintosh that isn't using Works. Most word-processing programs have utilities that let you convert files from the program's standard format to regular-text format. If you want to send a word-processor file including its format commands or a spreadsheet or database file complete with its formulas and formatting, use the Send File... command.

To send a text file:

- ☐ Choose the Send Text... command from the Communications Menu. A list of files on the current disk drive will be displayed, like this:

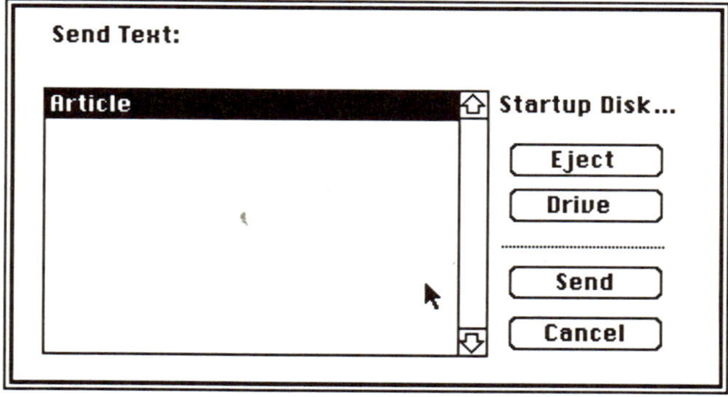

- ☐ Double-click on the name of the file you want to send. The contents of the file will be displayed on your screen as it is transmitted. When you see the last of your file displayed, you can then type further messages or send another file.

To send a formatted Works file, a Works word-processor file that contains a drawing, a MacPaint file, a BASIC program, another Mac program, the contents of a Scrapbook file, or another non-text file:

- Choose the Send File... command from the Communications menu. A list of all the files on the current disk drive will be displayed, like this:

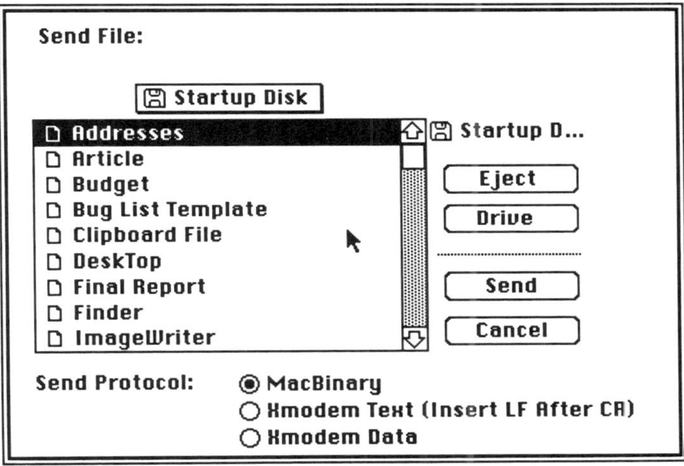

- Click on the Send Protocol option you want. The MacBinary protocol, the default, ensures error-free transmission of files between Macs using MacBinary. If you want to communicate with a computer other than a Mac or with one that isn't running software that has the MacBinary option, you need to use the Xmodem Text or Xmodem Data protocol. The Xmodem Text protocol is for transmitting text only; the Xmodem Data protocol is for transmitting text and formatting information (such as the specific layout of a word-processor, spreadsheet, or database file).

- Double-click on the name of the file you want to send, and the file will be sent. Instead of displaying the contents of the file on the screen, Works displays a status box that shows how much of the file has been transmitted, like this:

```
Transmitting Scrapbook File with MacBinary Protocol

Press "⌘" plus "." to abort the transfer.

Total Blocks:          29
Blocks Completed:       0     Retransmissions:      0
```

As the file is sent, the number of blocks transmitted increases until the number of blocks completed matches the total number of blocks to be sent. When the transmission is finished, you can type further instructions or send another file.

Receiving files

In addition to sending files, you can also set up your Mac to receive files from another computer. Because you receive text and binary files differently, there are two different commands for receiving files in Works: Capture Text... and Receive File.... Usually, you will use Capture Text... to receive text files, which contain only continuous streams of letters, numbers, or symbols. When you communicate by modem, the text you see on your screen isn't saved to a file on your Mac unless you tell Works to save it by using the Capture Text... command. Saving text files you receive is called capturing files, because Works is capturing the data you see on your screen and putting it into a file, rather than allowing it to simply scroll across your screen and disappear.

To capture a text file:

- Choose the Capture Text... command from the Communications menu. A dialog box will appear, asking you to type the name of the file in which you want to save the captured text.

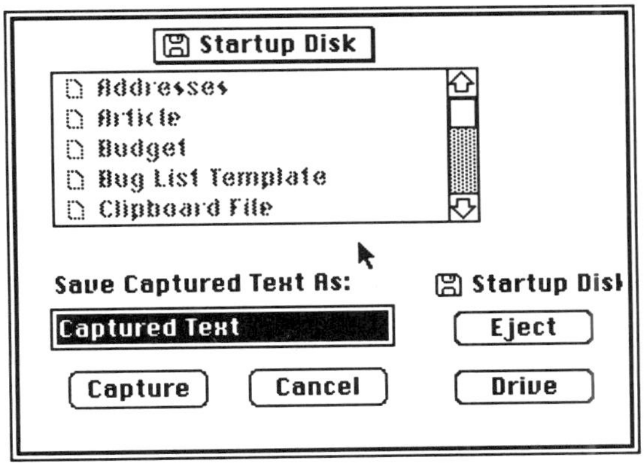

- Type a name for the file. If you don't type a file name, Works will save the file with the name Captured Text.
- Click the Capture button or press the Return key. The dialog box will disappear, and you'll be returned to the communications screen. Everything that appears on your screen from this point on will be saved to a file on disk under the name you specified.

Works does not begin saving text to a file until after you choose the Capture Text... command and name the file. Data on your screen at the time you issue the Capture Text... command will not be saved. Therefore, it's important to set up a captured-text file soon enough to capture everything you want. For example, if you want to capture an entire article from an information service, you need to choose the Capture Text... command before you begin displaying the article. As a rule, it's a good idea to set up a captured-text file right after you begin communicating, unless you're sure you won't want to save anything from the session. You can always delete captured-text files later.

Once you've captured all the text you want (once you receive all of an article or electronic mail message, for example), you must close the captured-text file. The file can then be opened as a Works word-processor file, which allows you to review or edit its contents. To close a captured-text file:

- Choose the End Text Capture command from the Communications menu. Works closes the text file and lets you continue with your communications session.

Closing a captured-text file does not end a communications session. If you wanted, you could capture some text, end the text capture, capture text to a new file, end the text capture, and so on, without disconnecting. If you wanted to capture three separate articles from an information service, for example, you might want to save each article in a file with a different name. You can open and close one captured-text file after another without ending the communications session. However, you can't open a captured-text file with the Works word processor until you have ended the text capture with the communications program.

Sometimes, you may want to receive a non-text file, or a text file that includes formatting, spreadsheet formulas, or database layouts. A friend may want to send you a BASIC program or a MacPaint drawing, for example. To receive a non-text file:

- Before the other computer begins sending the file, choose the Receive File… command from the Communications menu. A dialog box will appear, letting you specify the name of the file in which you want to save the incoming information.

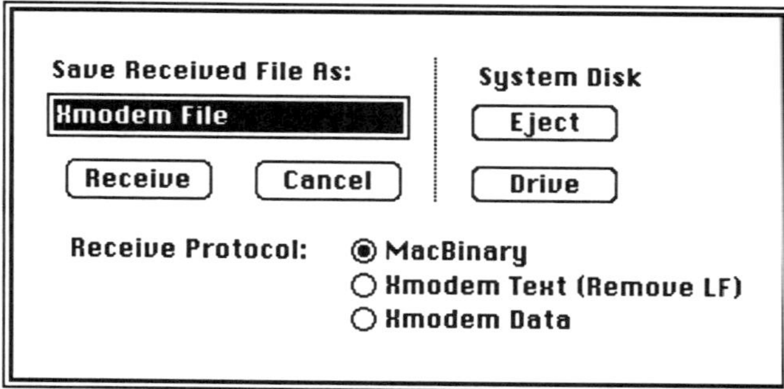

- Type a file name for the receive file, and choose a Receive Protocol option.
- Click the Receive button.
- Once you specify the file name, a status box appears, showing the total number of blocks in the incoming file and the number of blocks received as they come in.

When you've finished receiving a file, you must end the receive operation by choosing the Cancel Receive command from the Communications menu or by pressing the Command and period (.) keys at the same time.

- ☐ Choose the Cancel Receive command from the Communications menu (or press Command-.). The receive file will be closed.

As with capturing text, you can't work with a received file until you close it. Also, closing a receive file doesn't disconnect you from the remote computer.

Ending a communications session

To end a communications session, you must hang up the phone, just as you do at the end of a telephone conversation. To do this:

- ☐ Choose the Hang Up command from the Communications menu. The screen shows the message *Hanging Up. . .* , and then displays the message *OK* once the phone has been disconnected. Whenever the phone line is disconnected, for whatever reason, the screen displays the message *NO CARRIER*, to let you know that you're no longer in contact with the remote computer.

When you're calling another personal computer, ending the session is simply a matter of hanging up. However, when you call a commercial information service or electronic-mail utility, it's best to log off the service before you hang up. Each commercial service has a special log-off command you type (such as *BYE*, *EXIT*, *LOGOFF*, or *QUIT*), which lets the remote computer know you are ending your session. Most services have a time-out feature that automatically disconnects if you have not issued any commands for a few minutes. But if you don't log off such a service, you may be charged for the few minutes between the time you hang up and the time its time-out feature tells it to disconnect from you.

Answering an incoming call

You can set your Mac to answer a phone call from somebody else's computer. To do this:

☐ Choose Answer Phone from the Communications menu.

The following message will appear on the screen:

Setting modem to answer calls

This message tells you that your modem will automatically answer the phone.

WHAT YOU CAN DO WITH WORKS COMMUNICATIONS

Sometimes, integrated programs cut corners with their communications programs as a way to save space on the program disk. But that isn't the case with the Works communications program: It does most of the things you would want to do.

You can store all the telephone numbers you want

You can store an unlimited number of telephone numbers with the communications program. You can store up to eight telephone numbers with each communications document, and the number of communications documents is limited only by the amount of disk space you have. Even if you're storing eight names and telephone numbers with a communications document, one document occupies only 4K of disk space, so you can store dozens of documents on one Mac disk. Having all of your phone numbers on disk means you can have Works dial any of them automatically with your modem.

You can choose from three error-checking protocols

Works gives you the choice of Xmodem Text, Xmodem Data, and MacBinary error-checking protocols when you send files. Each of these protocols is suited to a particular communicating situation. As mentioned earlier in this chapter, Xmodem Text and Xmodem Data are for sending data to computers that don't have communications software with the MacBinary protocol. MacBinary transmission is better when you're communicating with another Mac that also can use the MacBinary protocol. The MacBinary option lets you send files over telephone lines with fewer errors than the Xmodem protocols do.

You can communicate while you're doing something else

Works has a feature called background communications—the ability to communicate with another computer while you're working with a file on your Mac. Other integrated programs for the Mac won't let you do anything else while you're communicating. With Works, you can call another computer, begin sending or receiving a file, and then work with another Works spreadsheet, word-processor, or database document while the transmission proceeds. When you go back to the communications document, you'll still be connected to the other computer. The background communications feature lets you make better use of your time.

You can send Works files without converting them to a particular format

Stand-alone communications programs usually require that you convert files to a standard text format before you send them. With Works, you can send any spreadsheet, word-processor, or database file as text without converting it. Works makes the conversion when you use the Send Text... command. If you'd rather send files with their formatting information and formulas intact, you can use Works' Send File... command instead.

WHAT YOU CAN'T DO WITH WORKS COMMUNICATIONS

The Works communications module performs all the major personal computer communications functions, but its designers left out a few convenience and performance features in the interest of fast, simple operation.

You can't store log-on sequences

Every commercial information or electronic mail service you can access with a personal computer requires a log-on sequence, typically a user identification number or name, a password, and perhaps some other identifying information. Some communications programs let you store these sequences so that they are automatically transmitted after you dial a commercial service's phone number. Works lets you store only names and telephone numbers, not log-on sequences. You must always type log-on sequences manually. If you always transmit the same information to a specific service or person, you can store it in a separate file and then transmit it when necessary. But log-on sequences usually require that your computer wait for certain prompts from the service you're calling before transmitting specific bits of data. Works can't be programmed to wait for certain prompts before transmitting data.

You can't automatically re-dial numbers

If you use a commercal service such as MCI Mail, you may find that your local telephone access number is often busy. With some communications programs, you can instruct the program to re-dial a phone number a specific number of times. Works has no such feature. If a number you call is busy, Works will disconnect after a few seconds, and then you must re-dial the number by choosing the Dial... command.

You can't emulate mainframe computer terminals

MacTerminal and some other communications programs have options that set up your modem to transmit in a format that mimics the data formats of popular mainframe data terminals such as the DEC VT-52 and VT-100, and the IBM 3270. Microsoft Works has no such option.

You can't import phone numbers from the database

Works is an integrated program, so you might expect that you can use telephone numbers stored in database files when working with a communications document. In fact, you can't. Any telephone numbers you want to use or store in a communications document must be typed into the telephone list by hand.

You can't edit or scroll text in a communications document

You can't alter the appearance of incoming or outgoing text while it is displayed on the screen when you are receiving or transmitting in the communications module. There are no editing or printing facilities in the communications module to let you reformat the text on the screen, change the font size, or print it. All text is displayed in 9-point Geneva type. Using the Edit menu commands, you can copy or paste text between a communications document and the Clipboard, and from there to other Works applications, but you can copy or paste only data that's visible on the screen.

You'll notice that the communications document window doesn't have any scroll bars—once text has scrolled off the screen, you can't re-display it in the communications module. To be able to review text that has scrolled off the screen, you have to have captured it into a word-processor file, where you can look at it after you've ended your communications session. If you don't plan ahead by capturing incoming text, it's gone once it scrolls off the screen.

You can't have more than one communications document open at a time

Works assumes that the only reason you'll have a communications document open is to communicate. The Macintosh can communicate information through only one port at a time. So it can't communicate with two different computers at once, even if you have two modems hooked up. For this reason, Works doesn't allow you to have more than one communications document open at a time.

COMMUNICATIONS TIPS AND TROUBLESHOOTING

Communications is a complex application that can present a number of problems. Sometimes, the problems are the result of your errors, and sometimes they're beyond your control. Here are a few tips and suggestions to make your communications as trouble-free as possible.

Check your modem before attempting to communicate

Make sure your modem is connected to your Mac, that it's connected to a telephone line, that it's plugged into an AC outlet (if necessary), that its switches are set correctly, and that it's turned on when you want to use it. If you attempt to dial out or receive a call and nothing happens, most likely one or more of your modem's cables are disconnected or the modem is off. If everything is connected, make sure the correct port (the one to which your modem is connected) is indicated in the Communications Settings dialog box.

Check your communications settings

If you can dial out but are unable to connect to a remote computer, you probably have the wrong baud-rate setting in your communications document. Use the Settings... command to display the Communications Settings dialog box, change the baud rate, and try calling again. If you are able to dial out but you or your communicating partner sees garbled characters on the screen, or if the remote computer hangs up right away, the first thing to check is the other communications settings. The Data Size, Stop Bits, and Parity settings in your communications document must match those settings on the remote computer. Otherwise, you won't communicate clearly.

Test your connection by using the keyboard

When you connect to a commercial information service's computer, you will receive a prompt from that computer asking for a password or identification number. If you can clearly read the prompts, and if the other computer responds to your typed information, then everything is fine. When you call a friend's computer, however, there are no prompts to let you know how the call is going. Before trying to send a file, type something like *Hello* to determine whether your partner can read your transmission. Then ask your partner to type something so you can make sure you are receiving properly. Once you're sure the communications link is working properly, you can safely transmit or receive your files.

Don't forget to use the Capture Text... or Receive File... command

Remember, text displayed on your screen as it comes in will be lost forever when it scrolls off the screen. To make sure you store all the data you receive, use the Capture Text... or Receive File... command immediately after establishing a connection. That way, you'll be sure that everything you receive is saved to a file on disk. You will probably end up capturing some extraneous text, such as a commercial service's prompts or the messages you send to verify a good connection, but you can always delete these extra bits of data when you open the received file with the Works word processor.

Don't forget to stop capturing text or receiving a file

Even though the entire file has been received, you have to tell Works to stop capturing text. As was mentioned earlier in this chapter, the Capture Text... command changes to End Text Capture when you begin receiving a file, and you must choose the End Capture Text command to close the receive file before you can work with it. Likewise, the Receive File... command changes to Cancel Receive when you begin receiving a binary file, and you must use the Cancel Receive command before you can work with the file.

Capture long files instead of reading them on-line

A commercial information service such as The Source charges you for each minute you're connected. It's easy to run up quite a bill if you spend time browsing through various articles stored on the system. One way to save money is to capture, or download, the text of articles so that you can review them later. Instead of reading an article while you are connected to a service (and paying for the time), set up a captured-text file and display the text as quickly as possible. If the text goes on for several screens, a prompt at the bottom of each screen will ask you to press the Return key to display more text. This is to allow you time to read each screen. To display (and therefore receive) the article as fast as possible while you're capturing it, press the Return key as soon as this prompt is displayed. Once you've got the whole article on disk, log off from the service. You can then open the captured-text file and read it at your leisure without incurring connect-time costs.

Use one document for several phone numbers

As mentioned earlier, you can store up to eight telephone numbers in each communications document. To conserve disk space and avoid confusion later, try to store all the names and telephone numbers that use the same communications settings with one document. That way, you can call any of several computers by using just one document.

The reason for having separate communications documents is to allow you to store documents with different baud rates, data formats, or other protocol settings as separate files. You can give each file the name of the person you call with it or the group of settings it stores. If you regularly call a friend named Joe Jones, who has a Mac and communicates at 1200 baud, for example, you could store one communications document called Joe Jones, which has the baud rate set to 1200 and the Xon/Xoff Handshake setting selected. If you communicate frequently with a Telex service, you could have another document called Telex, with the speed set to 300 baud. Of course, if more than one of your regular communications partners require the same settings, you can simply store more than one phone number on the same document.

Work with another file during long transmissions

Works lets you send or receive a file with a communications document while you are working with another spreadsheet, database, or word-processing file.

While you're working with another file, Works continues to send or receive data "in background," so you don't waste time staring at the screen and waiting for a file to be completely received or transmitted. When you want to check on the progress of your transmitting or receiving operation, you can use the Window menu to redisplay the communications document. Working on one document while you're connected to another computer can save you a lot of time when files take several minutes to transmit. Remember, though, you can have only one communciations document open at a time in Works.

COMMUNICATIONS SPECIFICATIONS

Here are some specifications you may want to refer to as you use the communications module:

Maximum size of sent and received files: Limited by the amount of available disk space

Maximum number of stored telephone numbers per document: 8

Error-correcting protocols available: MacBinary, Xmodem

Default Font: 9-point Geneva

Number of fonts available: 1

CHAPTER 9

Using Works as a System

Each of the Works applications is powerful by itself, but you can use these applications together to perform more complex tasks. You can easily move data from one Works application to another—or between Works and other programs—to create a data-handling environment that lets you work with information in the format and with the tools that best suit you. In this chapter, we'll cover the basics of moving data between applications, and then we'll look at several examples that show how this capability can help you.

MOVING DATA WITH WORKS

You can move data from one Works application to another, or between Works and other programs in three ways: by cutting and pasting data through the Clipboard; by merging database data into the word processor; and by exporting or importing files. Let's look at each of these methods in general before we see how they can be used to perform a variety of personal and business tasks.

Using the Clipboard

The simplest way to move data from one Works application to another is to use the Clipboard. The general procedure is the same, no matter which two applications you're using.

- ☐ Open the file from which you want to copy data (or activate that file, if it's already open on the desktop).
- ☐ Select the data you want to copy by holding down the mouse button and dragging the pointer across it.
- ☐ Choose the Copy command from the Edit menu. This copies the data to the Clipboard.
- ☐ Open or activate the file to which you want to copy the data.

- ☐ Move the insertion point or selection to the place in the file where you want the data to appear.
- ☐ Choose the Paste command from the Edit menu. The data will be inserted into the file.

You can use either the Copy or Cut command to place data on the Clipboard (except in spreadsheet charts and communications documents, where only the Copy command is available). As mentioned in earlier chapters, the Copy command places a copy of the selected text on the Clipboard, leaving the original data intact in the file. The Cut command removes the original data from the file and places it on the Clipboard. Each Works application handles data copied from other applications a little differently, as we'll see next.

Moving data to the word processor

The word processor is the most logical place to integrate or combine data from other Works applications because it has the most formatting flexibility. When you paste spreadsheet, database, or communications data into the word processor, the data appears in the format it had in the original file. For example, the word processor inserts tab stops to separate columns of numbers or data from the database or from the spreadsheet.

When you insert data between two blocks of word-processor text, the lower block of text moves down to accommodate the inserted data. Inserted data always appears in 9-point Geneva type, because this is the only font and size available in spreadsheet, database, and communications files. So, if the surrounding text is in a different font, size, or style, and you want the insert to match, you need to reformat it.

Once data is pasted into a word-processor file, you can edit it just as you would any other word-processor text. The data you paste becomes text, and any mathematical relationships, formulas, data attributes, or calculated fields from spreadsheet or database documents disappear when the data is moved to the word processor. If you copy a column of spreadsheet numbers containing a Sum formula into the word processor, for example, the formula will disappear, and the column will no longer recalculate automatically if you change one of the column's values, as it would in the spreadsheet.

Along with this change in the nature of the data, the format of pasted data is a consideration in the word processor. Data you paste into the word processor from the spreadsheet or database may be wider than the word processor's current line-width settings allow. (After all, spreadsheets or database files can be dozens of columns or fields wide.) If that's the case, the data will be inserted, and the line-width setting in the word processor will change to accept the new data. If you have a word-processor document set for 6½-inch-wide lines and you paste in spreadsheet data that is 11 inches wide, for example, the formatting in the section containing the inserted spreadsheet data will adjust itself to an 11-inch line. However, the word processor allows documents only up to 15 inches wide. So, if the spreadsheet or database data you insert is wider than 15 inches, the data will wrap around on the word-processor screen, like this:

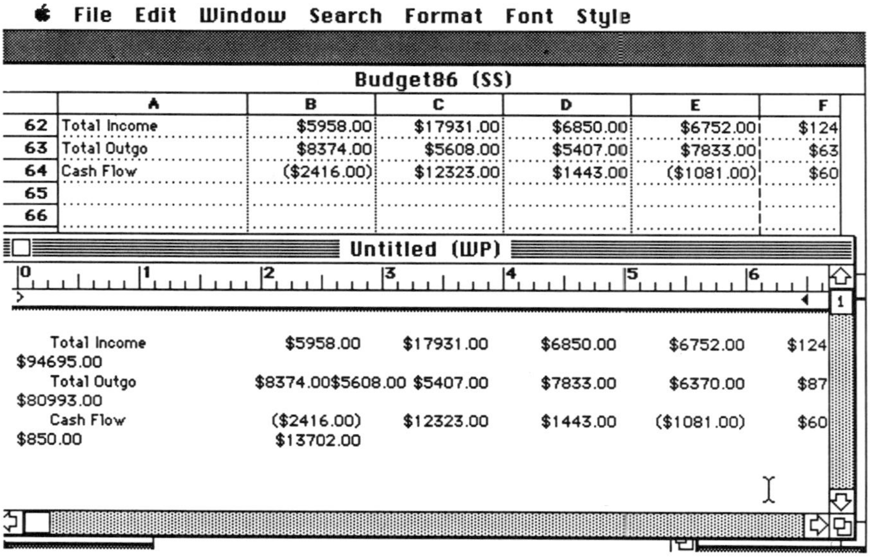

File Edit Window Search Format Font Style

Budget86 (SS)

	A	B	C	D	E	F
62	Total Income	$5958.00	$17931.00	$6850.00	$6752.00	$124
63	Total Outgo	$8374.00	$5608.00	$5407.00	$7833.00	$63
64	Cash Flow	($2416.00)	$12323.00	$1443.00	($1081.00)	$60
65						
66						

Untitled (WP)

```
    Total Income          $5958.00     $17931.00     $6850.00     $6752.00     $124
$94695.00
    Total Outgo         $8374.00$5608.00 $5407.00     $7833.00     $6370.00     $87
$80993.00
    Cash Flow             ($2416.00)   $12323.00     $1443.00     ($1081.00)   $60
$850.00                   $13702.00
```

If the data is wider than the maximum width of a word-processor document, you can't make more room for it by widening the line. To make the data fit, you have to reformat the data itself so that it takes up less space. You may be able to delete some of the space between columns.

But in some cases, there will simply be too much data to fit into the word-processor document properly, and you'll have to delete some data from the pasted selection.

To delete space between columns, move the insertion point into the line in which you want to eliminate space between columns, and then drag the tab stops in the ruler closer together. (The word processor inserts tab stops to maintain the original columnar formatting of the spreadsheet data.) As you drag the tab stops closer together, the columns will move closer together.

When you copy database data to the word processor, it's best to copy from the list window, where you can select several records or several fields by highlighting them before you use the Copy command. You can copy only one field of data at a time from a form window. When you copy data from a database file, the data from each field appears with the appropriate field name above it in boldface, like this:

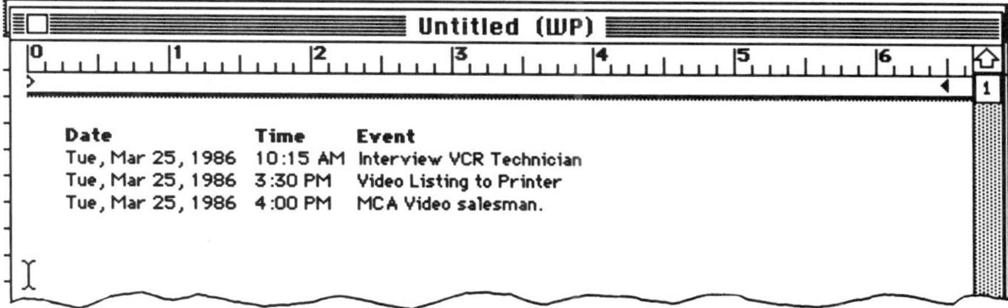

You can also paste individual cells, columns, rows, or blocks of spreadsheet data into the word processor. In addition to spreadsheet data, you can also copy spreadsheet charts to the Clipboard for use in the word processor. To copy a chart:

- Open or activate the spreadsheet file.
- Create a new chart or use the Draw Chart... command from the Chart menu to draw a chart.
- Choose the Copy command from the Edit menu (you can't use the Cut command in a chart window). This copies the chart to the Clipboard.

- Open or activate the word-processor file.
- Move the insertion point to the place in the word-processor document where you want the chart to appear.
- Choose the Paste command from the Edit menu. The chart will be inserted into the word-processor document, like this:

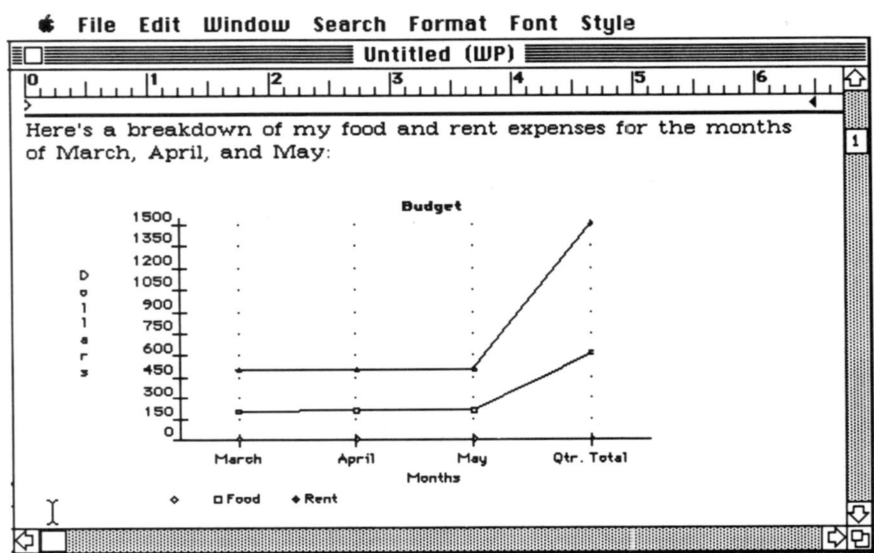

Unlike spreadsheet data, spreadsheet charts are not converted to word-processor text when you paste them from the Clipboard. Instead, they're treated as drawings. You can't edit the contents of a chart you've pasted into a word-processor document, even if the chart itself contains some text (horizontal or vertical titles, for example). Another difference between pasting text and pasting charts is that when you insert a chart between two blocks of text, the lower block of text does not move down to make room for the incoming chart. Instead, the chart appears on top of any text that is in its way, like this:

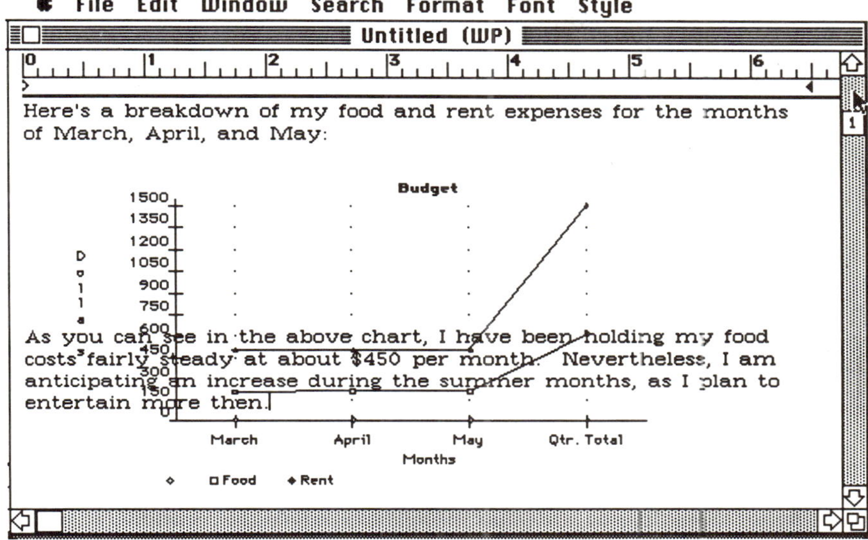

To remedy this situation, you can move the insertion point to the beginning of the overlapping text and then press the Return key a few times to move the text down and out from under the chart.

Pasting to the spreadsheet

In most cases, you'll want to paste only spreadsheet data into a spreadsheet. But there may be times when you'll want to move database or word-processor data to the spreadsheet format. If you begin a file in the database and then realize you want the additional calculating flexibility the spreadsheet offers, for example, you can move the data to the spreadsheet.

When you paste any kind of data into the spreadsheet, it is always inserted at the selected cell (or in the upper-left corner of a selected block), extending down and to the right of the selected cell. For example, if you select cell B3 in a spreadsheet file before pasting data, the data will be inserted into cell B3 and will fill some of the cells below and to the right of B3, depending on how much room is necessary. Of course, you can also select rows, columns, or blocks in a spreadsheet as the destination for pasted data.

One possible complication with pasting data into the spreadsheet, unlike pasting into the word processor, is that existing data doesn't move out of the way to accommodate data you're pasting in. If you select an occupied cell as the place for inserting data, or if cells are filled in the area where pasted data will appear, Works will display this warning message:

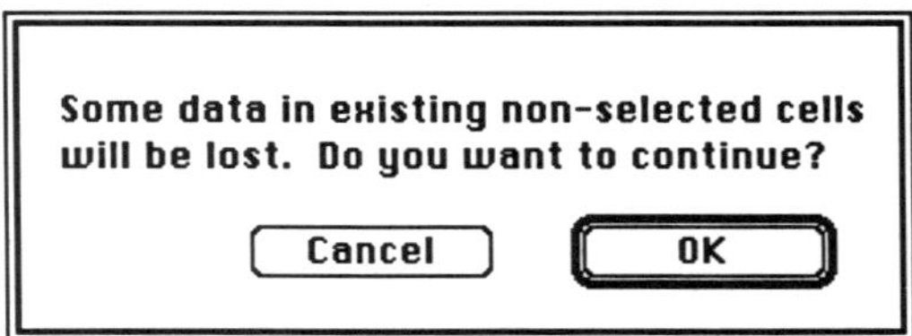

If you proceed with the paste operation, the existing data will be overwritten (replaced by the pasted data). When you paste data into the spreadsheet, therefore, make sure there are enough empty cells in the area where you're pasting.

When you copy data from the word processor to the spreadsheet, text is treated as label data, and numbers are treated as values. Because you are copying from a file that has lines containing words of varying lengths into a spreadsheet with strict cells, rows, and columns, you have to format the word-processor data so the spreadsheet knows where to place it. Any word-processor text separated by tab stops will be placed in separate cells in the spreadsheet, and any text separated by carriage returns will be placed in separate rows in the spreadsheet. Suppose you copy text and three columns of numbers from a word-processor document that looks like this:

File Edit Window Search Format Font Style

Untitled (WP)

These are the figures:

230 325 450

If you select cell A1 in the spreadsheet and then paste the data from the Clipboard, the spreadsheet will arrange the data like this:

File Edit Window Select Format Options Chart

Untitled (SS)

	A	B	C	D	E	F
1	These are the figures:					
2						
3		230	325	450		
4						
5						

The first line of text is treated as one label entry, so it all goes into one expanded cell. Long lines of pasted text will expand into as many spreadsheet cells as are necessary. Because two carriage returns separate the text line from the numbers, the numbers are inserted two rows down. And since the numbers have tab stops between them, each number is placed in a separate column. Also, there's a tab stop before the row of numbers in the word-processor document, so the spreadsheet begins inserting the numbers in column B.

When copying data from the database, make sure the list window is showing before you select the data. As mentioned earlier in this chapter, the list window lets you select any combination of fields or records from the file, and its row-and-column setup matches that of the spreadsheet. When you paste database data into a spreadsheet, each entry in a field becomes one cell, and each record becomes a row in the spreadsheet. The database data appears along with the boldface field names. You can delete the field names from the spreadsheet by selecting the cells in which they appear and using the Clear command. Information that was text in the database becomes label data in the spreadsheet, and numbers from the database become values.

Pasting to the database

The database treats incoming data from other applications as text, unless you've specified a particular data type (using the Set Field Attributes... command) for a certain field. If you have specified alternate data types (date, time, or numbers), the incoming data must match that data type. If you are pasting spreadsheet numbers into a database file and two of the fields are set up for date and time data, for example, Works will display a dialog box warning you that the data transfer into the date and time fields can't take place:

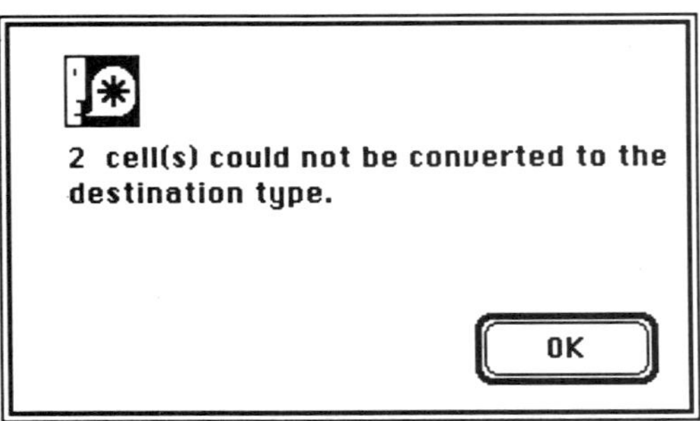

When you paste data into a database file, the data also is accepted or rejected according to the amount of room available. Data from spreadsheet columns is placed in fields in a database file, and data from rows is placed in records. If there aren't enough fields in a database file, not all of the pasted information will transfer. If you try to copy five columns of spreadsheet data into a database file that contains only three fields, the rightmost two spreadsheet columns won't be transferred. And, if you try to paste data into a place where it will overwrite existing data in a database file, Works will display a warning.

You can inadvertently arrange a database file so there are not enough available fields for pasted data to go into, even if the file contains enough fields. Suppose you want to copy these three columns of numbers from a word-processor file:

123	234	345

And let's suppose that the database file where you want to paste these numbers contains three fields, like this:

First Number	Second Number	Third Number

If you select the First Number field in the list window as the insertion point before pasting the data, then all three numbers will be pasted into a new record in order. The number 123 will go into the First Number field, 234 will go into Second Number, and 345 will go into Third Number. But if you select the Second Number field, the first two numbers will go into the Second Number and Third Number fields, and the third number will be left out.

When you move word-processor text to a database file, the database treats the text just as the spreadsheet does: All text separated by tab stops is placed in separate fields, and text separated by carriage returns is placed in separate records. If you had a database file containing two fields (Name and Phone), for example, you would have to format word-processor text like this to transfer it properly:

Joe Jones	555-4545
Ed Smith	555-1111
Al Green	555-2342

Here, the names and phone numbers are separated by a tab stop, and each name/phone number (or record) is on a separate line (separated by a carriage return). You have to be careful about how word-processor text is formatted if you want it to transfer properly to the database file.

Merging database data with the word processor

The second way to move data from one Works application to another is by merging. This feature is available only for merging data from a database file into a word-processor document. To merge data, you must have two files open on the desktop—both the database file from which you want to get the data and the word-processor file into which you want to merge the data. You select fields from the database file to merge with the word-processor document, and all the work is done in the word-processor document by the Prepare to Merge... command. The procedure is described in detail in Chapter 3.

As we'll see in the examples that follow this overview, the merge feature can be quite powerful. You can merge data from several database files at once (as long as they're all open on the desktop), and you can use the database's record-selection features to merge data only from certain records. If you want to send a form letter to all of your customers who are past due in their payments, for example, you can merge the name, address, and payment amount fields from a database file and then use the database file's record-selection features to merge data only from the records of delinquent customers.

Importing and exporting text files

The Works applications can make use of files created by other programs by importing them, and you can format Works files so that they can be used by other programs by exporting them. The word processor and database can both import and export text files. If you want to use a file that was created with MacWrite or Microsoft Word as a Works word-processor file, or if you want to use a file created with Microsoft File as a Works database, for example, you can import it. The importing procedure is simple:

- Choose the Open... command from the File menu.
- Click the Word Processor icon.
- Click the Import File box. You will see a listing of all the text files, MacWrite files, and Microsoft Word files on the current disk.
- Double-click on the name of the file you want to import. The file will be converted to a new, untitled Works word-processor file, which will then be displayed.

In the database, this procedure is a little more complicated. The database also works with text files, but text files don't have a row-and-column format like the database. So you must tell the database how to treat the incoming text data. When you try to import a text file into a new database file, Works displays a dialog box that asks you to specify the format of the incoming text file, like this:

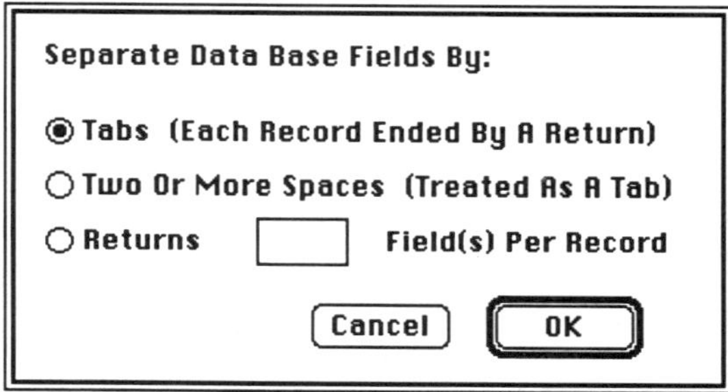

As you can see, Works separates text information into fields and records according to how each word or group of words is separated from the others. The Tabs option tells Works that data separated by tab stops in the text file should be placed in separate fields in the database file. The Two Or More Spaces option tells Works that groups of data separated by two or more spaces should be placed in separate database fields. The Returns option means that groups of data separated by carriage returns should go in separate fields. When you use the Returns option, you must tell Works how many database fields to create from the information. When a file's data is separated by carriage returns, the database needs some way of determining where one record ends and the next one begins. To see why, let's look at the following list of two addresses:

Joe Jones
123 1st St.
Morris, CA 95003
Fred Smith
383 Alvin Dr.
San Carlos, CA 94504

Each line in this list ends with a carriage return, so Works will put each line into a separate field if you don't tell it otherwise. In this case, you want two records with three fields in each record, so you need to specify the number of fields in the Field(s) Per Record box.

In many cases, you won't know the exact format of a text file you're importing. If you don't, try the three different format options. If the format of the resulting database file isn't right when you choose one format option, close the file without saving it and try another format option.

When it comes to exporting text files or transferring Works text files to other programs, both the word processor and the database work the same way:

- Choose the Save As... command from the File menu. The Save As dialog box appears.
- Click the Export File box.
- Type a name for the file that is different from the name of the standard Works file.
- Press the Return key. The file will be exported or saved as text, and it can then be loaded by another program that uses text files.

When you save a database file as text, Works separates field entries by tab stops, and it separates records by carriage returns. Also, the database saves the field names as the first record in the file.

Importing and exporting spreadsheet files

You can import or export spreadsheet files either as SYLK files or as text files. SYLK is a special file-transfer format developed by Microsoft for its products that lets you exchange data between Works and other Microsoft software, such as Multiplan and Microsoft Excel. SYLK files contain text and numbers, but they also contain formulas. Thus, you can import a SYLK file made from a Microsoft Excel spreadsheet, for example, and begin working with it right away, as if it had been created with Works.

Microsoft Excel and Multiplan have some features that Works doesn't, however. If you've used some of these extra features in files you've imported from Microsoft Excel or Multiplan, they won't work in the Works spreadsheet. When Works is unable to use a Multiplan or Microsoft Excel formula, it places quotation marks around the formula and presents it as a label. Appendix B of the Works Reference Manual has more information about the limitations of using Multiplan or Microsoft Excel SYLK files with Works.

Text files can contain numbers, words, and formulas. If you import a text file, Works will place all the data separated by tab stops in separate columns and all the data separated by carriage returns in different rows. Numbers are automatically converted to values in the spreadsheet; text becomes labels. If text is written in exactly the same format as a formula, such as =C3+C4, Works converts such text into a formula in the spreadsheet.

To import a text file or a SYLK file into the spreadsheet:

- ☐ Choose the Open... command.
- ☐ Click on the Spreadsheet icon.
- ☐ Click the Import File box. A list of SYLK and text files on the current disk drive will be displayed.
- ☐ Double-click on the name of the SYLK or text file you want to load. A dialog box will appear, asking you whether you are importing a SYLK file or a text file. Click the appropriate option.
- ☐ Press Return or click the OK button, and a new Works spreadsheet file containing the converted text or SYLK data will open.

When you export a file from the Works spreadsheet, you have three options. You can export the file as a SYLK file, for use in Microsoft Excel or Multiplan; you can export it as a text file with labels and values only; or you can export it as a text file with labels, values, and formulas. To export a file:

- ☐ Choose the Save As... command from the File menu.
- ☐ Click the Export File box. A dialog box will appear, asking you to choose one of the three possible formats for the file.
- ☐ Click the export format option you want (SYLK, text with labels and values, or text with labels, values, and formulas).
- ☐ Type a name for the file that is diffferent from the original Works file's name (so you don't overwrite your original spreadsheet file with the exported text file).
- ☐ Click the OK button or press the Return key to save the file.

Now, let's look at some examples of these data-movement techniques in action.

EXCHANGING WORD-PROCESSOR FILES BETWEEN WORKS AND MACWRITE

Suppose Al Chroma and a friend are working on a screenplay together, and Al is using the Works word processor while his friend is using MacWrite. If Al wants to use his friend's MacWrite files in Works, he'll have to import them. To do this:

- ☐ Load Works.
- ☐ Click on the Word Processor icon.
- ☐ Click the Import File box. A list of MacWrite, Word, and other text files on the current disk will appear. If the file you want isn't on this disk, either click the Eject button and insert the correct disk or click the Drive button to view the directory of the disk in the other drive.
- ☐ Double-click on the name of the file you want to import. Works loads the file and opens it as an untitled word-processor document.

If Al wants to save one of his Works word-processor files in a format that his friend can use in MacWrite, he can export the file. To export a file:

- Open the file you want to export.
- Choose the Save As... command from the File menu. The Save As dialog box will appear, asking you to type a name for the file.

If you want to save the exported file on a disk other than the one in the current drive (you might put the file on a blank disk so you can mail the disk to your friend, for example), you can insert another disk or change drives and save the file with the name it already has. But if you're saving the exported file on the disk containing the original file, give the file a different name so that you don't overwrite the original.

- Type a name for the file.
- Click the Export File box.
- Click the Save button or press the Return key to save the file. The file will be saved in a text format that can be read by MacWrite.

You can share your Works files with many other word-processing programs on the Macintosh or with other computers by exporting them. If you are sharing the file with a person who has a modem, you can transmit the file as a communications document with the Send Text... command. Word-processor files you transmit by using the Send Text... command have the same format as files you export onto a disk.

USING A TEXT FILE IN THE DATABASE

Now let's suppose Al Chroma has been elected secretary/treasurer of the Classic Film Club. When he took over his duties with the club, he had to get the membership file from Ed Green, the outgoing secretary/treasurer, who had maintained them with a database program on a different kind of computer. Al wants to use Ed's database so that he doesn't have to type the membership list into his Mac. Fortunately, Ed has stored the file as text, so he can transmit it to Al via modem. For the purposes of this exercise, we'll simulate the file Ed transmits to Al by creating a text file from a database file that's very much like a text file Ed might transmit to Al via modem. Once we have the text file, we'll use it to create a new database file. The database file we'll use is shown in Figure 9-1.

Name	Last Dues Paid	Address	City	State	Zip	Phone	Member #
Nancy Bischel	Feb 27, 1985	339 Pardee St.	Hayward	CA	94022	415-555-6666	00031
Steve Marshall	Mar 18, 1985	7790 Jacob Way	So. San Francisco	CA	94011	415-555-9900	00025
Fran Maple	Apr 14, 1985	353 Country Lane	Redwood City	CA	94459	408-555-7925	00018
Jan Hutchinson	Apr 17, 1985	459 Stag St.	Larkspur	CA	93434	415-555-0006	00008
Otis Rushmore	Apr 19, 1985	1432 Universe Dr.	Palo Alto	CA	94408	415-555-7863	00013
Madelyn Korbut	May 15, 1985	957 Oak Park Dr.	Saratoga	CA	95500	408-555-0121	00011
Kelly Stiern	May 30, 1985	4402 Bandley St.	Los Altos	CA	95505	408-555-4445	00026
Sandy Taylor	Jun 1, 1985	14 Carlick Drive	Palo Alto	CA	94330	415-555-6771	00035
Gary Carlston	Jun 12, 1985	23 Palou Ct.	San Rafael	CA	94599	415-555-7810	00029
Floyd Kefir	Nov 22, 1985	9976 Castro St.	San Francisco	CA	94405	415-555-4675	00017
Linda Feldman	Nov 30, 1985	11223 S. Hindry	Redwood City	CA	94459	415-555-2891	00039
Paul Cohen	Dec 4, 1985	1265 Borrego St.	San Francisco	CA	94403	415-555-4599	00038
Ken Cholaro	Dec 18, 1985	1490 Stevens St.	Redwood City	CA	94436	415-555-0090	00040
Bob Barron	Dec 22, 1985	332 George St.	Mountain View	CA	95500	415-555-1110	00027

Figure 9-1. *A membership file might look like this printed sideways on the page.*

- ☐ Create a new database file, and define fields for Name, Last Dues Paid, Address, City, State, Zip, Phone, and Member #.
- ☐ Type in the 14 records shown in Figure 9-1.
- ☐ Choose the Save As... command from the File menu, click the box marked Save Text Only, type the file name *Members.text*, and then click the Save button to save the file to a disk.
- ☐ Save the new database file you created with the name Members, and close it.

We'll use this file again later.

- ☐ Choose the Open... command, click the Word Processor icon, click the Import File box, and then select Members.text from the list of files that appears. The database data will open into a word-processor file, like this:

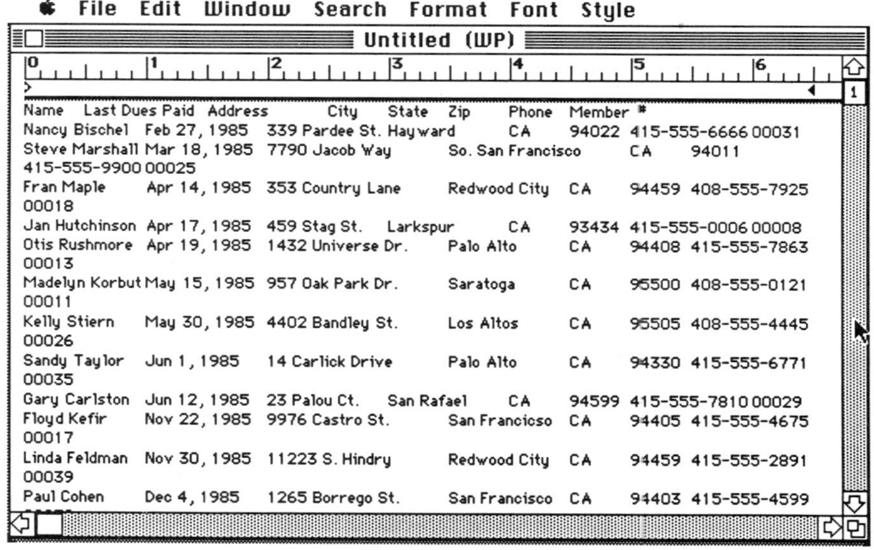

This new text file is much like the one Al Chroma would receive via modem from Ed Green, so we can use it to continue this exercise.

Before we do, though, let's go over the steps Al would take to actually receive the text file using Works' communications function.

- ☐ Open a new communications document.
- ☐ Make sure the communications settings match those being used by the other computer.
- ☐ Turn on your modem, and make sure it's connected to the telephone line and your Mac.
- ☐ If your communications partner is calling you, set your Mac to receive the call by choosing the Answer Phone command from the Communications menu. Otherwise, choose the Dial... command, enter the other person's phone number, and then click the Dial button.
- ☐ When you make contact with the other computer, the message *CONNECT* will appear. You and your partner should type a few words back and forth to make sure you're communicating properly.
- ☐ Choose the Capture Text... command from the Communications menu (you can accept the default file name, Captured Text, by pressing the Return key when the dialog box appears).
- ☐ Type a request for the other person to begin transmitting the text file.
- ☐ When you've received all of the text file, choose the End Text Capture command from the Communications menu. The file, automatically named Captured Text, is stored on the current disk.
- ☐ Type a sign-off message to let the other person know you're about to hang up, and choose the Hang Up command from the Communications menu.
- ☐ Click the close box on the communications document.

Now, we're ready to convert the text file for use in the database. When we open the file, we'll open it as a word-processor document, remember. So we'll need to open the document, export it as a text file onto our disk, and then import that text file into the database. Here's the procedure:

- ☐ Open the file Captured Text. It opens as an untitled word-processor document, just like the one we created for this exercise. If that file isn't on your screen now, display it.

Notice that there's very little formatting in this document. Depending on the computer that sent the file, the formatting of a data file you receive could look different from this example. The individual entries in the original database file (name, date, address, and so on) are separated by tab stops, rather than by spaces or carriage returns. Notice, too, that the end of each record is indicated by a carriage return (each Name entry begins on a new line). The method used to separate the entries is important: You have to tell Works which method was used when you convert the file to a database file.

- ☐ Choose the Save As... command from the Edit menu.
- ☐ Click the Export File box.
- ☐ Type a new name for the file.

This is only a temporary file (you won't need this exported file once the data is converted to a database file), so give it a simple name, such as Text.

- ☐ Press the Return key to save the file.
- ☐ Close the untitled word-processor document without saving it.

Now that the file is in text format again, you can create a new database file with it.

- ☐ Choose the Open... command from the File menu.
- ☐ Click on the database icon.
- ☐ Click the Import File box.
- ☐ Double-click on the file name Text. A dialog box opens, asking you how Works should identify individual entries in the imported file. Click the Tabs option, and then press Return.

- The new database file opens, with the entries divided into appropriate fields.

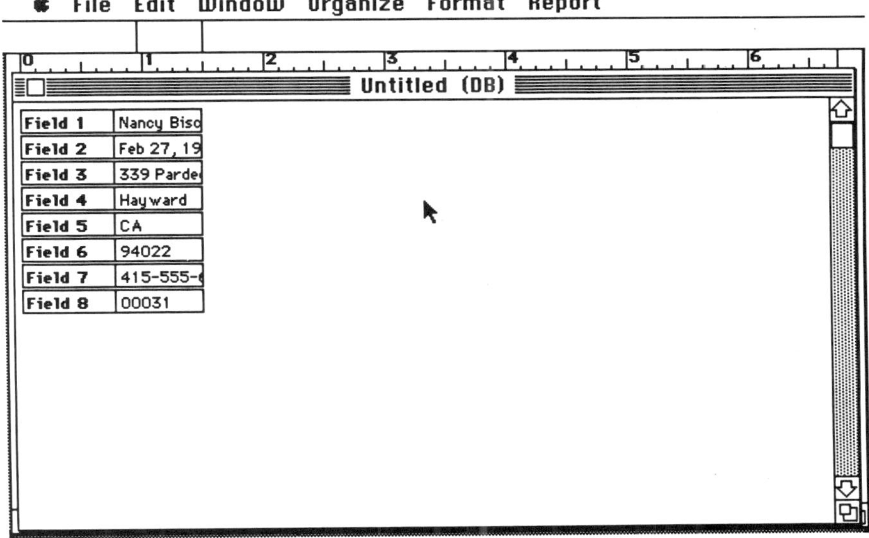

As you can see, each entry separated by a tab in the original text file has been placed in a field in the database. If you look at the list window, you'll see that each record is separated properly, too. Now we can re-name the fields with the Change Field Name... command, make the fields wider so they show all the data they contain, and then add more fields or arrange the information to suit ourselves. Before we close the new file, though, we want to be sure to save it with a descriptive new name, such as Members. Also, we can delete the Text file we exported from the word processor as well as the Captured Text file we received from Ed Green, because we won't need either file anymore.

Text files created by different database programs will have their individual entries separated in different ways. Remember, if you choose one option for separating entries when you open a database file and the data isn't formatted properly, just close the file without saving it and try another option. If for some reason none of the three options produces a database file with the right format, you'll have to open the text file with the word processor and put the data into a format that is acceptable to the Works database, by separating the entries either with tab stops or with spaces.

THE FILM CLUB REPORT

One of Al's duties at the Classic Film Club is to prepare a monthly newsletter reporting on the club activities. Since Al has a Macintosh with Works, he can combine data from several files into one document. Al plans to create the report itself in a new word-processor document, incorporating data from a financial spreadsheet, the membership database he got from Ed Green, and a database that's a calendar of club events. In this month's report, Al wants to discuss the club's finances for the first three months of the year, particularly March expenses, and he wants to remind delinquent members to pay their annual dues. After that, he'll add a list of upcoming club events.

☐ To start, create and load all the necessary files to the desktop: the Club Finances spreadsheet shown in Figure 9-2, the membership database file you created in the last exercise, and the Club Calendar database file shown in Figure 9-3. Then, open a new word-processor document.

	Classic Film Club – 1986 Finances		
	Jan	Feb	Mar
Income			
Dues	360	120	180
Film Rentals	500	275	350
Events	0	335	260
Total Income	860	730	790
Expenses			
Projector Rentals	120	120	120
Popcorn	35	85	125
Utilities	28	34	30
Soda Pop	15	35	52
Candy	20	40	35
T-Shirts	150	55	0
Supplies	75	121	68
Total Expenses	443	490	430
Cash Flow	417	657	1017

Figure 9-2. *The Club Finances spreadsheet lists expense and income sources for the Classic Film Club.*

File Edit Window Organize Format Report

Club Calendar (DB)

Date	Time	Event
Jan 2, 1986	7:30 PM	Club Meeting, San Carlos Clubhouse
Jan 18, 1986	11:00 AM	Fox Theatre Tour, San Jose, 11-5
Feb 6, 1986	7:30 PM	Club Meeting, San Carlos Clubhouse
Feb 15, 1986	1:30 PM	Private Screening of Potemkin, San Carlos Clubhouse
Feb 22, 1986	7:30 PM	Public Screening of Intolerance, San Carlos Clubhouse
Mar 6, 1986	7:30 PM	Club Meeting, San Carlos Clubhouse
Mar 22, 1986	7:30 PM	Public Screening of Twentieth Century, San Carlos Clubhouse
Apr 3, 1986	7:30 PM	Club Meeting, San Carlos Clubhouse
Apr 12, 1986	11:00 AM	Paramount Theatre Tour, Oakland, 11-5
Apr 19, 1986	7:30 PM	Public Screening of The 39 Steps, San Carlos Clubhouse
Apr 25, 1986	8:00 PM	Disney Studios Weekend Begins
May 1, 1986	7:30 PM	Club Meeting, San Carlos Clubhouse
May 24, 1986	7:30 PM	Public Screening of Potemkin, San Carlos Clubhouse

Figure 9-3. *The Club Calendar database lists the activities of the Classic Film Club.*

☐ To begin the report, create a simple banner, or heading, containing the newsletter's title and publishing information. Then use the Draw… command to put a box around the banner.

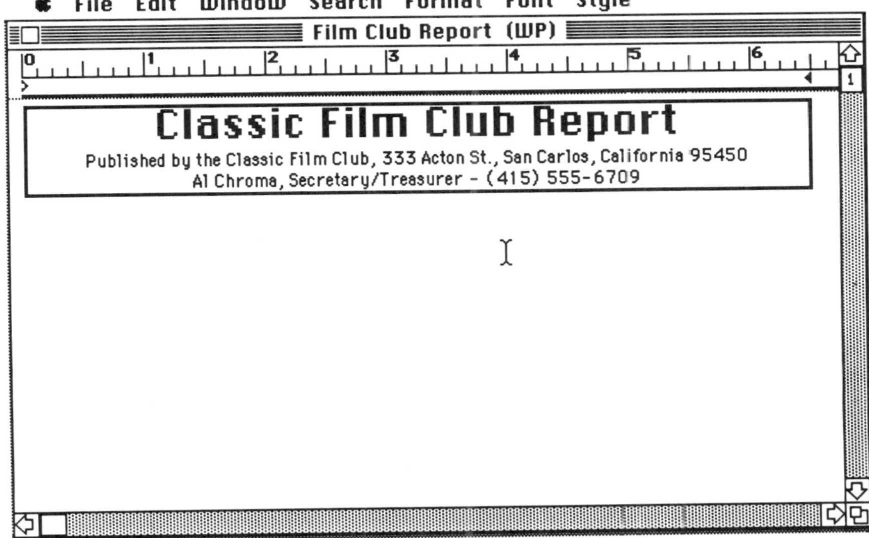

☐ Type the introductory paragraph, a heading for the finance section, and these introductory sentences:

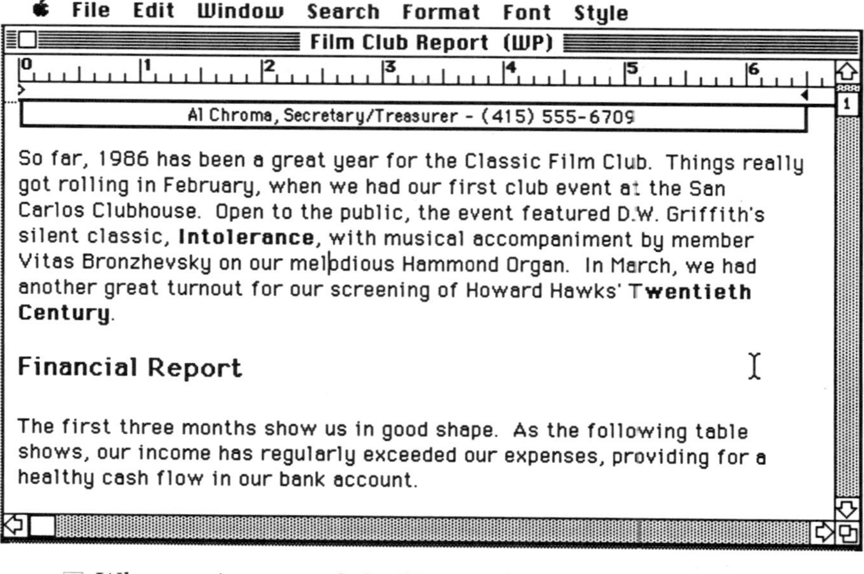

☐ When you've created the file, save it with the name Film Club Report.

Now, we want to paste in some rows from the Club Finances spreadsheet.

☐ Choose the Club Finances spreadsheet file from the Window menu to activate it.

The only rows of data we're interested in right now are the Total Income and Expense rows and the Cash Flow row at the bottom. These three rows are not next to each other, so we'll have to copy them to the word-processor document one at a time:

☐ Select the Total Income row by clicking in the blank to the left of cell A10, and copy the row to the Clipboard.

- ☐ Choose the Film Club Report file from the Window menu.
- ☐ Place the insertion point at the end of the introductory finances paragraph, and then press the Return key twice to move it down two lines.
- ☐ Choose the Paste command from the Edit menu. The row of income figures appears in the word-processor file.

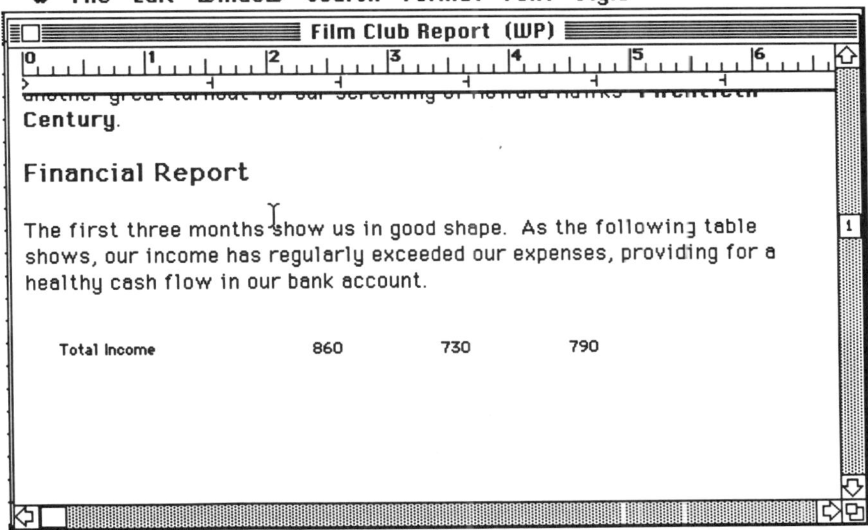

- ☐ Next, copy the Total Expenses and Cash Flow rows from the spreadsheet to the word-processor file in the same way, placing them below the Total Income row. There will be extra spacing lines between each line of figures, but you can delete them by selecting the blank lines and pressing the Delete key. The data looks like this:

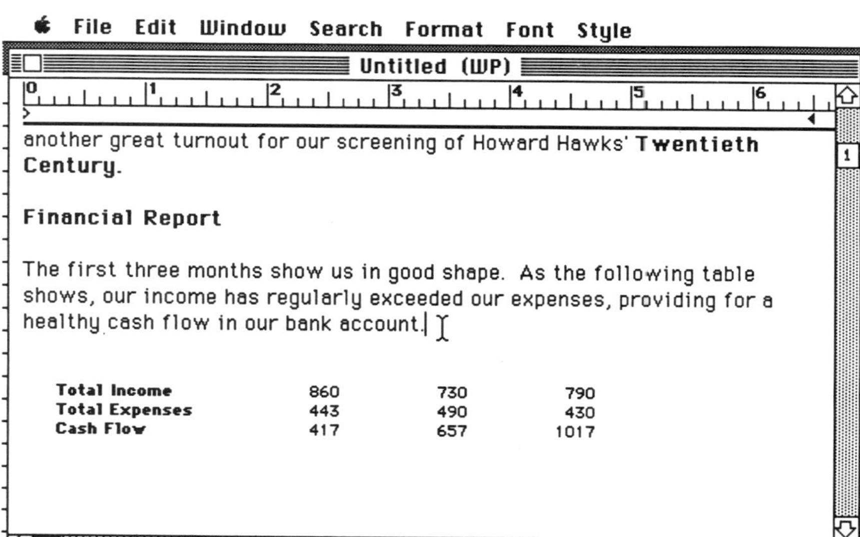

- Now, insert labels for the months January, February, and March above the columns. Tab to the proper positions.

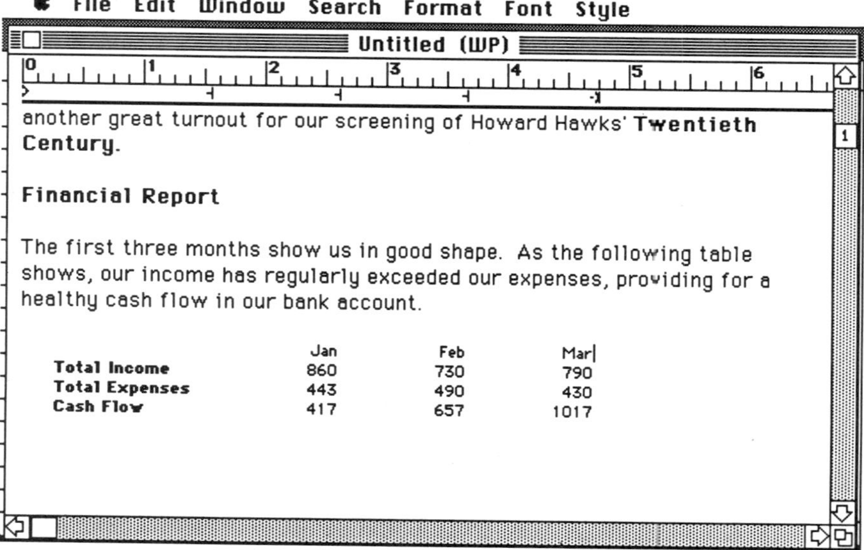

At this point, the insertion point is at the end of the last label we typed. The inserted text changed the document's font size to 9 point (the spreadsheet's size), so you'll have to change the font size back to 12 point before you continue typing text.

☐ Choose 12 Point from the Style menu.

Now, we can type some more text. The next topic we want to bring up is a problem with popcorn expenses. We'll want to support our assertion about high popcorn expenses with a pie chart for the club's March expenses.

☐ Type the additional text shown here:

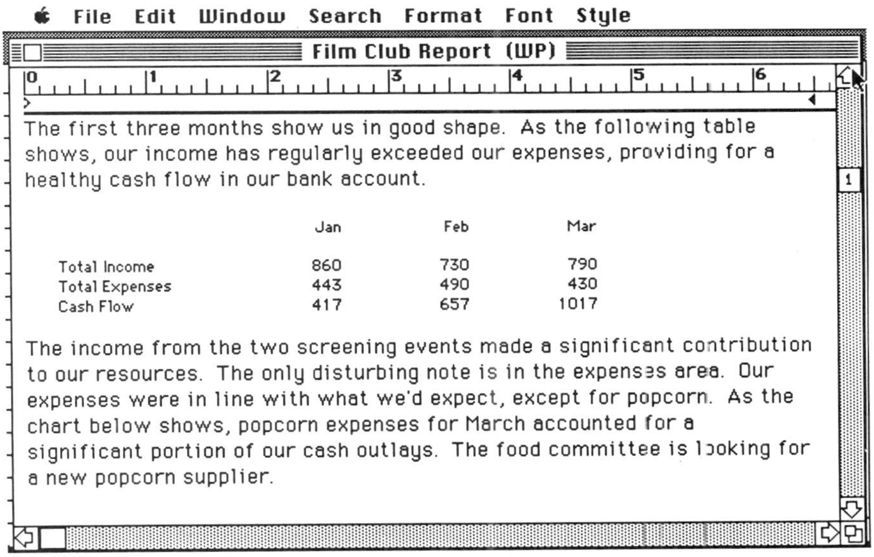

 File Edit Window Search Format Font Style

Film Club Report (WP)

The first three months show us in good shape. As the following table shows, our income has regularly exceeded our expenses, providing for a healthy cash flow in our bank account.

	Jan	Feb	Mar
Total Income	860	730	790
Total Expenses	443	490	430
Cash Flow	417	657	1017

The income from the two screening events made a significant contribution to our resources. The only disturbing note is in the expenses area. Our expenses were in line with what we'd expect, except for popcorn. As the chart below shows, popcorn expenses for March accounted for a significant portion of our cash outlays. The food committee is looking for a new popcorn supplier.

☐ After you type the text, press the Return key twice to move the insertion point down a couple of lines, and then choose the Club Finances spreadsheet from the Window menu.

Next, Al creates an expenses chart for March, called Club Finances Chart 1. We'll create this chart by activating the Club Finances file, defining a new pie chart that plots the values in column D from row 11 through row 17 with the titles taken from column A. When we've entered these row and column designations in the pie-chart definition window, we'll click the Plot It! button to draw the chart.

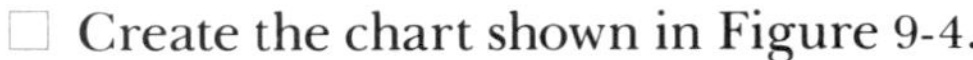

☐ Create the chart shown in Figure 9-4.

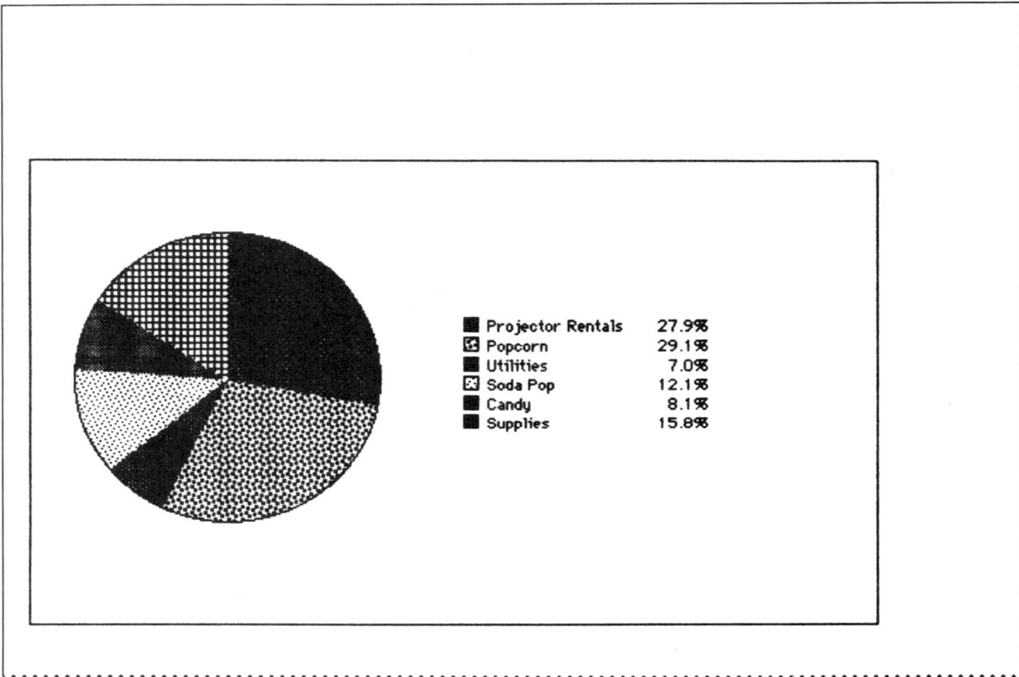

Figure 9-4. *A chart created with the spreadsheet's chart feature graphically illustrates a breakdown of expenses.*

Now all we have to do is copy the chart to the word-processor document.

☐ Choose the Copy command from the Edit menu to copy the chart to the Clipboard.

☐ Choose the Film Club Report file from the Window menu to display the word-processor document.

When the document appears, the insertion point should be in the proper position (because we put it there before drawing and copying the chart).

☐ Choose the Paste command from the Edit menu. The expenses chart appears in the report file.

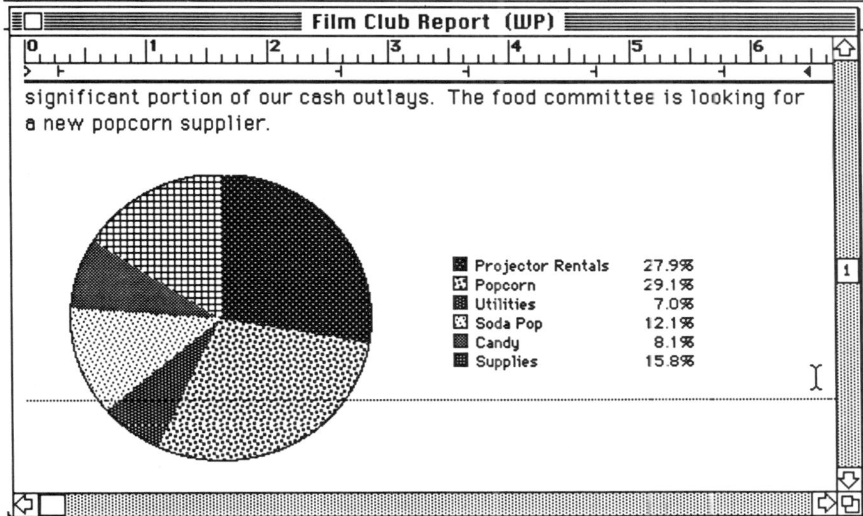

As you can see, the chart has been pasted into the report document, but there's a page break (the dotted line) right in the middle of it. We'll have to move the page break up so that the entire chart is printed on one page.

☐ Click in the space above the chart to move the insertion point there.

☐ Choose the Insert Page Break command from the Format menu. The page break moves up above the chart.

Now we can move to the membership section of the report, which Al has called Member Notes.

- ☐ Type a heading for the membership section similar to the one before the financial section, and type the introductory sentences shown here:

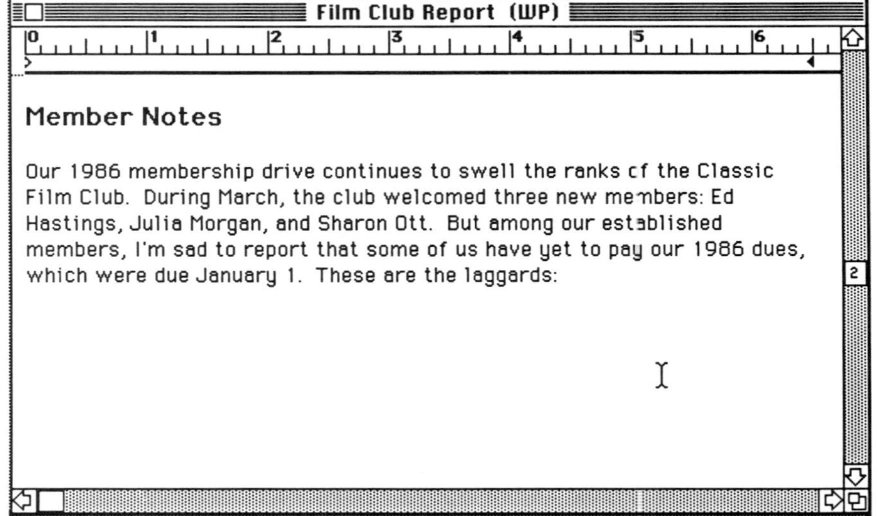

Now, the stage is set for another data transfer, this time from the Members database file.

- ☐ Move the insertion point to the end of the introductory Member Notes text.
- ☐ Press the Return key twice to move the insertion point down two lines.
- ☐ Choose the Members file from the Window menu. The Members file appears.

The membership section of the report will contain a list of members who haven't yet paid their dues for 1986. (Al figures that anyone who hasn't paid any dues since before September, 1985, is delinquent.) To select these members' names from the file and paste them into the report:

- ☐ Choose the Record Selection... command from the Organize menu.

- Install a record selection rule that selects records where the Last Dues Paid entry is less than (earlier than) September 1, 1985, and then select these records. The Members database window now contains only those records of members who haven't paid dues since before September 1, 1985.
- Select only the names from the records displayed by dragging the mouse pointer over the Name field.
- Choose the Copy command from the Edit menu to copy the names to the Clipboard.
- Choose the Film Club Report file from the Window menu.
- Choose the Paste command from the Edit menu. The names appear, along with the field name in boldface, below the Member Notes text.

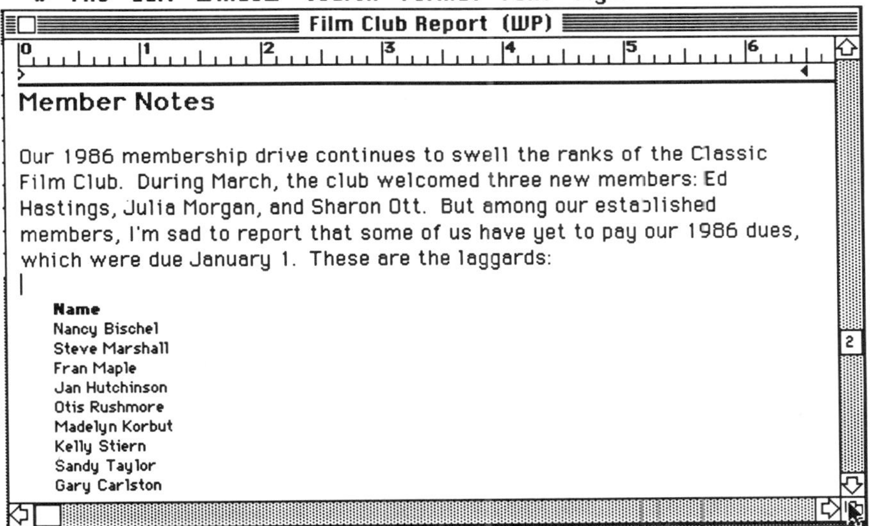

Now that the data is in the word-processor document, we can delete the field name, change the type size of the names to match the rest of the text, and reformat the names so that they follow one another at the end of the paragraph, like this:

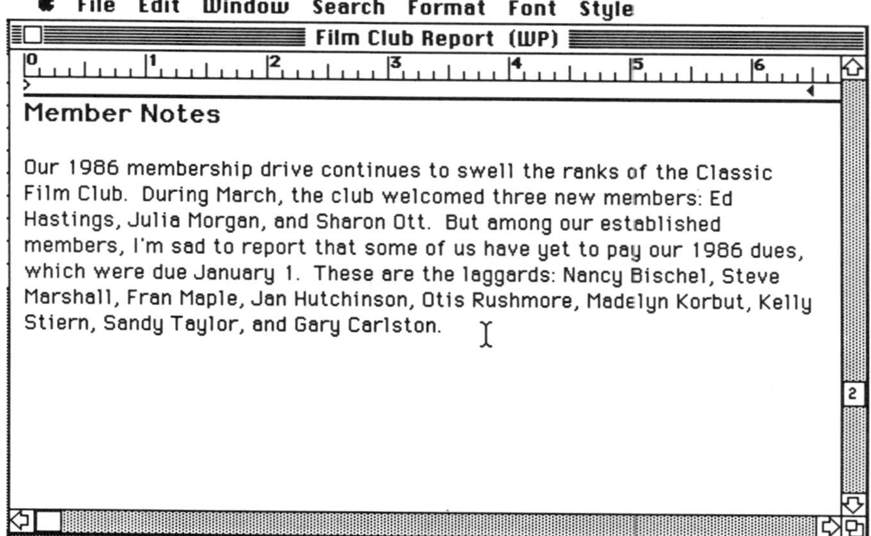

- To reformat the names, place the insertion point at the beginning of the first name and press the Delete key to remove the unwanted spaces. Repeat this process for each name on the list.

The only section remaining in the report is the calendar of events. After typing some introductory text, we'll use the Club Calendar database file as the source of information for this section.

- Type the introductory text as shown here:

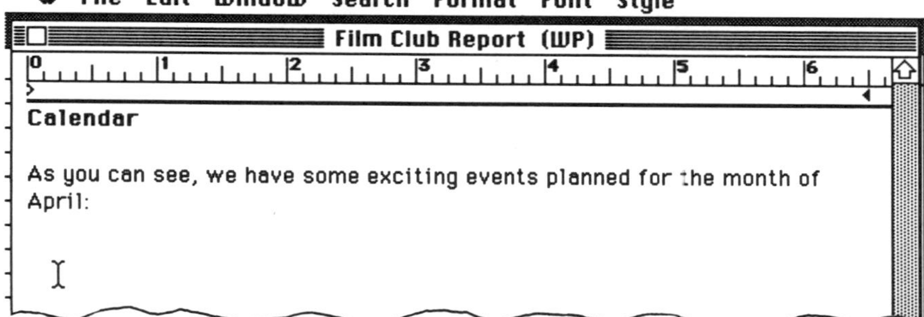

- Choose the Calendar file from the Window menu.
- Select the records for the month of April.
- Copy the records to the Clipboard.
- Choose the Film Club Report file from the Window menu.
- Move the insertion point to the line below the introductory text.
- Choose the Paste command from the Edit menu. The calendar listings for April appear in the file.

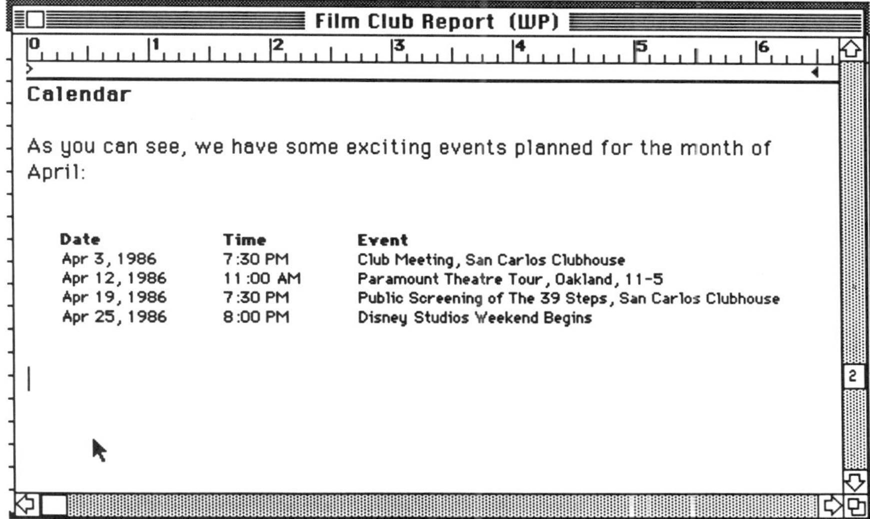

- To finish this section, select the pasted text and change the font size to match the other text in the document.

Before printing this file, we'll want to scroll back through the document and make sure that no page breaks are in inconvenient places. If we find a page break in the middle of a section, we can move the page break to the space above the beginning of the section, so the entire section prints on one page. The report is then ready to print.

As this example shows, it's easy to move data from one Works application to another, and the word processor is a good place to combine data from different files, because you can reformat the data easily once it has been transferred.

A REAL-ESTATE-LISTING REPORT

Al's wife, Claudia Chroma, sells real estate. She's been using a Works database file to keep track of her house listings. (One record from the file is shown in the form window in Figure 9-5.) Claudia would like to be able to print a report on an individual house to give to a prospective buyer. But she can't, because Works reports are only as wide as a list window and the Houses file contains more fields than can appear in a list window, as you can see by the following:

File Edit Window Organize Format Report

Houses (DB)

Address	City	Zip	Phone	Bedrooms	Bathrooms	Dining
335 Cedar Lane	Belmont	94505	415-555-1313	3	2.5	Formal
18 Beulah Dr., #27	Redwood City	94405	415-555-9870	2	2	Area
49 Windbreak Ave.	Brisbane	94042	415-555-6784	3	1	Area

The only way to display the data in all of the fields is by merging the database with a word-processor document. Using the Prepare to Merge... command in the word processor, we can pull all these fields from selected records into individual pages of a word-processor document, and then we can print the word-processor document.

To follow along with this exercise, you'll have to create a database file called Houses.

☐ Open a new database file by clicking the Database icon and then clicking the New button.

- ☐ Using the form window, define 29 fields with the names shown in Figure 9-5.
- ☐ Once you've named all the fields, type in the first record's data, using the data in the form window shown in Figure 9-5.

If you like, you can create two more records to create a three-record file, but you really only need one record to complete this exercise.

- ☐ Choose the Save As... command and save this new database file as Houses. Leave the new Houses file displayed on the screen.

Now, you're ready to merge this data into a form created with a word-processor file.

- ☐ Open a new word-processor document.

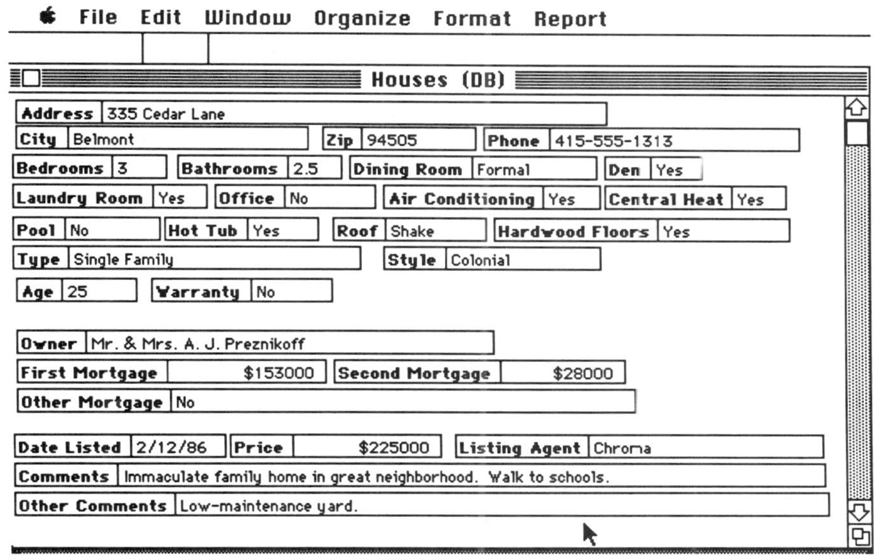

Figure 9-5. *The Houses file contains a database of real-estate listings.*

Working with the word processor, we can design a one-page form called House Form to display the information from the Houses file. To help us remember all the data fields in the database file, we can use the Print Window command from the database's File menu to print a copy of the form window from the Houses file that we can refer to as we create the form. Because of the formatting flexibility in the word processor, we can rearrange the information any way we want.

☐ Create a word-processor document that looks like this:

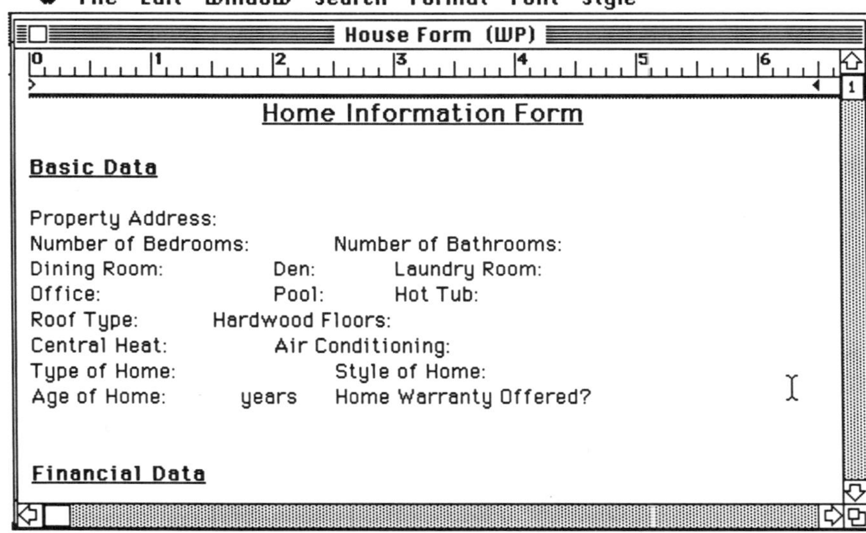

☐ Use the Save As... command to name the file House Form.

Headings will help customers identify each item of information, and the blank spaces will contain the merged data. To merge the information, we'll simply move the insertion point to each blank space in this document, and then use the Prepare to Merge... command to merge the appropriate field from the Houses database file.

☐ Make sure the Houses database file is on the desktop.

☐ Display the House Form file.

☐ Move the insertion point to the blank space after the Property Address heading.

- Choose the Prepare to Merge… command from the Edit menu. A dialog box will appear showing the database files available on the desktop. If the Houses database isn't the only open database file, choose the Houses file from the list on the left by clicking on it.
- Choose the Address field from the Houses database file from the list of fields displayed on the right.
- Click the Merge button. The dialog box disappears, and a merge-data box, a placeholder for data from the Address field, appears in the House Form after the address heading.

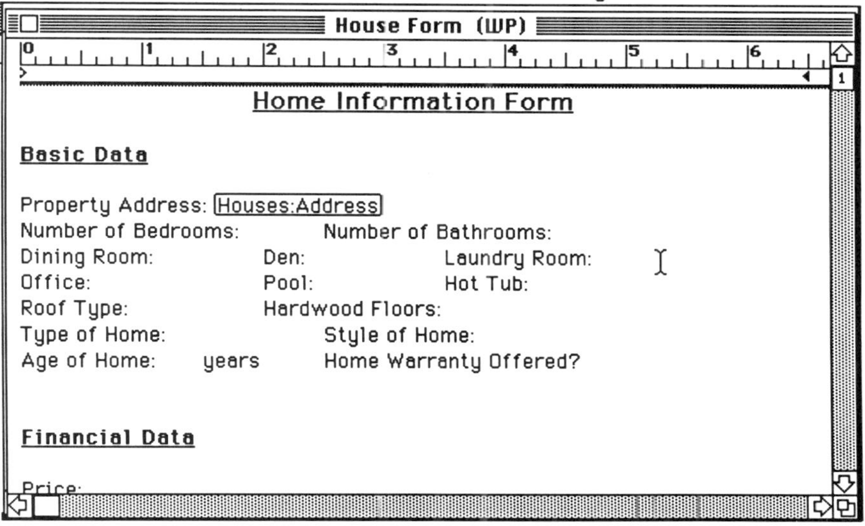

The insertion point is now blinking to the right of the Address field's merge-data box.

- Type a comma (because you usually put a comma after a street address), and then make one blank space by pressing the spacebar.
- Merge the City field from the Houses database on the same line.
- Put a comma and a space after the City field's merge-data box.

☐ Merge the Zip field on the same line. The form looks like this:

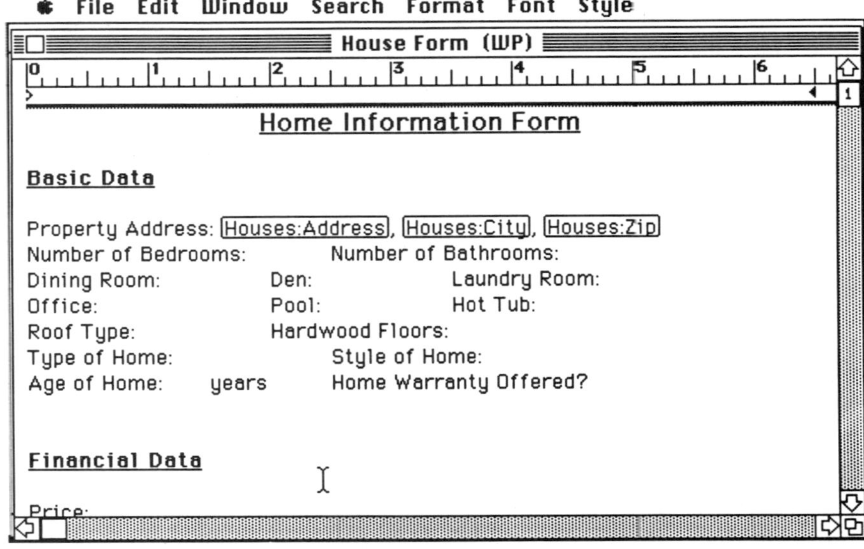

Now we can merge the rest of the fields from the database in the appropriate positions in the form.

☐ Complete the basic data part of the form to look like this:

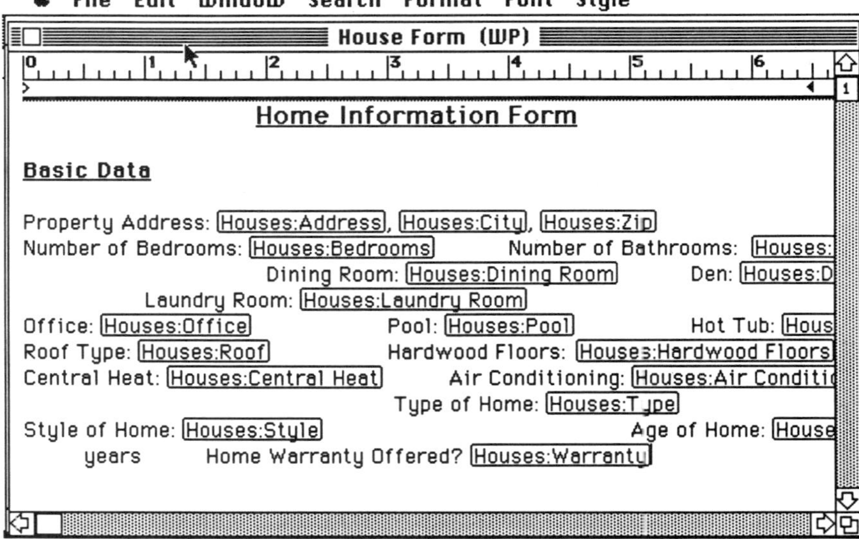

Notice that some of the data headings have moved to the right or to the line below because we inserted merge-data boxes between them. Although the text headings move to accommodate the merge-data boxes when the boxes are displayed, the text will move back to its original positions when the actual data is inserted. If you want to see this, you can choose the Show Field Data command from the Edit menu. The merge-data boxes will be replaced by actual data from the currently selected record in the Houses file, and the text headings will return to their normal positions, like this:

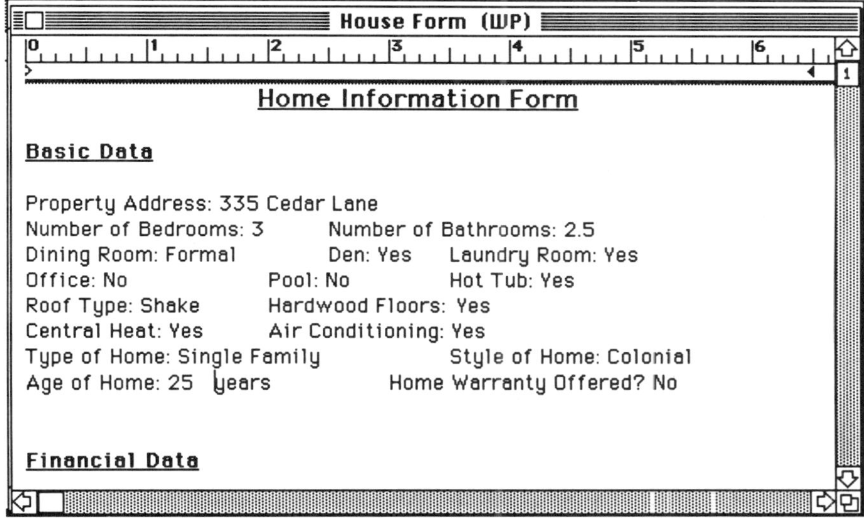

In fact, using the Show Field Data command is a good way to make sure the text in the form is exactly where you want it to be. When Works inserts data into a merge document such as this one, it creates as much space as is needed for each piece of merged data. If the data being inserted is longer than the amount of space you've left in the form between two text headings, the heading to the right moves farther to the right (or even wraps around to a new line) to make room. In this example, the data in most of the blanks (except the Address and

Comments fields) will be about the same length in each record, so we don't have to worry about having text wrap down to a new line because the merged data is too long.

Once we're happy with the layout of text in the House Form, we can use the database's record-selection features to print out only selected records. For example, if one of Claudia's customers wants to look only at traditional-style houses with 3 bedrooms and 2 bathrooms costing between $100,000 and $150,000, she can set up record-selection rules in the Houses file to select only houses that meet these criteria, and then use the House Form to print them out.

Remember, use the Print Merge... command to print merged documents in the word processor. If you use the normal Print... command, the merge-data boxes will be printed, not the merged data.

By using word-processor forms and merging data from the database, you can create database reports in just about any format. So although you're limited to row-and-column layouts of data when you create reports within the database itself, you can use the word processor to gain a lot more formatting flexibility. You can also use the word processor's Font and Style menus (options the database doesn't have) to customize the appearance of text or merged data.

CONVERTING AN INVENTORY SPREADSHEET TO A DATABASE FILE

The main reason for pasting spreadsheet data into a database file (or database data into a spreadsheet, for that matter) is to be able to work with data in the different ways that another application allows. For example, the spreadsheet is fine for totaling numbers in columns, but it isn't very good at producing reports of selected inventory items and their values. When you look at a spreadsheet file, you look at the whole file; when you look at a database file, however, you can look at selected groups of records.

To illustrate these two different ways of looking at data, let's suppose Al has the inventory spreadsheet shown here:

File Edit Window Select Format Options Chart

INVENTORY (SS)

	A	B	C	D	E
1		Videotape Inventory			
2					
3	Title	Quantity	Cost	Total Value	
4					
5	Adventure				
6	Blazing Bullets	1	$34.95	$34.95	
7	Jungle Fever	2	$32.95	$65.90	
8	Six Gun City	1	$22.95	$22.95	
9	The One-Eyed Assassin	3	$34.96	$104.88	
10	The Spy Who Said No	3	$28.95	$86.85	
11	Two Guys In Trouble	2	$34.95	$69.90	
12					
13	Subtotal Adventure	12		$385.43	
14					
15	Aerobics				
16	Aerobic Profit-Taking	4	$34.95	$139.80	
17	George Will's Yoga Fun	1	$22.95	$22.95	
18	Tip O'Neill's Workout	2	$19.95	$39.90	

You may recognize this spreadsheet—it's the same inventory spreadsheet we created in Chapter 5. If you've already created this spreadsheet, use it to do this exercise. Otherwise, refer to the inventory exercise in Chapter 5 and create the spreadsheet before continuing.

By looking at this file, Al can quickly tell the value of videotapes in a certain genre subgroup. But the file leaves out a lot of information, such as the format of each tape and the distributor. Al wants to transfer this information to a database file, where he can add fields to display more types of data and then sort records out of the file more flexibly. Here's what to do:

- ☐ Open the Inventory file. Make a note of the number of columns in the file and the type of information they contain.

Remember, Works will transfer all the data in each spreadsheet column into a field in the database, and it will make each row of spreadsheet data a separate record in the database. The Inventory file has four columns (called Title, Quantity, Cost, and Total Value), but we don't need the Total Value column in the new database file (we can calculate the total value of each tape title with a calculated field in the database).

- ☐ Open a new database file, and specify three fields: Title, Quantity, and Cost. Then, click the Done button in the Field Name window. The list window in the new file looks like this:

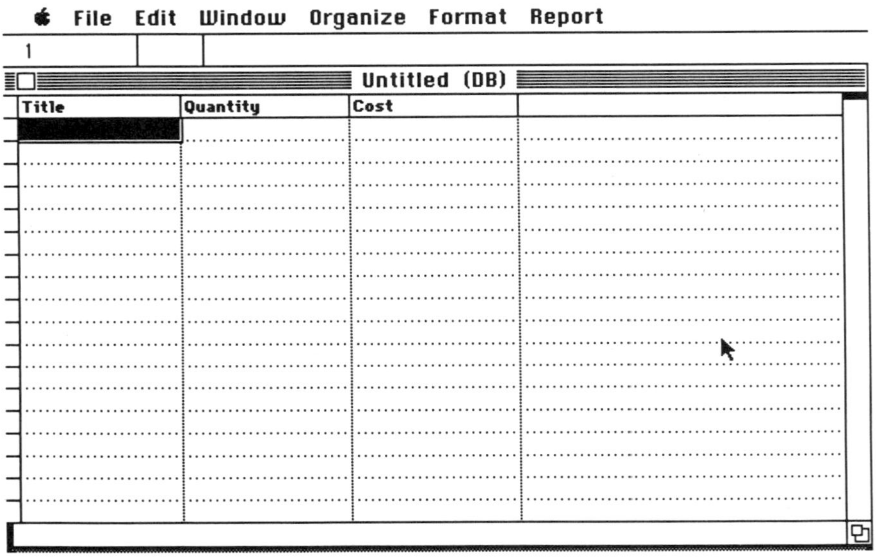

Before we transfer the data from the spreadsheet, we need to use the Set Field Attributes... command to make the Quantity and Cost fields numeric. We also need to make the Quantity field General in format, and format the Cost field for Dollars with two decimal places. This way, the data will be properly formatted when we paste it in, and (by identifying the data as numeric) we can use these fields to create a calculated field that shows the total value of each title in inventory. To set the field attributes:

- ☐ Click on the Quantity field name to select this field.
- ☐ Choose the Set Field Attributes... command from the Format menu, and click on the Numeric Type option.
- ☐ Click the OK button to return to the list window.
- ☐ Repeat the first two steps with the Cost field.

- Click on the Dollar Display option to specify dollar display for the field's numbers.
- Click the OK button to return to the list window.

To move the data from the spreadsheet:

- Choose the Inventory spreadsheet from the Window menu.
- Select all the titles, quantities, and costs of the tapes in the Adventure category. (You don't want to transfer the Total Value column, the Adventure heading, the column headings, or the Subtotal Adventure row; so don't select them).
- Choose the Copy command from the Edit menu to copy this data to the Clipboard.
- Choose the Untitled database file from the Window menu.
- Click on the Title field in the top record in the list window to select it.
- Choose the Paste command from the Edit menu. The spreadsheet data is pasted to the database file, and the data is formatted properly, as you can see here:

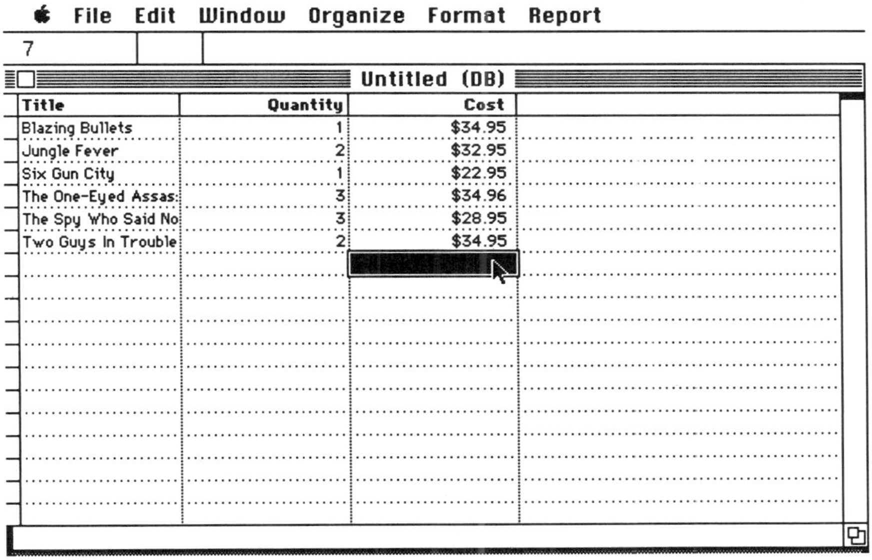

File Edit Window Organize Format Report

7

Untitled (DB)

Title	Quantity	Cost
Blazing Bullets	1	$34.95
Jungle Fever	2	$32.95
Six Gun City	1	$22.95
The One-Eyed Assas:	3	$34.96
The Spy Who Said No	3	$28.95
Two Guys In Trouble	2	$34.95

Some of the titles aren't completely visible in the Title field.

- ☐ Drag the field boundary between the Title and Quantity fields to the right until all the titles are showing.
- ☐ Paste in the rest of the videotape titles, quantities, and costs.

Once we have transferred all the data from the spreadsheet, we need to save the database file.

- ☐ Choose Save As... from the File menu, type the name *Tape Inventory*, and click the Save button.

Now, we can add new fields to store more specific information about each tape, such as the genre category, the format, the distributor, the copyright date, the rental price, and so on. Using the database's reporting features, we can create reports with subtotals that show the number and value of tapes in each category, as we did earlier in the database section.

When you paste data from the database to a spreadsheet file, the procedure is much the same, except you don't have to specify a certain number of fields for the spreadsheet file. Each field of data copied from a database file's list window will become a column of data in the spreadsheet. So, it's easy to move data between these two applications whenever you want to work with text or numbers a little differently.

INTEGRATION TIPS

Taking advantage of Works' integration features is largely a matter of using the Clipboard, the import/export and merge features, and some imagination. Here are some general tips to keep in mind as you work with several files on the desktop at once and move data between them.

Group files in folders by project

The disks on the Macintosh can hold dozens of files, so it can be hard to locate a specific file if the files are jumbled together in one window. By organizing your files into folders, you can reduce the number of items in a disk window and make it easier to locate individual files. If you use several files for a specific project, for example, you can find them more easily if you group them together in a folder on a disk and then label the folder with the project's name. If Al Chroma works with a calendar, a membership database, and a financial spreadsheet for his monthly Classic Film Club report, for example, he can put all these files into a folder called Film Club. To create a new folder in a disk window, choose the New Folder command from the File menu in the Finder.

Use the Resume Works feature

Another organizational tool you can use in Works is the Resume Works feature. Resume Works is a special file that stores a particular desktop, which lets you pick up right where you left off the last time you used Works. It remembers which files you had open on the desktop when you chose Quit, and opens Works with that specific collection of files (or desktop) when you double-click on the Resume Works icon from the Finder. The Resume Works icon looks like this:

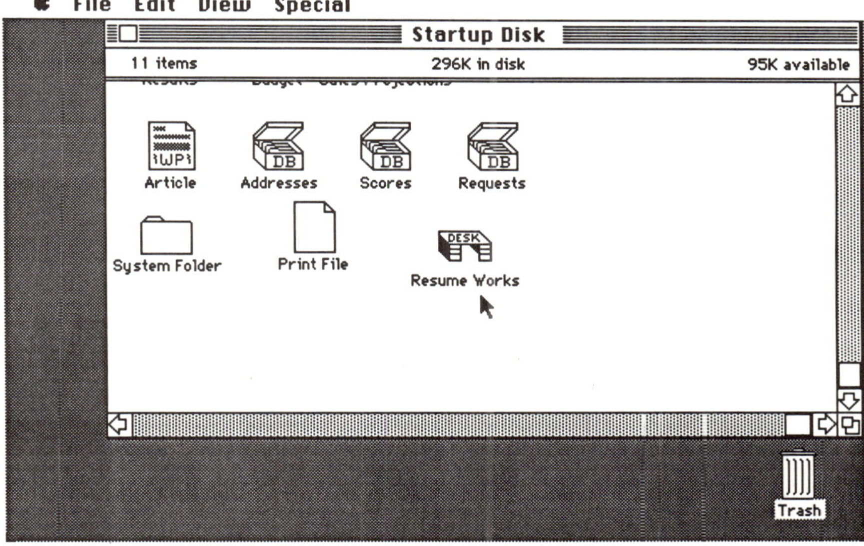

If you close all of the files on the desktop when you quit Works, nothing is stored in the Resume Works file. If you quit Works with files open on the desktop, however, Works stores the state of the desktop in the Resume Works file on the system disk you are using to run Works at the time.

The Resume Works icon acts like any other file icon in the Finder. You can select it and change its name to make it more descriptive. You can move the icon around in a disk window or copy it to another disk or folder. By renaming the Resume Works icon, you can store several different desktops for different projects. For example, if you create a regular sales report that requires you to use a spreadsheet, a database, and a word-processor document, you can quit with those three documents open and then rename the Resume Works icon as Sales Report. Then, whenever you need to do the sales report, you can double-click on the Sales Report icon, and the files you need will be loaded automatically. If you don't rename the Resume Works icon, the file will be overwritten each time you quit Works with files open on the desktop.

Or, suppose you have five different projects, which we'll call Monday, Tuesday, Wednesday, Thursday, and Friday. Each week, you do these five different projects on five different days. To create a desktop file for each project with the Resume Works feature:

- ☐ Load Microsoft Works, and then load all the Monday files.
- ☐ Quit Microsoft Works. Your new Resume Works file will now appear in the system disk window.
- ☐ Rename the Resume Works file *Monday*.
- ☐ Load Works again, and then load all the Tuesday files.
- ☐ Quit Works. The Resume Works file will appear again (the Monday file will also appear).
- ☐ Rename the Resume Works file *Tuesday*.
- ☐ Repeat these same steps for the Wednesday, Thursday, and Friday files.

At the end, you'll have five desktop files, one for each day's project. When you want to start work each day, open the appropriate day's desktop file, and all the files you need will be loaded to the desktop.

Each Resume Works file will open no more than ten files, since you can't have more than ten files open at once in Works.

Avoid disk clutter

If you import and export a lot of files or capture a lot of text files with the communications module, you should keep in mind which files are meant to be stored permanently and which ones represent data that's merely in transit from one program or application to another. If you receive a file from a friend via modem, for example, that file might be named Captured Text. But if you open that file with the word processor, you'll create a new, untitled file, and the Captured Text file will still be on disk. Once you save the word-processor file, you no longer need the Captured Text file, and you can delete it from your disk.

Every now and then, you should examine your disk's contents and delete any temporary files. By keeping your disk free of needless clutter, you'll be able to find the files you want more easily.

Check data destinations in the spreadsheet and database

When you paste data into a word-processor document, any existing data in the file moves to make room for data you're inserting. In the spreadsheet and database, however, the data you paste in will overwrite any existing data in its path. Works will warn you when you're about to overwrite data in the spreadsheet or database when you try to paste from the Clipboard. You will avoid the warning message, though, if you get into the habit of pasting data at the end of a database file, or at the bottom or right edge of your existing data.

YOU'RE ON YOUR WAY

Armed with the explanations and exercises in this book, you should now have a solid understanding of how to use Microsoft Works and some ideas about what you can do with this program to simplify your business and personal life. The more you put these tools to your own use, the more you'll understand about how to use them better. Remember, you may be at the end of this book, but you're only at the beginning of what promises to be a long and productive partnership.

APPENDIX

This appendix describes some enhancement products for your Mac that will help you get more out of Microsoft Works. Some of the products are sold by Apple Computer, and some are sold by other vendors. The product descriptions include approximate retail prices. These prices (and even the products themselves) can change rapidly, so you should check your local computer retailer, user group, or your favorite computer magazine for updated prices and product descriptions. Products are listed alphabetically by product group.

HARD DISKS

A hard-disk drive is a great convenience when it comes to storing a lot of files in one place. A hard disk can store 10 to 20 million bytes (10 to 20 megabytes) of data, while a floppy disk can hold only 800,000 bytes (800K). What's more, with a hard disk, you don't have to swap disks in and out of a disk drive.

Hard disks also speed up the operation of most programs on the Mac, including Microsoft Works. A hard disk can transfer data to your Mac about five times faster than a floppy disk, so programs and data files load much more quickly. Most of the Works program loads into your Mac's memory when you first start Works, but there are some parts of the program (including the Print, Page Setup, and Search dialog boxes and the Help file) that remain on disk, and load into memory only when they're needed. If you have the Microsoft Works program on a hard disk, these extra program segments load into your Mac's memory much more quickly when you need them. Also, data files of all kinds can be loaded and saved much more quickly with a hard disk than with floppy disks. So, having a hard disk means you'll be able to get your work done more quickly.

Each of the five hard-disk drives described in this appendix represents a slightly different approach to adding a hard disk to your

Mac. There are several other Mac hard disks on the market, but these are representative of the different types of products available.

Macintosh Hard Disk 20, *Apple Computer, Inc., 20525 Mariani Avenue, Cupertino, CA 95014, (408)996-1010.*

Apple's own hard disk for the Macintosh is a slim box that fits underneath the Mac and has the same length and width as the Mac's base. It stores 20 megabytes of data. Unlike most other hard disks, the Hard Disk 20 connects to the Mac through the external-disk-drive port. Data transfer between the Hard Disk 20 and the Mac is slightly slower than the data transfer to and from hard disks that connect to the Mac's SCSI (Small Computer Systems Interface) port. The SCSI port on the Macintosh Plus is located on the rear of the computer next to the printer, modem, external-disk-drive, and mouse ports. The Mac was designed to start up from either its internal or external floppy drive, so a hard disk connected to the external-disk-drive port can be used to start up the Mac. Older Mac hard disks connect to the printer port, and can't be used to start up the Mac. The Hard Disk 20 comes with a 90-day warranty and retails for $1,495.

Bernoulli Box, *Iomega Corporation, 1821 West 4000 South, Roy, UT 84067, (801)778-1000.*

Technically, Bernoulli Boxes aren't hard disks. Instead, they use removable cartridges containing flexible mylar disks that spin much faster than traditional floppy disks. Bernoulli Boxes come in various sizes: 5-, 10-, and 20-megabyte single-drive units, as well as two-drive systems with 10-megabyte or 20-megabyte drives in them (for totals of 20 or 40 megabytes, respectively). The major advantage of a Bernoulli Box is that it uses removable media. You can store data on one Bernoulli Box cartridge, and then put in a new cartridge to store some other data. It's impossible to run out of storage space because, when the old cartridge is full, you simply put in a new one. The two-drive Bernoulli systems also make it easier to back up your data, because you can save files onto each of the two drives, so you always have two copies of your data. The Bernoulli Box connects to the SCSI port of the Macintosh, which allows you to start up the Mac from it, rather than from a floppy disk. Bernoulli Boxes cost from $1,795 for a 5-megabyte single-drive system to $4,495 for a 40-megabyte dual-drive system.

HyperDrive, *General Computer, Inc., 215 First Street, Cambridge, MA 02142, (617)492-5500.*

The HyperDrive is unique among Mac hard-disk drives in that it is installed inside your Macintosh and connects directly to your Mac's internal circuit board. HyperDrives come in 10- and 20-megabyte sizes. The direct connection to the Mac's internal circuitry means that a HyperDrive transfers data to and from your Mac as quickly as possible, and you don't have to have an extra box sitting on your desk. HyperDrives are popular with people who want a lot of storage but don't want to have to carry an extra box around with them. Once a HyperDrive is installed, your Mac starts itself up from the HyperDrive. HyperDrives are shock-mounted for reliability, and they come with an internal fan, which helps your Mac run a little cooler. These drives must be installed by a dealer. The HyperDrive 10 (10 megabytes) costs $1,695, and the HyperDrive 20 (20 megabytes) costs $2,195.

AST-4000, *AST Research, Inc., 2121 Alton Avenue, Irvine, CA 92714, (714)863-1333.*

The AST-4000 is a very large hard-disk drive for those who need lots of storage. The AST-4000 is a 74-megabyte hard disk that comes with a built-in 60-megabyte cartridge tape-backup unit. The tape-backup unit is very handy because it saves you the trouble of swapping floppy disks in and out of your Mac when you want to back up your data. The AST-4000 hard disk can be expanded with external units to a total capacity of 370 megabytes. Like the Bernoulli Box, this drive connects to the computer through the SCSI port, so you can start up your Mac from the hard disk. The AST-4000 retails for $6,995.

LoDOWN hard disks and tape-backup devices, *LoDOWN, P.O. Box 5146, Pleasanton, CA 94566, (415)426-1747.*

One of the low-price leaders in hard disks for the Mac, LoDOWN offers 10-, 20-, 40-, and 80-megabyte hard disks, as well as 22- and 60-megabyte tape-backup units. These units connect to the Mac through the SCSI port. LoDOWN claims its hard disks are faster than any other, including the HyperDrive 10 and 20. Also, you can connect up to eight LoDOWN drives to one Mac Plus, so you can add extra storage as you need it. The tape-backup units can be used to back up any other Mac hard disk, as well. LoDOWN hard disks cost from $795 for the 10-megabyte model to $3,995 for the 80-megabyte model. Tape-backup units are $895 for the 22-megabyte unit and $1,795 for the 60-megabyte unit.

MODEMS

If you want to use the communications features of Microsoft Works, you'll need a modem. All modems use pretty much the same technology: They all connect to your Mac the same way, and they all work the same way. One big difference is speed. A couple of years ago, 1200-baud modems were all priced at $500 or more, and many people bought 300-baud modems, because they were cheaper. Now, you can buy a 1200-baud modem for about $200 (although the prices still range up to about $500), and almost everybody uses a 1200-baud modem. So presumably, if you're in the market for a modem, you're looking for a 1200-baud modem, too. If so, your buying decision will be based on the cost of the modem, the modem's compatibility with your software, and any special features you want the modem to have.

You can also buy faster modems, which run at anywhere from 2400 baud, or bps (bits per second—twice as fast as 1200 baud) up to 9600 baud. These modems send your data much faster, and thus cut down on the amount of time you are connected and paying for a call or for access to an information service. The hitch with using a faster modem is that the other computer must also be transmitting at the higher speed. Currently, most other individual users are working with 1200-baud modems, and only some of the commercial services are using 2400-baud modems. You should keep an eye on the developments in this area, though. As the rest of the world begins using faster modems, maybe you should, too.

If you were using another brand of computer, you'd have a choice between an internal modem (one that fits inside the computer) and an external modem (one that's packaged as an extra box that sits on your desk). But because you're a Mac owner, you don't have that decision: All Mac modems are external. However, you still do have to decide whether you want a modem with one or two telephone jacks. Most external modems have two phone jacks. You plug the cord from the wall into one jack, and you plug your own telephone into the other, so everything is connected to the wall jack with only one cord. If your modem has only one jack, you'll need either two telephone outlets (one for your phone and one for your modem), or you'll need to buy a "T" adapter that lets you connect two lines into one wall jack.

There are many special features you might want to consider. Any modem you're likely to buy is what is called an intelligent modem—it receives commands from your computer's software and knows how to automatically dial a number, answer the phone, and detect whether it is getting a dial tone and when a number being called is busy. All modems these days can dial on either pulse or tone-dialing systems, too. And most plain-vanilla modems have a speaker that allows you to hear the progress of your call. But some modems go well beyond these capabilities. Some have indicator lights or even alphanumeric displays that tell you if a call is connected, or if the line is busy.

Some modems have built-in error-correcting circuitry that helps overcome noise on the telephone line by checking the accuracy of data transmissions. Many modems can automatically re-dial busy numbers. A few modems even offer an internal clock that lets you set the modem to dial a number without your intervention, or a built-in memory buffer that lets the modem send or receive information even while your computer is turned off. If you don't do much communicating, you'll probably be happy with a relatively simple, inexpensive modem. The more communicating you do, though, the more you'll appreciate some of these advanced features.

The following are some representative modems. These haven't been specifically tested for use with Microsoft Works, but Works is designed to work with all Hayes-compatible modems. Since these modems all work fine with other Macintosh Hayes-compatible communications software, they should cause no problems with Works.

Apple Personal Modem, *Apple Computer, Inc., 20525 Mariani Avenue, Cupertino, CA 95014, (408)996-1010.*

The Apple Personal Modem is a Hayes-compatible modem that transmits at either 300 or 1200 baud. Most external modems have a separate power transformer that plugs into the wall and is connected to the modem by a cord. The Apple Personal Modem has a built-in power transformer, and the modem itself plugs into the wall. With this modem, you avoid the nuisance of a power cord, and, since the modem itself plugs into the electrical socket, you don't have the modem cluttering up your desk.

The Apple modem has fairly basic features. It allows automatic dialing and answering, and has two phone jacks, so you can hook your telephone to it. It also has a built-in speaker so you can hear the progress of your call when you dial. The Apple Personal Modem retails for $399, but to connect it to your Mac, you'll have to buy a Mac-to-modem cable for another $29.95.

Hayes Smartmodem 1200, *Hayes Microcomputer Products, 5923 Peachtree Industrial Boulevard, Norcross, GA 30092, (404)449-8791.*

The Hayes Smartmodem is the industry standard for personal-computer modems. It was the first widely-sold personal-computer modem, and it still is the best-selling one. All personal-computer communications-software makers strive to make their products work with Hayes modems, so most modem makers try to make their modems Hayes-compatible. Microsoft Works is designed to work with Hayes and Hayes-compatible modems.

The Hayes Smartmodem is an external unit that has all the features you would expect from an intelligent modem. It will dial a number and answer the phone automatically, and it has a built-in speaker and status lights that tell you how your call is progressing. If you buy a Hayes, you are buying a modem with an excellent reputation for quality. In exchange for the standard features, the unimpeachable Hayes compatibility, and the excellent reputation, you can expect to pay more than you would for a competitive product. The Hayes Smartmodem 1200 retails for $599, and although it is frequently discounted to around $400, that's still a lot to pay for a 1200-baud modem these days.

MACMODEM 1200 and MACMODEM 2400, *Microcom, Inc., 1400A Providence Highway, Norwood, MA 02062, (800)322-3722.*

The MACMODEM 1200 is a 300/1200-baud external modem that comes with its own communications software. The modem is Hayes-compatible, however, so it should work with Microsoft Works. The MACMODEM features two telephone jacks (so you can connect your phone to the modem), a speaker, and a set of indicator lights that show you the progress of each call. The MACMODEM's claim to fame is its built-in error-correcting circuitry. Microcom has an error-correcting method called MNP (Microcom Networking Protocol), which gives you error-free transmission when you communicate with another system that is also using MNP. You might want to start out with the 1200-baud MACMODEM 1200 and then upgrade later to the 2400-baud MACMODEM 2400. The MACMODEM 1200 is priced at $699, and the MACMODEM 2400 is $999.

ProModem 1200 and ProModem 1200G, *Prometheus Products, Inc., 4545 Cushing Parkway, Fremont, CA 94538, (415)490-2370.*

The ProModem 1200, an external modem that sits on your desk, is the only modem in this sampling that can be expanded with extra features as your communications needs grow. Even in its normal state, though, it offers a lot of capabilities beyond basic communications. The ProModem is Hayes-compatible, and can transmit at either 300 or 1200 baud. It can automatically answer or dial, as most modems can, but it can also automatically re-dial busy numbers. It automatically senses whether to use tone or pulse dialing (so if you happen to choose the wrong setting with Works, this modem will correct your mistake as it dials). It also has a built-in speaker, and two telephone jacks, so you can hook it between your telephone and a phone jack. This "basic" ProModem retails for $495, but you can find it for less than $300 from mail-order firms.

As your communications needs grow, the ProModem 1200 can grow with you. A $99 alphanumeric display that attaches to the front of the modem gives you visual messages about the date or time, or the progress of your call. A $149 communications buffer lets you program transmissions to take place in the future, or build security features into your modem. If you want to send or receive messages when you're not around, you can set the ProModem to dial out or receive calls on its own, even if your Mac is turned off. Outgoing or incoming messages are stored in the communications buffer. The basic buffer has only 2K of RAM—not enough for serious message-sending or reception—but you can expand it to 512K by plugging in inexpensive memory chips.

The buffer also has security features. You can set the buffer so incoming callers need to enter a password to access your computer. You can even set the modem for a security call-back: The incoming caller enters a password, your ProModem hangs up, matches the password with a telephone number, and, if the password is valid, calls the person back to make the connection. Security procedures such as the ProModem's help prevent unauthorized people from accessing your computer via the telephone.

In all, the ProModem can be a highly sophisticated communications center, and the price is quite reasonable. If you're really shopping for a bargain, though, you might look at the ProModem 1200G, a non-expandable version of the ProModem that retails for $299.

Both the ProModem 1200 and ProModem 1200G come without a data cable for your Mac. Prometheus doesn't sell a Mac-to-modem cable by itself, but if you buy the ProModem 1200M ($549 retail), you'll get the modem, a cable, and Prometheus' own communications software for the Mac. Otherwise, you can buy a Mac-to-modem cable from your Apple dealer for about $30.

PRINTER ADAPTERS

Your Mac was designed to print either on an Apple ImageWriter or on a LaserWriter. For one reason or another, though, you may want to print on a different brand of printer. For instance, you may want the typewritten look of a daisy-wheel printer, or you may have another brand of dot-matrix printer that you also use with another computer. As it is, you'll have a hard time printing on a non-Apple printer with your Mac and Microsoft Works. But there are some hardware and software products that help you make the connection.

Universal Card, *Hanzon Data, Inc., 18732 142nd Avenue NE, Woodinville, WA 98072, (206)487-1717.*

The Universal Card is a serial-interface card for Epson FX, RX, LX, and MX printers that lets you run an Epson printer with your Mac. You install the card by plugging it into the expansion connector inside an Epson printer. Once it is installed, it converts incoming data from your Mac so that the Epson can print it. The card has two modes: One mode passes all data to the Epson printer and prints it with the Epson's normal print, and the other mode translates data intended for an ImageWriter to the Epson's data format, making the Epson act like an ImageWriter. The interface automatically changes from one mode to the other under control from the software you're using. The Universal Card costs $130.

Start software, *SoftStyle, 7192 Kalanianaole Highway, Suite 205, Honolulu, HI 96825, (800)367-5600.*

Start software is a family of programs that let you print from a Macintosh onto a variety of printers. Normally, the Mac comes with only two printer-control programs (or drivers, as they're often called)—one for the ImageWriter and one for the LaserWriter. The Start software programs are drivers for other brands of printers: Epstart ($45) is for Epson printers; TI-start ($75) is for Texas Instruments printers; Toshstart ($45) is for Toshiba printers; Jetstart ($45) is for the Hewlett-Packard ThinkJet printer; and Laserstart ($95) is for the Hewlett-Packard LaserJet printer. Once you install one of these drivers on your Works Startup disk, you can then select a different printer with the Chooser desk accessory. If you install the Epstart driver, for example, the Epson printers are then listed as optional printers on the Chooser's printer list.

PRINTER BUFFERS AND SPOOLERS

When you print from Microsoft Works, your Mac sends data to your printer much faster than your printer can print it. So there's a bottleneck while your Mac waits to send additional data until your printer catches up with what's been sent. And while your Mac is waiting, you can't use it for anything else. To eliminate this bottleneck, you can buy a printer buffer or spooler.

A printer buffer is a box containing external memory. Your Mac sends the data to be printed into the buffer's memory, and the buffer's memory feeds the data slowly to your printer. In the meantime, your Mac has emptied its own memory of the data to be printed, so you're free to do other things.

A print spooler does much the same thing, except that a spooler is a software program that uses part of your Mac's own memory to store the data to be printed, but leaves the rest of the Mac's memory for other jobs. Because print spoolers use part of your Mac's own memory, they diminish the amount of available memory space when you use them. With a 512K Mac or a Mac Plus, however, you will probably have plenty of memory to use a print spooler. And because print spoolers are software programs rather than hardware, they are far less expensive than printer buffers. Printer buffers, on the other hand, do not use up any of your Mac's memory, and they can usually store larger documents than spoolers can. Here are some examples of each type of product:

MacBuffer, *Ergotron, Inc., 1621 East 79th Street, Minneapolis, MN 55420, (800)328-9839.*

The MacBuffer is an external printer buffer that comes in 256K, 512K, and 1-megabyte sizes. It stores outgoing printer data from your Mac and feeds it to your printer so the Mac can move on to other jobs. The buffer allows your Mac to transfer data to it six times faster than it normally could, so you can regain the use of your Mac that much quicker. You can also connect two Macs to this buffer, which allows two computers to share one printer. The MacBuffer can also make multiple copies of data you send to it, so you can print several copies of a document from the buffer, even though you only transmitted one copy of the document from your Mac. The MacBuffer is priced fairly reasonably at $299 (256K), $449 (512K), and $699 (1 megabyte).

MicroSpooler, *Consolink Corporation, 1275 South Sherman Drive, Longmont, CO 80501, (800)525-6705.*

The MicroSpooler is an external printer buffer that comes in various memory sizes, from 16K up through 256K. You can start out with a small buffer if you like, and then enlarge its memory later. The MicroSpooler works with either serial or parallel printers, and has a couple of features that make using a buffer more convenient. One of the problems with using some buffers (particularly internal buffers) is that once you send data into the buffer, it will be printed—there's no way to change your mind. If you begin printing a 30-page document and then decide you forgot to include something, you can't abort the printing process. With the MicroSpooler, there's a reset switch on the front of the unit that clears the buffer's memory and resets it. So you can cancel a printing job at any time. Another feature is a copy switch, which lets you print up to 99 copies of a document automatically (on the 64K model). You send just one copy of a document from your Mac to the buffer, and then the buffer takes care of printing the extra copies by itself. MicroSpoolers cost from $259 (16K) to $595 (256K) for the models in which the memory is expandable. There's also an economy 16K model that isn't expandable, which sells for $139.95.

Printer Optimizer, *Applied Creative Technology, Inc., 10529 Olympic Drive, Suite 101, Dallas, TX 75220, (214)358-4800.*

The Printer Optimizer is an external printer buffer that has a lot of intelligence, which you can use to connect your Macintosh to different printers or to connect to more than one printer. The unit comes with connections for one parallel printer. You can also add extra interfaces for as many as two more serial or parallel printers. So, you could use the Printer Optimizer to switch between, say, an ImageWriter, a LaserWriter, and a daisy-wheel printer from your Mac.

The Printer Optimizer has the ability to translate your Mac's data into the format required by any printer on the market. You could tell Works you're printing a word-processor document on an ImageWriter, for example, and the Printer Optimizer would convert the ImageWriter printer data to data for a Diablo 630 daisy-wheel printer connected to the Optimizer's parallel interface.

Along with the data-conversion features, the Printer Optimizer has a very flexible data-buffering system. You can print multiple copies of a document from the buffer's own memory. You can also store more than one document in its memory and print stored documents in any order you want. And, if you're in the process of printing a lengthy job from the buffer and you have another printing job you want to get out immediately, you can bypass the buffer and print directly from your Macintosh.

You can even set up the Printer Optimizer as a modem buffer—that is, you can have it receive and store data from a modem without having to leave your Macintosh running. If you want to receive data from another computer in the middle of the night, for example, you can set up the Printer Optimizer with a modem to receive the data. Then, whenever you're ready, you can transfer the data from the Printer Optimizer to your Mac.

You can control all the Printer Optimizer's functions through a front-mounted numeric keypad, and you can issue commands directly from your software. In all, the Printer Optimizer is a very versatile unit that does much more than buffer data. The basic Printer Optimizer with 64K of memory retails for $428. Memory modules with an additional 64K are $59, and 256K memory modules are $179. Extra serial and parallel interfaces are $79 (for two parallel output interfaces), $99 (for one extra serial input and output), and $149 (for one extra serial input and two serial outputs).

ShuffleBuffer, *Interactive Structures, Inc., 218 Great Valley Parkway, Malvern, PA 19355, (215)644-8877.*

The ShuffleBuffer is an external printer buffer offering some additional features that can be very handy if you do a lot of heavy-duty printing with your Mac. Like any buffer, the ShuffleBuffer can store several pages of text and print them from its own memory. It comes in 32K, 64K, and 128K sizes, and the smaller-sized models can be upgraded to expand their memories. The ShuffleBuffer can also print multiple copies of a document (up to 254 copies) from its own memory, and it has a reset switch that allows you to empty the buffer if you start a printing job, then change your mind and want to stop printing.

In addition to these standard features, the ShuffleBuffer has two alternate operating modes that give you more flexibility when printing: Random Access Printing and Bypass. When you use the buffer's Random Access Printing mode, you can store several print jobs in the buffer and then select the order in which you want data printed from the buffer. Using Bypass mode, you can interrupt a job being printed from the buffer and print something directly from your Mac.

With these printing mode options, the ShuffleBuffer gives you a lot of printing flexibility. As you might expect, however, the extra built-in intelligence that makes the ShuffleBuffer so versatile also makes it more expensive. The 32K model retails for $349, the 64K model is $399, and the 128K model is $499. These prices include a set of cables to connect the buffer, your Mac, and your printer.

TopDesk, *Cortland Computer, P.O. Box 9916, Berkeley, CA 94709, (415)845-1142.*

TopDesk is a set of additional desk accessories for your Mac that you can install on your Works system disk. Once you install these accessories, they appear on the Apple Menu when you're using Works (or any other program where you've installed them on the system disk). One of the accessories is a print spooler, called Back Print. Back Print lets you select up to 30 pages of text, begin printing, and then continue doing other work while the printing continues from a part of your Mac's memory. Unlike an external buffer, which has its own memory, Back Print uses a portion of your Mac's own memory to store data being sent to your printer.

Along with Back Print, TopDesk features six other accessories: Launch, which lets you start up another program from a currently-running program (saving you the delay of having to quit the first program before starting the second one); MenuKey, which lets you assign combinations of Command and other keys as shortcuts for choosing commands from menus (even within programs such as Works); View, which lets you look at a second MacWrite document on the screen while you have another MacWrite document open (you don't need this feature with Works, because Works lets you have as many as 10 documents open at a time); Shorthand, which lets you store strings of text under keyboard combinations (so you can enter long, often-repeated phrases by pressing a couple of keys); Encrypt, which lets you encrypt your data files so others can't open or use them; and Blank, which turns off your Mac's screen automatically when you don't use your Mac for several seconds or minutes. With the exception of View, all of these accessories can enhance the operation of Works in one way or the other. TopDesk sells for $69.

SPELLING PROGRAMS

The Works word processor makes it easy to enter text, but it doesn't assure that the text you enter is accurate. A spelling program can help by examining a word-processor file and comparing the words in the file with words stored in a part of the program called a dictionary. Whenever a spelling program finds a word that is not in its dictionary, it marks the word so you're aware of it. Most spelling checkers locate each unmatched word in the context of a document, and then let you take one of four actions: correct the spelling manually, add the word to a personal dictionary, automatically correct the spelling with a correct spelling suggested by the program, or skip over the word.

These options are important because spelling programs aren't always right. If you use technical terms or a lot of proper names in your text, the spelling program may highlight these words as misspelled simply because they aren't in the spelling program's dictionary. But if you continue to add such words to the program's personal dictionary, you can build up a personal list of technical terms or proper names, and as you do, the spelling program will highlight fewer and fewer words as "misspelled." A program's ability to suggest alternate spellings also is handy, because it saves you from reaching for a dictionary when the program finds a misspelled word and you aren't sure how to spell it. Being able to skip over highlighted words is important, too, because although a word is correct, you might not want to permanently add it to a personal dictionary. And finally, showing you the words in context is important, because sometimes words may be incorrect in one context and correct in another. These features are all good things to have in a spelling program.

Most Mac spelling programs are designed to work with a specific word-processing program. Since Works is a brand-new program, there may not be any spelling programs that work directly with it in the first few months Works is on the market. Several Works-compatible spelling programs are said to be in development, including Spellswell from Greene, Johnson; MacSpell+ from Creighton; and MacLightning from Target Software. When they become available, these programs will let you check the spelling of normal Works files. If you want to use a spelling program with Works before these Works-specific programs come out, you'll have to export Works files as standard text files (see Chapter 9), and then use a program such as Hayden Speller, which is capable of checking standard text files.

Hayden Speller, *Hayden Software Co., 600 Suffolk Street, Lowell, MA 01853, (617)937-0200.*

The Hayden Speller uses an approach to spelling that's slightly different from typical programs. Most spelling programs compare the words in a file against a large dictionary, on the theory that the larger the dictionary, the more thoroughly the document will be checked. But larger dictionaries also take more time to scan, so it takes longer to check a document against a big dictionary than a smaller one. The Hayden Speller uses only a 22,000-word main dictionary and lets you add words to one or more personal dictionaries to check for proper names, technical terms, or other personal words, if you like. The point in having such a small main dictionary is that the program can check files more quickly (it can scan just about any document in less than two minutes). The dictionary has been carefully chosen, Hayden claims, so it is said to contain 95 percent of the commonly used English words.

Like most spelling programs, the Hayden Speller shows you misspelled words in context and lets you correct them on the spot. It will also suggest correct spellings of words. The program sells for $79.

INDEX

D

E

F

G

H

I

K

L

M

T

ABOUT THE AUTHOR

Charles Rubin has been writing about microcomputers since 1981. He is a contributing editor for *A+* magazine. His work has also appeared in *Personal Computing, PC Week, LOTUS, InfoWorld,* and *Macworld* magazines. His books include the best-selling ***Appleworks, Command Performance:*** *AppleWorks*, and *The Endless Apple,* published by Microsoft Press, and *Thinking Small: The Buyer's Guide to Portable Computers.* Charles lives in Oakland, California.

The manuscript for this book was prepared and submitted to Microsoft Press in electronic form. Text files were processed and formatted using Microsoft Word.

Cover design by Becky Geisler-Johnson

Interior text design by Microsoft Press

Principal typography by Russell H. Steele

The high-resolution screen displays were created on the Apple Macintosh Plus and printed on the Apple LaserWriter

Text composition by Microsoft Press in Baskerville with display in Futura Bold, using the CCI composition system and the Mergenthaler Linotron 202 digital phototypesetter.